The Nature of Magic

The Nature of Magic

An Anthropology of Consciousness

Susan Greenwood

BERG

Oxford • New York

First published in 2005 by
Berg
Editorial offices:
1st Floor, Angel Court, 81 St Clements Street, Oxford OX4 1AW, UK
175 Fifth Avenue, New York, NY 10010, USA

Paperback edition reprinted in 2006

Berg is the imprint of Oxford International Publishers Ltd.

Library of Congress Cataloging-in-Publication Data
Greenwood, Susan.
The nature of magic : an anthropology of consciousness / Susan Greenwood.
  p. cm.
Includes bibliographical references and index.
ISBN 1-84520-095-0 (pbk.) — ISBN 1-84520-094-2 (cloth)
1. Nature worship–History. 2. Nature–Religious aspects. I. Title.
BL2520.G74 2005
201'.4—dc22

2005003346

British Library Cataloguing-in-Publication Data
A catalogue record for this book is available from the British Library.

ISBN-13   978 1 84520 094 7 (Cloth)
          978 1 84520 095 6 (Paper)

ISBN-10   1 84520 094 2 (Cloth)
          1 84520 095 0 (Paper)

Typeset by JS Typesetting Ltd, Porthcawl, Mid Glamorgan
Printed in the United Kingdom by Biddles Ltd, King's Lynn

www.bergpublishers.com

For Henry Arthur LaRiviere
(1883–1958)

Contents

Preface

The black of the night enveloped me as I lay alone in a shavan, an Iranian nomadic tent, by the side of a noisy rushing stream on a Snowdonian hillside of North Wales. My aim was to communicate with the spirits of the dark and elemental nature. The waters cascaded over the large stones in the stream and I let them enter my awareness of the place when the feelings of fear had subsided a little. I had come back to Cae Mabon, a 'stunningly beautiful elemental centre on the edge'[1] with an eclectic shamanic magical group called 'Mad Shamans'. The previous year a group of us had climbed Mount Snowdon, and as it had been my birthday, it had particular significance for me. At the end of our stay at Cae Mabon I had danced the spirits of the mountain and its waters as they surged through me. I felt very connected to the place – the wild mountain had become a part of me: 'external nature' had become internalized, and a change had occurred in my consciousness. This year I wanted to return; it was like returning to a part of myself. As I lay in the shavan I consciously opened myself up to the dark and the further change that I knew would occur. The experience of the dark of the night in the shavan and the thunderous, cascading Snowdonian river had left me with a feeling that I had to let the past and the non-essential go. On the way home I had my luggage stolen from the train; this seemed to me to be a very real confirmation of my communication with the Snowdonian elements.

This work is an anthropological study of magic and consciousness conducted through an examination of nature spiritualities. Often collectively termed 'nature religion', nature spiritualities are concerned with developing intense personal relationships with nature, as demonstrated by my own encounter with the Snowdonian elements above. In Western cultures, nature, the earth, or 'the environment' as it is now frequently called, has been progressively devalued by some dualistic conceptions of the universe that separate humans from nature. A definition of the environment as 'all material entities which exist on planet Earth but which are not human' reveals the fundamental separation between humans and the natural world (Simmons, 1993:1). The central theme of this work is to examine how practitioners of nature spiritualities overcome this cultural alienation and relate with nature as a living and inspired cosmos.

The sociologist Max Weber observed that the 'fate of our times' was characterized by rationalization, intellectualization and, above all, by the 'disenchantment of world' (1948:155). Through the use of Friedrich Schiller's disenchantment pł he was referring to the degree in which rationalization had displaced ma elements in modern Western societies (Gerth and Wright Mills, [1948] 1970:51). Non-Western cultures have not been so affected and the anthropologist Victor Turner has astutely noted that African thought, which consists of autonomous linked world-views, 'embeds itself from the outset in materiality', but this materiality is 'not inert but vital' (1975:21). To a great extent Western cultures have lost a sense of material vitality (although it must be emphasized that some aspects have been maintained through forms of empirical naturalism as well as commonsense understandings and see Chapter 1). Re–enchanting the world for practitioners of nature religion means learning to see nature as alive and also as having a spiritual dimension; this particular type of thinking is not possible within a cosmology that conceives of the world as de-spirited or as a machine. Reciprocity between inspirited beings has to be developed to establish communication; this is what I call 'magical consciousness'. 'Magic', a term used widely to mean many different things, is here employed to refer to a participatory and expanded aspect of consciousness awareness such as my Snowdonian experience already described. I shall argue that magical consciousness is an aspect of consciousness, a part of nature; it is natural rather than supernatural, and participatory rather than individual.

Nature religion is a response to a certain specific loss of relationship with the natural world. This book is not the place for a detailed examination of the history of the process of that loss; rather it is an exploration of the recovery of relationship, primarily through the development of magical consciousness. The work has two main aims within the general theme of reconnection to nature: the first is to examine magical consciousness as a de-centred perception, a natural aspect of mind, that enables an awareness of participation with other phenomena in the cosmos; and the second, which follows on from the first, is to look at some inherent paradoxes and contradictions and ask whether nature spiritualities are necessarily ecological in outlook. Nature religion has developed within a specific historical and cultural context of the Western Hermetic or Mystery tradition. Consequently, there are philosophical and ideological influences that reflect attention away from the natural world and encourage a focus on 'inner' nature and anthropomorphic deities; this tends to shift awareness away from a more ecological view. Some of the ambiguities of practice will be explored within the general context of participating in nature.

Why study nature religion? Some claim that movements such as the New Age (a component of nature religion – see below) are 'inchoate and barely studied' (Vitebsky 2003:287); and they have often been dismissed as 'plastic' or 'flaky' and not taken seriously by academics, especially anthropologists who frequently view such spiritual practices of Westerners with a suspicion, and sometimes ridicule, that would never be tolerated against non-Westerners. In my opinion, this is all the more reason to investigate this rich ethnographic area. Why focus on consciousness? Studies of nature religion have tended to focus on socio-cultural explanations rather than cognition, and anthropologists have rarely studied consciousness in the making (Comaroff and Comaroff, 1992: 236–237; Glucklich 1997). By contrast, this work is an anthropology of consciousness in the making as an awareness of the relatedness of all things.

So, what is nature religion? Catherine Albanese, in her epilogue to *Nature Religion in America*, says that it is an elusive form of religion, 'Unorganized and unacknowledged as religion, it is – given the right places to look – everywhere apparent.' It is also a form of religion that 'slips between the cracks of the usual interpretative grids – or that, more slippery still, evades and circumvents even adventurous ways to name it' (Albanese, 1991:199). The reason why it is so elusive, she concludes, is because it contains its own pluralism within. Nature religion in the United States is really nature religions. Given this, Albanese has looked for significant cultural pathways in key historical contexts, offering a 'kind of plot' to her readers. I intend to follow Albanese's lead in providing cultural pathways through the rich diversities of nature spiritualities. For ease of analysis, I use the term 'nature religion' as an analytical construct that incorporates this diversity; I do not seek to homogenize differing nature spiritualities but simply to make analytical distinctions.

Nature religion comprises a number of spiritual ontologies, all of which have different conceptions of nature, but most share the view that there is an interconnected and sacred universe. This universe is usually viewed primarily in animistic terms. 'Animism', a term coined by nineteenth-century anthropologist Edward Tylor, stems from the Latin word *anima* meaning 'breath', 'life' or 'soul' (Andrews, 1998:12) and expresses the idea that the world is inspirited. There is a multiplicity of psycho-spiritual practices, magical groups, occult societies, transpersonal therapies and organizations that may be said to comprise nature religion. However, as with all analytical abstractions and generalizations, the divisions between groups are often arbitrary, and practitioners may move in and out of the various organizations feeling, perhaps, that each 'path' offers a different dimension or approach to the same goal. This does not mean that there is an unending amount of freedom or flexibility, and the boundaries of some practices – especially those that involve initiation, such as in some forms of witchcraft – are often clearly demarcated and actively maintained. Nevertheless, the uniting theme beneath all the apparent diversity is a connection with, and a valuing of, nature experienced through magical consciousness.

There is considerable debate amongst practitioner/academic email lists, for example Natrel (the nature religion scholars' list), on the definition and practice of nature religion, and there is no commonly agreed definition. The fact that nature religion is described as 'religion' with connection with the natural world raises the question of whether a religious attitude is appropriate. The word 'religion' derives from the Latin *religio* signifying the need for duties and reverence in the maintenance of a harmonious relationship with divinity (Hutton, 1999:3), but this does not necessarily equate with an ecological view that is more concerned with relationship with the natural world rather than reverence to divinity, even if nature is the source of that divinity. A broader definition of religion is required to account for the diverse forms that it takes in the world. Theologian Ian Markham argues – utilizing Wittgenstein's view that it is a mistake to search for the essence of a 'thing' that includes everything within a certain definition – that religion is a way of life that embraces a total world-view, certain ethical demands, and certain social practices (Markham, 1997:5–6).

Unfortunately, for those seeking precise definition, nature religion does not embrace one world-view, and it is important to note from the outset that there is little homogeneity of practice apart from the overarching need to reconnect with nature. For the purposes of analysis, I shall demarcate three very broad categories of spiritualities that are sufficiently different from each other to warrant some comparison, whilst noting that there are many similarities amongst these categories – both in terms of beliefs and practices. The categories are Paganism, New Age, and Western Shamanism, although it must be emphasized that these are not discrete; they overlap with each other, often merging into a more general category of 'earth mysteries'. There are New Age shamans, Pagan shamans, Pagans who adopt New Age healing therapies and New Age practitioners who venerate a pagan goddess.

'Paganism' is an umbrella term for a number of different world-views, epistemologies, and systems of belief ranging from high magic (which incorporates elements of esoteric Christianity), contemporary witchcraft or Wicca (developed in the 1940s), feminist witchcraft or Goddess tradition, Druidry, Norse magic or Heathenism, Egyptian magic, and in some cases also Chaos Magick as well. Paganism is part of a sustained occult tradition largely originating in the Renaissance rather than deriving from folk beliefs. The New Age movement is a counter–cultural form of spirituality that also originated in Western esoteric traditions (Hanegraaff 1998) and emerged in America as a self-conscious social movement in 1971 (Melton, 1986). The New Age was originally millennial and world-denying in its search for a new order based on spiritual enlightenment. The earth was seen to be entering a new cycle of evolution marked by a new human consciousness that would give birth to a new civilization – the 'Age of Aquarius'. This would overcome the present corrupt culture by cataclysm and disaster. The idea of a New Age, according to David Spangler, one of its foremost proponents, came from the predictions of Nostradamus, the American psychic Edgar Cayce, the Theosophical Society, the Lucis Trust, Rudolf Steiner's anthroposophy, prophecies found in the spiritual traditions of Mayan, Aztec and Hopi Indians, and also from the 'Judeo-Christian belief in the second coming of

Christ' (Spangler, 1984:17–19). When the anticipated apocalypse did not arrive there was a 'turn inward' and nature became a source of revelation rather than something that obscured real spirit (Sutcliffe, 1998). Many Western shamanic practices merge with the New Age, while others seek to emulate or recreate native and indigenous spirituality. There are many different practices ranging from so-called Native American medicine wheel teachings (which derive more from New Age aspects of Shamanism) and Core Shamanism (a practice that concentrates on techniques of soul retrieval and healing for Westerners) to specific Celtic, Anglo-Saxon, heathen or Romany gypsy traditions. These are developments of what is probably an ancient human method of contacting the spirits of game animals and ancestors.

All in their different ways seek to kindle an awareness of different possibilities within sacralized views of nature. Beneath the heterogeneity of approaches lies the notion of magic as an alternative world-view. Anthropologist Ariel Glucklich says that the word 'magic' works too hard, 'we reach for it frequently, to describe wildly different things' (1997:vii). As a historical category magic is constantly created and recreated; it is understood in relation to religion and to science, often in oppositional terms. In the past magic has been rejected as non-religion, today it is often condemned as non-science (Ankarloo and Clark, 2002:x). However, increasingly the tripartite division between magic, religion and science is breaking down. Magic is frequently viewed by its practitioners as a religion and as a science (it has its own laws which will, one day, be discovered by science), as well as a form of spirituality. Above all, it comprises a 'holistic' alternative way of seeing the world, one that is frequently rooted in an awareness of the spirituality of the everyday, the earth, the body with all its attendant thoughts, feelings and emotions, and a sense of the interconnectedness of it all. This is magical consciousness, the conception that has the capability of 're-enchanting the world' for those who experience it.

The methodology that I adopt for this research is one of direct involvement. I have dealt at length with the complexities of conducting anthropological fieldwork from a participatory approach in previous works. This is notoriously difficult when studying magic due to the varying and often derogatory attitudes to what is seen as the non-rational and non-logical in Western social science. I do not intend to repeat the arguments already made but would instead refer the reader to my ethnography on high magic and witchcraft, *Magic, Witchcraft and the Otherworld* (2000), and also to some reflections on the morality and ethics of an anthropology of magic (Greenwood 2003). Most of my research data was gathered through participant observation – putting myself in similar situations to other practitioners and experiencing what happened. I also spoke to many people, had long involved conversations, and made a number of close personal friendships in the process. I attended workshops, healing sessions, sat around a fire in a Pagan protest camp, and took part with other practitioners in an anti-war demonstration in London. I took extensive notes, occasionally used a tape-recorder (with permission); sometimes I asked people to send me their reflections which I then incorporated, with their agreement, into the final text.

Growing out of my earlier book, this work, like its predecessor, has challenged me to try and write academically about magic – the experience of the otherworld. Virginia Woolf once wrote that the main thing in beginning a novel was not to feel that you could write it but that it existed 'on the far side of a gulf, which words can't cross' (Banks, 1989:238). This was a little how I felt about writing about magical consciousness. After sharing experiences of magic with many practitioners I knew that magical consciousness existed – intuitively I had 'known' about this as a child – but trying to put it into words was like crossing a chasm or an abyss to bring the meaning through, and then only incompletely. The problem was how to express the inexpressible, or what psychologist William James termed 'the ineffable'. Woolf thought that the novel had to be 'pulled through' in 'breathless anguish' (ibid.), but when I was writing the bulk of this book – during one 'mad' summer – it felt not as though I was pulling it through but that it was creating itself through me. Surely no one admits to writing anthropological fieldwork in this way; this approach is much too subjective. However, magical consciousness *is* subjective and I was engaged in intense 'participant observation' at the time, working with Romany gypsy shaman Patrick 'Jasper' Lee and his herbalist assistant Lizzie Gotts-Lee.[2] 'The field' and my own life came into what seemed like a crash collision: after a healing ritual and some sound advice from Jasper I experienced a profound feeling of communication with my ancestors and came to realize what many non–Western peoples know – that the dead and the living are intrinsically linked in life. This was a major turning point in my research and I started to explore it using the notion of magical consciousness.

After I had sent my completed typescript to the publishers I came across Ariel Glucklich's *The End of Magic* (1997) when looking for a text to give my undergraduate students studying altered states of consciousness at the University of Sussex. As I read the introduction to Glucklich's work, I realized that we had both come to the same conclusion about the academic study of magic: that many psychological and sociological theories explained magic away. Indeed we had both employed the term 'magical consciousness' in order to bring the experience of magic back into theoretical consideration. Consequently, it was with great pleasure that I read his work and incorporated it into my analysis in the final draft of this present volume. That we should independently come to the same conclusions using different 'data' is affirming of our idea that magic is a natural process of the human mind.

Many people are due thanks in helping to bring this work to publication. I am grateful for so many thought–provoking conversations with Brian Morris whose influence on my thinking is obvious, although we may well agree to disagree on some issues. I have been extremely fortunate to have taught two undergraduate courses on Shamanic Consciousness and Altered States of Consciousness instigated by Brian Bates at the University of Sussex. Teaching these wonderful courses (the latter over a number of years) allowed me to explore consciousness in a way that would have been impossible under different circumstances. Brian's wit and wisdom, as well as the students at Sussex, have taught me so much and I am deeply appreciative. I also thank Gordon MacLellan for his critical and profound reflection on a whole range of issues to do with magic; for his friendship, and for his support when things got tough, which they often did.

I am privileged to have had the enormous benefit of many stimulating and wide-ranging 'mycelium' discussions on magic, shamanism, and Paganism with Geoffrey Samuel; and Annie Keeley has enriched my understandings of magic with her insights and observations from many years of experience. Thanks are also due to Graham Harvey who in asking me to teach a course on nature and religion at King Alfred's University College in Winchester set the whole project in motion. I would also like to thank Pat Caplan for continuing support and for encouraging me to reflect more on magic and the politics of knowledge through contributing to her edited book on morality (Caplan 2003) whilst writing this work. Justin Woodman invited me to give a paper on work in progress – now Chapter 6 on the Wild Hunt – at a University of London Intercollegiate Seminar; this helped develop my thinking. Many people read draft chapters and gave valued critique and suggestions: Geoffrey Samuel, Brian Morris, Gordon MacLellan, Jenny Blain, Annie Keeley, Jasper Lee, Lizzie Gotts-Lee, and Adrian Harris have all helped me to see with fresh eyes. Andy Letcher, Ruth Smith, Anne Barrowcliffe, Annie Keeley and Jo Crow offered reflections on magical experiences; Derek Duparcq enriched my understandings of the New Age with his treasured vignettes of early New Age life in Australia. I am also deeply grateful to the anonymous reviewer at Berg for insightful suggestions, Ross Wignall for looking over the typescript, and to Jo Crow for helping with the index.

I also want to thank Jo Crow for shared journeys 'into the carpet'; Phil Hine, Maria Strutz and the other Mad Shamans; Scottie Eadie for diving wing–deep into magic; my cousin Jax Handford for her amazing sense of humour and for being a great Empress; and of course my son Adrian and daughter Lauren for being who they are.

Finally, I leave the last acknowledgement to be exprssed by poet and philosopher Susan Griffin: 'These words are written for those of us whose language is not heard, whose words have been stolen or erased, those robbed of language, who are called voiceless or mute, even the earthworms, even the shell-fish and the sponges, for those of us who speak our own language...' (*Woman and Nature*).

Notes

1. This description comes from a 2001 Cae Mabon promotional leaflet.
2. When I was conducting fieldwork Lizzie's name was May-Gotts.

Introduction

On one occasion at Beltane (1 May) on Old Winchester Hill, an Iron Age hill fort on the South Downs in Southern England, a gathering of ten New Age practitioners attuned to the natural energies of the earth. Using a combination of chanting, walking, singing, dowsing, and dancing around a maypole, the aim was to bring healing and balance to each person as well as to the environment by the alignment of inner energies with the ley lines and chakras[1] of the earth. Up and down the country assorted groups of witches celebrated the coming of summer in various ways, some as the rebirth of the young King of the Greenwood and his union with the Goddess as the embodiment of nature; while other Pagans were encamped in a wood in Kent to prevent it being turned into a leisure centre. During the same period in the same county, a group of local school children, guided by shaman environmental educators, created an imaginative world of animals, plants and fairies in a bluebell wood for a May Fair. What motivates and connects these events is a spiritual revaluing of the natural world and the regaining of a sense of unity with nature. One well-known Pagan said to me: 'For modern people the world has been intentionally deprived of significance, and so you have to reconnect.' Connection with the natural world is thus the basis of nature spiritualities.

How is it that the human mind comes to 'disconnect', to 'renounce its sensuous bearings isolating itself from the other animals and the animate earth' (Abram, 1997: 261)? Historian Catherine Albanese, in her study of nature religion in America, observes that historically religious reflection in Western cultures, which has been primarily conducted through the 'Judeo-Christian tradition', has been preoccupied with three symbolic centres: God, humanity, and nature. God has been paramount, and humans and nature, as creatures of God, have shone – but only in reflected light, leaving nature as a symbolic centre largely unnoticed. By contrast, what she terms 'nature religion' focuses on nature as source of the sacred (1991:7–9). Disconnection is largely due to the fact that in Western history there has been a progressive withdrawal of divinity from the natural world accompanied by a devaluation of human experience. This started in the period of Late Antiquity between the accession of Marcus Aurelius and the conversion of Constantine to Christianity (Dodds, 1990:37). Aided by Copernicus's transferral, in 1543, of many astronomical functions previously attributed to the earth to the sun, a fundamental change was made regarding human relationships to the universe and to God, creating the transition from a medieval to a modern Western view (Kuhn, [1957] 1974:1–2). The Copernican revolution facilitated the seventeenth – century mechanistic conception of nature developed by philosopher René Descartes (1596–1650) who separated the thinking mind from the material world and thus laid the ground for an objective science; this contributed to the view that human relationships to the world were in opposition to nature.

It has been suggested that the notion of nature as a mechanical inanimate system may be comforting for some, giving the idea that human beings are in control of nature and confirming the belief that science has risen above primitive animistic beliefs (Sheldrake, 1990:3). However, this view comes at a cost. A superior sphere of reason was constructed over a sphere of inferiority; the former was a privileged domain of the master, while the latter, which formed a category of nature, comprised a field of multiple exclusions created by racism, colonialism and sexism. Racial, ethnic and sexual difference were cast as closer to the animal and the body, a lesser form of humanity lacking full rationality or culture (Plumwood, 1993:4). During the seventeenth and eighteenth centuries discourses on the animality of negroes, American Indians, the Irish, infants, women, the poor, the ignorant, the irreligious and the mad prevailed (Thomas, 1984: 42–44).

The mechanistic conception of the world was combined by some philosophers with a particular Protestant rationalized belief system that viewed God as an omnipotent clockmaker standing outside and apart from his creation. The element of design in mechanistic philosophy did not arise from 'the "natures" of things but from the properties with which God endowed them' (Hooykaas, 1977:14). A divine creator implies a dependence of the created on a creator, and also a differentiation between creator and created. Human beings had a special role to play due to being made in God's image; this further emphasized their separation from the rest of creation. The development of capitalism promulgated the view that nature was a commodity or a resource to be used (Merchant, [1980] 1990:51–56; Morris, 1996:20). Although mechanistic theories did not go unchallenged, particularly by Vitalism, a radical analysis by Paracelsus of the activity in nature whereby matter and spirit were unified into an single, active, vital substance (Merchant, [1980] 1990:117), and also by the academic disciplines of botany and zoology (Sheldrake, 1990:41), Descartes' views have been influential. Historian Keith Thomas notes that Descartes' explicit aim was to make men lords and possessors of nature; other species were inert and lacking any spiritual dimension and this created an absolute break between man and the rest of nature, a 'transcendent God, outside his creation, symbolized the separation between spirit and nature'. Indeed, Thomas goes further by saying that 'Man stood to animal as did heaven to earth, soul to body, culture to nature' (Thomas, 1984:34–35). The result has been described as a spiritual alienation from the natural world. This work is not a history of this alienation, rather it seeks to examine nature religion as a spirituality that seeks to find a unity in Nature; it has emerged as a 'backlash' to the general historical and philosophical context that has separated mind from nature. As anthropologist Clifford Geertz has noted, our brains are in the world, 'And as for the world, it is not in our brains, our bodies, or our minds: they are, along with gods, verbs, rocks, and politics, in it' (Geertz, 2000:205).

Not surprisingly, the term 'nature' has a history. In early Greek philosophy, nature was the essence of a thing that made it behave the way it did (Morris, 1996:27). This oldest meaning the term was dominant into the thirteenth century when it denoted an essential quality, an innate character. A century later it came to mean a vital or inherent force that directed the world of human beings. At the time of the sixteenth and seventeenth centuries, nature was viewed as a physical power causing phenomena of the material world. The changing meaning of nature reflected the changing structure of society, and in the seventeenth century nature was observed and studied as the work of God. By the eighteenth century, with the establishment of a scientific world-view, nature was seen to be governed by laws; nature became increasingly synonymous with the material world and science was involved in interpreting its universal laws. At this time, nature was a clear authority: the laws of nature were the laws of reason. Nature had become rationalized (Marshall, 1995:222–223). Inevitably, there was a reaction to scientific rationalism and it took the form of the Romanticism movement with its view of nature as pastoral landscape and immanent mysticism. More recently, four contemporary discourses on nature have been outlined: the first is as a science where nature is seen in objective and abstract terms; the second is as an economic resource – nature is a source of productive wealth; the third views nature as a source of emotional identification, relationship and tradition; and the fourth is through nature mysticism whereby nature has spirit and is worthy of reverence and awe (Ivakhiv, 2001:37). Nature spiritualities draw on the last two discourses: nature is viewed as a source of emotional identification and spirituality; practitioners immerse themselves in nature.

Catherine Albanese calls the immersion in nature a 'quantum dance of religious syncretism' in which the different movements 'move freely together, mixing and matching, bowing to new partners'. The centrality of nature, Albanese observes, provides a language to express cosmology and belief; it forms the basis of understanding and practising a way of life; supplies material for ritual symbolism, as well as drawing a community together (Albanese, 1991:154–156). Nature religion does not exist as a definite and identifiable religious tradition such as Buddhism or Christianity, but, as Peter Beyer notes in his sociological analysis, the term refers to a range of religious and quasi-religious movements, groups and social networks in which practitioners consider nature to be the embodiment of divinity, sacredness, transcendence, or spiritual power (Beyer, 1998:11). Beyer, who analyses nature religion in terms of globalization, points out that nature religion comprises a counter-cultural strategy – a religious critique of institutionalized social structures and normal consciousness. He is concerned to show how nature religion fits into a global context through the use of 'nature' as a powerful counter-structural symbol representing resistance to dominant instrumental systems. Using anthropologist Victor Turner's ([1969] 1974) analysis of the anti-structural components of religious ritual, Beyer argues that nature religion is counter-structural – stressing oppositional aspects – rather than being anti-structural (1998:18). He notes certain critical features that characterize nature religion: a comparative resistance to institutionalization and legitimization in terms of identifiable socio-religious authorities and organization; a distrust of politically oriented power; a faith in charismatic and individual authority; a strong emphasis on individual path; a valorization of physical place; a this-worldly emphasis with a search for healing, personal vitality, and transformation of self; a strong experiential basis; a valuing of non-hierarchical community; a stress on holistic conceptions of reality; and a conditional optimism regarding human capacity and the future. This is certainly the case in radical Pagan protest against the destruction of nature for road development etc. However, magical consciousness is not necessarily counter-structural. Some movements within nature religion – such as the New Age – are alternatives to Christianity, incorporating many mystical elements of Christianity, and may be said to be supportive of mainstream social structure, particularly regarding capitalistic enterprise.

Also viewing nature religion in terms of globalization, anthropologist Piers Vitebsky, in a comparison of Sora shamanism in tribal India and ethnic revival shamanism in Arctic Siberia, claims that indigenous knowledge loses its holistic world-view when appropriated by New Age neo-shamanists; when transplanted it becomes global rather than local cosmological knowledge (2003:295–296). An alternative approach is to see nature religion not as a counter-cultural movement, or as an expression of a form of global knowledge, but as an expanded form of consciousness that is common to all humans. I shall argue that if nature religion is studied in terms of magical consciousness then holism, a central defining feature of indigenous knowledge, is not lost but just expressed in a different cultural and physical context.

Magical Consciousness

So, a connection with nature concerns less a form of counter-cultural resistance – although this may be the case in more radical forms of Pagan protest – and more a development of magical consciousness. Using the term 'magical consciousness' creates a definition that is doubly ideologically loaded – both 'magic' and 'consciousness' are broad concepts that are notoriously difficult to define. Facing a similar dilemma over a definition of 'globalization', the historian A.G. Hopkins notes that holistic concepts may be a source of confusion as they invariably carry conflicting ideological messages, but abolishing them would not remove the difficulty. He recommends that when using general terms to describe broad issues, definitions should be explicitly stated and framed to match the purpose in hand. With this in mind I shall define magical consciousness as a specific perception of the world common to practitioners of nature religion. Before that, however, it will be necessary briefly to consider both consciousness and magic.

Although consciousness has been of modern philosophical concern since Descartes' *cogito* 'I think therefore I am' shifted the focus from the cosmos to the individual human being (Rapport and Overing, 2000:65), a single definition of consciousness is evasive. The study of consciousness is problematic, not only for neuroscience and psychology due to its subjective and constantly changing character (Edelman, 1992:111), but also for anthropology, which has only belatedly come to find consciousness relevant, having taken it 'largely for granted, neglecting – even, perhaps, denying – its significance and relevance' (Cohen and Rapport, 1995:1). As John and Jean Comaroff have pointed out, anthropologists usually study consciousness and its transformations by examining its effects or expressions; its social and symbolic manifestations as *conscience collective*. Rarely is the nature of consciousness in the making, or its historicity examined. Consciousness itself is seldom scrutinized:

> Sometimes it is regarded as the mere reflection of a reality beyond human awareness, sometimes as the site of creativity and agency. But, almost invariably, 'consciousness' is treated as a substantive 'mode of' or 'for' the world, as so much narrative content without form. (Comaroff and Comaroff, 1992:236–237).

The classic work of psychologist William James (1890 [1950]) indicates why consciousness has been seen to be so formless and so difficult to pin down. James's notion of mind as a 'theatre of simultaneous possibilities' views consciousness as a process that compares, selects and suppresses data, much as a sculptor works on a block of stone, extricating one interpretation from the rest. He writes that '[m]y world is but one in a million alike embedded, alike real to those who may abstract them. How different must be the worlds in the consciousness of ant, cuttle-fish, or crab!' (ibid.:288–289). Consciousness, says James, is also like a stream or river (ibid.:239); it is a continuous and always changing process. The work of neuroscientist Gerald Edelman, in *Bright Air, Brilliant Fire*, draws on and develops James's ideas: consciousness depends on unique history and embodiment, it is constructed through social interaction, and meaning takes shape in terms of concepts that depend on categorizations (1992:170). The picture that emerges from these views is that there is a multiplicity of consciousnesses, or aspects of consciousness, rather than a single state.[2] The notion of consciousness as a stream of possibilities both overcomes the Cartesian emphasis on mind and reflective reasoning aspects, and opens up possibilities for alternative views of consciousness as process that is inclusive of body, as well as being more expansive to include other beings in nature, and even perhaps being an intrinsic quality of a wider universe.

Notwithstanding, anthropologist Michael Harner, who explored South American Indian shamanism and developed 'Core Shamanism' as a method that synthesized shamanic techniques for Westerners, differentiates between what he terms an 'ordinary state of consciousness' (OSC) and a 'shamanic state of consciousness' (SSC), referring to 'ordinary' and 'nonordinary' reality respectively. The shaman can move between states of consciousness at will (Harner, [1980] 1990: xix). Harner's distinction of OSC and SSC for Westerners belies the complexities of consciousness – such as aspects arising from imagination, emotion, cognition, and perception – and that people, whether shamans or not, are constantly shifting effortlessly from awareness to awareness or aspect to aspect; it is not always so easy to categorize consciousness in this manner.[3] This is not to deny that a shaman is nonetheless a specialist in one part of this process as a mediator of different realities.

Turning to magic we will see that it means many different things to different people. Magic, as anthropologist Ariel Glucklich points out, can refer to a moon-swept landscape, love, music, the occult, the extraordinary that defies the laws of nature, and gross superstition among many other things. It is, he claims, a 'decadent hodge podge of ideas from many sources'. We use the term so much, Glucklich argues, that it means too much and therefore hardly anything at all; we need a clear and definite understanding (1997:vii, 4–9). Historically, magic had a negative association in Roman times being viewed as a system that utilized powerful forces to control nature. Seen to be outside the ordinary course of nature in the fifth century (Flint 1993:3), it was rehabilitated in an exalted sense in the Hermetic tradition of the Renaissance when it was seen as a way to contact higher powers or God and was associated with neoplatonism (Solomon and Higgins, 1996:122). Magic, under this guise, was 'natural magic' or 'sympathetic magic' and involved the secret virtues of plants, stones and talismans for drawing down the powers of stars (Yates, [1964] 1991:2, 22). This was a form of esotericism based on the view that there were correspondences between the natural and celestial worlds, both seen and unseen (Faivre 1994:10–13; see p.29). During the Reformation, demonic magic, which was seen to rely on supernatural intelligences, was sharply demarcated from 'true' religion and science. The aspect of control – using preternatural or supernatural means to gain control over nature – was opposed to the religious attitude of reverence: an inclination to trust and to be in awe of powers superior to humanity. Magic is also concerned with the ritual working of unseen (occult) or subtle levels of reality in order to create change in the everyday world – such as casting a spell or raising energy to direct to a specific intention (see pp.29–30). Magic is, as Pagan Margot Adler observes in her influential study of Paganism (she calls it Neo–Paganism) in America, a convenient word for a whole collection of techniques that involve the mind, including the mobilization of the imagination and the ability to visualize; magic is a knowledge about how emotion and concentration can be used to change consciousness ([1979] 1986:8).

My use of the term 'magic' here concerns an aspect of consciousness that is primarily natural rather than supernatural or mystical, although it may be interpreted in those ways socially or culturally. A magical 'state of mind' must be experienced; it has an intrinsically subjective and sensory quality that is embodied and intuitive rather than purely reflective and intellectual, although the reflective and intellectual may be engaged *with* the intuitive and the embodied as there is no radical opposition. I want to make it clear that my use of the term 'magical consciousness' is not an attempt to reify an aspect of consciousness but rather to draw attention to a certain dimension of human experience. In my focus on magical consciousness I do not wish to suggest that magical consciousness should be opposed to rationality, neither do I want to create a dualism between science and magic (or religion) or between reason and imagination, but rather to highlight a part – or strand, or thread, or 'expanded' awareness – that is an important component of the whole process of consciousness central to how many practitioners of nature spiritualities experience the world. It is the development of this type of expansive awareness – one that actively develops the imagination in making connections between other beings both seen and unseen – that constitutes the basis of magical practice. Above all, magical consciousness concerns the awareness of the interrelatedness of all things in the world.

Anthropologist Bruce Kapferer, in his study of sorcery among Sinhalese Buddhists in Sri Lanka, argues that the magicality of human beings is in embodied, passionate relationships with others and in the way that realities are constructed; sorcery (as a psycho-social expression) accentuates vital dimensions of the ways that humans explicitly or implicitly construct their realities:

> Human life is magical in the sense that human beings span the space that may otherwise individuate them or separate them from others. Their magical conjunction with other human beings in the world – imaginative, creative, and destructive – is at the heart of human existence. (Kapferer,1997:2).

Magical conjunction, I suggest, is magical consciousness; it is not a category of thing in itself but an aspect of a particular experience of consciousness and a way of ordering reality. Magical consciousness is a dimension of human thought and action; it is not primarily individual nor can it be divorced from the wider social or environmental context – it is a participatory and holistic way of thinking.

Psychologist, biologist and anthropologist Gregory Bateson was a holistic thinker seeking an understanding of the human part in the whole living world (Rapport and Overing, 2000:102); he sought to overcome the Cartesian split between mind and body, and in *Mind and Nature: a necessary unity* (1985) he expressed a relational view of mind. Bateson thought that the mind should be seen as immanent in the whole system of organism–environment relations in which humans are enmeshed. The brain was in relation to the surrounding environment and the mind (as a processor of information) extended outwards into its environment along multiple sensory pathways; the perceiver was involved in his or her environment. Thus the mind was not just involved with the working of the human brain; it was viewed in much wider terms as a way of coming to understand the world by being in the world. Bateson tried to find a language of relationship to describe the living world as a dynamic reality. He thought that logic, a method for describing linear systems of cause and effect, was unsuitable for the description of biological patterns and that metaphor was the language of nature. Bateson attempted to find the underlying pattern in the structure of nature and the structure of mind in 'an ecology of mind'. The mind is concerned with thoughts and ideas about the world; it classifies and maps things. Mental maps organize connections and differences between things in a familiar pattern; and patterns connect. Bateson called this 'ideation'. By contrast, 'abduction' was the process of recognizing the patterns between different things through metaphor, dreams, allegories and poetry. Abductive systems link the body and the ecosystem: a meta pattern is shared (Bateson, 1985:16–17, 157–158; Rapport and Overing, 2000:102–108; Ingold, 2000:16–18).

Although Bateson did not discuss magic directly, his work on abductive systems employing dreams, poetry and metaphor links closely with conceptions of magic as relational thinking. He believed that knowledge always existed surrounded by an unknown that was penetrable to the ambitious investigator. Ideas could be drawn from many disciplines and he 'respected the mystic's approach to life as much as the scientist's' (Heims, 1977:150, cited in Lipset, 1982:201).[4] Creating relationship – in physical or spirit form – is the basis of magical consciousness. A de-centred part of the process of consciousness that is receptive to other beings both seen and unseen, magical consciousness is a perception that is able to move away from a primary focus on the individual; it is a consciousness that is aware of connections between phenomena and it is shaped by psycho-social experience and world-view. Magical consciousness may be explained in terms of mysticism, an experience of vastness, sometimes experienced as a union with an ultimate reality, cosmic consciousness, or God; it is also explained in more animistic terms. Ecologist and phenomenological philosopher David Abram says that the human mind is instilled and provoked by the 'tensions and participations between the human body and the animate earth'. He asserts that by acknowledging an inner psychological world and the surrounding world, psychology is loosened from the strictly human sphere to meet with other minds in oak, fir, hawk, snake, stone, rain, and salmon; all aspects of a place make up a particular state of mind – a 'place-specific intelligence' shared by all beings that live in the area (1997:262).

Magical consciousness requires a shift in perception from a so-called normal perception; this is akin to what the anthropologist Stanley Tambiah, drawing on philosopher Lévy-Bruhl, has termed 'participation'. An ancient construct in Western philosophy and theology, the term 'participation' accounts for the togetherness of diverse elements – how one thing participates in one or several others (Saler, 2003:50). Tambiah says that participation can be represented as occurring when 'persons, groups, animals, places, and natural phenomena are in a relation of contiguity, and translate that relation into one of existential immediacy and contact and shared affinities' (1991:107). Participation, according to Tambiah, uses the language of solidarity, unity, holism and continuity in space and time; it also engenders a sense of encompassing cosmic oneness (ibid.:109). Participation is contrary to causality, defined by Tambiah as quintessentially represented by the categories, rules and methods of positivistic science and discursive mathematico–logical reasoning (ibid.:105). Analytically separate, participation and causality intertwine in many combinations and Tambiah is careful to emphasize that they do not form a dualism; he points out various contexts and discourses where one or the other mode predominates, the different modes becoming increasingly difficult to separate in the scientific theory-making branch of modern physics (ibid:110). In fact, if consciousness is viewed as a process the problems of dualistic thinking are avoided. My experience on the Snowdonian hillside, already mentioned, is but one example of the participation required in developing magical consciousness. Experiences such as these are said to bring about a transformation of perception; changes may occur through the meeting of other practitioners for rituals, meditation, as well as specific practices of healing or environmental protest, for example. In the chapters that follow more examples will be given.

Part of the process of developing a magical consciousness is learning to see the natural world as vital and alive – seeing it in animistic terms. Edward Tylor used the term 'animism' to refer to the 'anima' or soul as the essence of a being or the 'animating principle'. For Tylor, animism was the earliest form of religion, coexisting with magic in 'primitive' societies (Tambiah, 1991:49–50). More recent anthropologists, such as Tim Ingold, take a phenomenological approach to animism, seeing it as a world-view envisaged from within a 'total field of relations whose unfolding is tantamount to the process of life itself'. Taking his cue from Bateson and drawing on ethnographic work on the hunter-gatherer Cree people of north-east Canada who say that the entire world, not just the human world, is saturated with powers of agency and intentionality. Ingold asserts, like Bateson, that mind should be seen as immanent in the whole system of the organism–environment relations;[5] the whole organism-in-its-environment is the point of departure of an indivisible totality (2001:13–19). There is no separation between mind and nature; mind is not added onto life but is immanent in intentional engagement of living beings within their environments (ibid.:107–108). David Abram takes this further when he argues that 'perception, in its depths, is truly participatory' (1997:91). He defines magic in its most primordial sense as participating in a world of multiple intelligences with:

> the intuition that every form one perceives – from swallow swooping overhead to the fly on a blade of grass, and indeed the blade of grass itself – is an *experiencing form, an entity with its own predilections and sensations, albeit sensations that are very different from our own.* (Abram,1997:9–10).

Abram draws on Merleau-Ponty's phenomenology and makes four points to illustrate this magical animistic world-view: firstly, perception is inherently interactive and participatory – there is a reciprocity between perceiver and perceived; secondly, spontaneous pre-conceptual experience is not dualistic in terms of animate/inanimate but forms relative distinctions between diverse forms of animateness; thirdly, perceptual reciprocity between sensing bodies and animate expressive landscape engenders and supports linguistic reciprocity – language is rooted in non-verbal exchange; fourthly, human languages are informed by structures of human body, human community and more-than-human terrain. Language is not specifically human: 'Experientially considered, language is no more the special property of the human organism than it is an expression of the animate earth that enfolds us' (Abram, 1997:89–90).

In views such as this magic is essentially a natural phenomenon, not mystical or metaphysical; it expresses a conceptual and perceptual world-view that creates meaningful connections between phenomena. To an extent, this is what Carl Jung meant when he said that, 'No man lives within his own psychic sphere like a snail in its shell, separated from everybody else, but is connected with his fellow-men by his unconscious humanity.' Jung saw this as a collective unconscious, a living reality; the pre-conscious aspect of things and a reservoir from which to draw – it was nature not something mystical. Here Jung draws on the Greek definition of psyche which, according to Aristotle, meant the 'principle of life' that animates a living thing. Psyche was a wider concept than mind or consciousness and was equivalent to soul, the 'first principle of living things' and the functional state of a living creature (Morris, 1994:44–46). For Jung, the psyche occurs in living bodies and in matter, but the original feeling of unity with the unconscious psyche has been lost due to the conscious mind becoming more and more the victim of what Jung saw as its own discriminating activity (Sabini, 2002:14, 72, 82).

Practitioners of nature religion may look back to a time of unity with nature, and psychologist Brian Bates's historically-based novel *The Way of Wyrd* ([1983]

1996) has been influential in this respect.[6] This work is an introduction to a shamanistic inspirited nature as told through a story of the initiation of Wat Brand, a Christian scribe, by Wulf, an Anglo-Saxon sorcerer. Wulf tells Wat that the soul is the essence of wyrd and is present in everything – even rocks have soul (psyche), the principle of life. Wat questions Wulf:

> 'Rocks do not breathe, Wulf. Surely then, they cannot have soul?' Wulf watched me steadily, through narrowed eyes.
> 'Rocks breathe,' he said evenly. 'But each breath lasts longer than the life and death for a man. Hills and mountains breathe, but each breath lasts a thousand human lifetimes.'
> (Bates, [1983] 1996:111)

Bates writes that the original Anglo-Saxon form of the word 'weird' meant 'destiny', 'power' and 'magic' or 'prophetic knowledge'. He points out that in Anglo-Saxon times all aspects of the world were seen to be in constant flux and motion, and a dynamic and pervasive world of spirits coexisted with the material world. The spirits were manifestations of the forces of wyrd and were invisible to most humans ([1983] 1996:6–7). Life force, or vital energy, permeated everything in this world-view; it was manipulated by the sorcerer, as the mediator of the spirit world and the human world, who 'connected individual human functioning with the pulse of earth rhythm' (ibid.:13).

Bates sees wyrd as a path to knowledge – of psychological and spiritual liberation; it is a way of being that challenges dominant notions of body, mind and spirit. All aspects of the world are seen to be in relationship in this view, and the totality is conceived of as a web. The web of wyrd is a view of the world conceived as a relationship of patterns (ibid.:12) and it offers a metaphor for connection – a European model for a cyclical process more visible in non-Western contexts. Bates himself likens it to the Chinese notion of Yin and Yang, but it also has parallels with much African thought in the sense that the material world is not seen as inert but vital. Bates employs a psychological approach to shamanism that is very popular amongst practitioners but problematic for some academics; I shall discuss this further in Chapter 8.

Theoretical Approach

As I have already indicated, magic is a difficult and complex area to study; it is fraught with different conceptions, misconceptions, prejudice and a certain amount of ambiguity. This is all the more reason to examine magical consciousness as an aspect of human thinking. I have chosen to focus on consciousness because it is so fundamental to how we come to know the world, as well as to conceptions of our place in nature, and it has not been dealt with adequately by anthropologists. Studying magical consciousness raises interesting problems for scholars in the social sciences. Western science has been shaped by the dominant philosophical theme of rationalism, a tradition stemming from Plato, which holds that knowledge is based on reason, and is associated with Descartes who had an ecstatic visionary experience during which the nature of the universe was revealed to him. Ironically, this convinced him that his mission in life was to seek truth through reason and he reformulated the rationalist tradition to argue that knowledge was derived from rational reflection on the world, rather than from empirical observation.[7] As noted previously, he adopted a mechanistic conception of the world and thought that ideas such as 'God', perfection, and infinity were derived from thinking itself. For Descartes, the mind was associated with the immaterial soul, and was a thinking substance capable of self-consciousness; the body, on the other hand, had materiality and was part of a mechanistic universe. Without a soul the human body was an automaton responding to inner and outer stimulation according to the rules built into its mechanism: it was without consciousness, and under the control of its emotions and external stimuli. By contrast, a soul without a body had consciousness, but only of innate ideas lacking sensory impressions of the world (Morris, 1991:6–14). Equating the mind with soul and thought, Descartes claimed that the mind produced ideas out of its own potentialities through a rational reflection on the world. Descartes' rationalism was enforced by the eighteenth-century Enlightenment when the 'light of reason' was to be shed on the dark mysteries of religious traditions: scientific research would overcome magic and superstition.[8] Magic came to be separated from both religion and science.

The split between magic, religion and science was reinforced by the dichotomy of mind and body, as well as self and other. Cartesian philosophy is responsible for the radical dualism between mind and body so prevalent in Western thought.[9] Despite the fact that since the Enlightenment there has been a repudiation of the ultra-rationalism of Descartes through an emphasis on experience,[10] his dualism of mind and body has had a profound effect on Western philosophy and thinking making it hard to envision alternatives.

Anthropologist Geoffrey Samuel claims that in modern Western societies the mind–body and self–other dichotomies are deeply entrenched (1990:135). Referring to the West African and African–American *orisha* cults, where possession of devotees by the spirit *orisha* is a central part of the practice, he notes that the language of immanent gods and spirits found in such cults is not completely unfamiliar to modern Westerners because it formed a way of thinking at one stage in European thought. However, Westerners have lost the ability to understand this kind of discourse, making it 'difficult to understand other cultures where such a language is still spoken' (ibid.:134). How do we analyse magical consciousness as part of a wider process of consciousness when our structures of thought have been shaped by a rationalism that does not recognize magical consciousness as a legitimate form of knowledge?

Facing similar problems, religious studies scholar Adrian Ivakhiv, in this study of pilgrims and politics in the New Age centres of Glastonbury and Sedona (2001), avoids a sterile dichotomy between, on the one hand, a scientific view which questions the 'reality' of contact with spirits of the land and spirits of ancestors (by questioning whether ideas about spirits are a screen for the projection of fantasies and unconscious desires) and, on the other hand, a religious view that totally accepts that particular landscapes harbour numinous powers experienced as real energies, by adopting a Geertzian hermeneutic–phenomenological position:[11]

> both of the opposite poles of these paired dichotomies emerge out of an interactive web that is tangled and blurred at its very origins. This is a tangled web within which the world is ever being created – shaped and constituted through the imaginative, discursive, spatial, and material practices of humans reflectively immersed within an active and animate, more-than-human world. It is a tangled web of selfhood and otherness, identities and differences, relations both natural and cultural; a web through which circulate meanings, images, desires, and power itself (the power to act, to imagine, to define, impose, and resist). I will argue and try to demonstrate that the Earth – the actual places, landscapes, and geographies – and imagination – the ways we conceive, narrate, and 'image' the world – are thoroughly intertwined within this tangled web of power – and desire-laden relations. (Ivakhiv, 2001:4)

Noting that science and mystical/religious means of knowledge production have different methods and draw on disparate ideas, he claims that both are a means of interpreting a reality which

> remains a protean tangled web, a reality whose nature is not known directly, but which is always mediated by signs and interpretative traditions. Scientists, scholars, New Agers, religious believers, postmodern philosophers are all interpreting subjects who spin webs of significance and meaning; these webs are conditioned by 'effectivities' or 'action capabilities' and desires and intentionalities both conscious and unconscious. (Ivakhiv, 2001:229–230)

Ivakhiv gives no guidelines on further analysis of this 'protean tangled web' and it remains unclear how specific meanings have arisen.

By contrast, Samuel has introduced a theoretical framework for social and cultural anthropology that reflects pluralistic and historical Western scientific thinking, and which is in harmony with a magical relational theme. His 'Multimodal Framework' (MMF) seeks to deliberately dissolve Cartesian dichotomies of mind and body, as well as individual and society: 'In philosophical language, the MMF is neither a form of "individualism" nor a form of "holism" (or "collectivism") as normally understood' (Samuel, 1990:8); it offers explanations in terms of both by seeking a new language within which scientific theories may be framed. Samuel's framework is anticipated in Aristotle's metaphysics, a higher order of science which connected different experiences – such as art and reasoning – in a scientific study of Being (Johnson, 2000:180–181). The MMF also covers informal and non-scientific knowledge where knowledge is not something contained in the mind but a 'patterning of mind and body as a totality' (Samuel, 1990:6). Rational thought is not opposed to 'symbolic' thought – there are a series of modes or states of human consciousness, all of which are rational and symbolic, individual and cultural (ibid.:37). Samuel's argument is for a new social science theoretical framework to reflect a pluralistic ideal of many ways of knowing – from commonsense, informal and non-scientific knowledge implicit in daily activities, to modes of operating within so-called traditional societies – that have been hard to incorporate effectively within Western rationalistic modes of knowing (ibid.:3–7).

Samuel is aware that any framework image chosen will necessarily impose some conceptual structure on reality, selectively including some aspects while ignoring others, but feels that the anthropologist Clifford Geertz's notion of a 'web' in which 'man is an animal suspended in webs of significance he himself has spun' (1973:5) is a reasonable one. Thus Samuel's model does not reject the interpretative tradition but sets it within a broader conceptual schema that seeks to break out of the 'hermeneutic circle' of meanings. Seeing hermeneutics as one of a variety of bodies of knowledge operating in the world, rather than a single all-encompassing and unified system, Samuel also uses the general metaphor of a web, but his intention is to provide an alternative explanatory framework. The MMF is a framework for the systematic testing of ideas (ibid.:26) and overcomes the problems inherent within the interpretative tradition of incoherence of general perspective (ibid.:31).

Whilst noting that webs are not purely individual – 'once spun, they take on a life of their own' – nor are they just social – 'they have spinners' (Scholte, 1984:540) – Samuel searches for a conceptual space that is neither individual nor social but within which webs might exist:

> These processes of spinning and being caught happen in time (through history), and if we are to describe them adequately, we should give time and explicit place within our image. Rather than speaking of 'webs of significance', therefore, I suggest that we view the structures of meaning and feeling in which and through which we live as patterns formed by the currents in the course of a vast stream or river. The direction of the stream is the flow of time. Geertz's 'webs' now correspond to semi-permanent currents, or to use William Blake's term, 'vortices', that have become established in the onward flow of the river. (Samuel, 1990:11).

At any point in the stream, which represents the dynamic and processual nature of life, we can draw a cross-section to see a structure of 'webs' laid across the surface. This model enables a 'particle and wave' approach developed using ideas inspired by Einstein's theory of relativity; it incorporates multi-dimensions – both 'stream' and 'web' are different perspectives on a wider whole[12] (cf. Grof 1993; Capra 1996; Glucklich 1997; Nettle 2001).

Thus the MMF also goes beyond the original non-scientific hermeneutic approach of Geertz; it is an approach that not only makes possible an examination of participation as a form of magical consciousness but one that also allows analysis of the discourses that have shaped contemporary thought and practice in nature religion. Magical consciousness, as examined within this framework, is represented (in Western cultures) as an informal way of knowing. In this view, knowledge is a patterning of mind and body in relation to a wider perceptual field. 'Nature religion', as a definable category, represents many eco-spiritual practices that recreate a relationship with nature. If we cut a cross-section through Samuel's theoretical river at the present point in history we can see a variety of practices shaped and informed by esotericism, romanticism and environmentalism; these are semi-permanent currents in the course of the process of life and will be explored in the following chapters. These currents provide the structure through which magical consciousness is experienced.

The question of whether nature religion is an eco-spirituality is one that specifically addresses questions concerning the place of human beings in nature, as well as the fundamental basis of consciousness. A comparison of these currents reveals inherent contradictions concerning religiosity and mystery (a discourse of esotericism) and ecology and connectedness (an organismic discourse), of which the paradoxes and implications will be examined in Chapter 8. Nature religion appears to be a 'widespread cultural response to the decay of main-line religions and to a widely felt awareness of ecological crisis' (Pearson, Roberts and Samuel, 1998:1). However, all is not as simple as it seems. Catherine Albanese, in an examination of Ralph Waldo Emerson's book *Nature* (1836), notes that within this work there is a confusion between a view of matter as 'really real', an embodiment of Spirit and the 'garment of God', and a view of matter as illusion, an unreality, a trap from which it is necessary to escape. In other words, nature might be sacramental, or it might be the subject of erroneous perception (Albanese, 1991:80–82).

This underlying tension, Albanese shows, is masked by Emerson, who moves between 'Nature Real' and 'Nature Illusory', 'telling us it isn't so even as he tells us that it is' (ibid.:83). The basis of the problem lies in the mysticism of nature, the occult union between humans and nature. Nature shows a correspondence between visible things and human thought, and can train the understanding to conform to the shape of things; it can also teach a moral law or discipline – nature is both mother and teacher. But Emerson doubts that nature exists outwardly and claims that the best and happiest moments of life are the 'delicious awakenings of the higher powers' and the 'reverential withdrawing of nature before its God' (ibid.:83–84). This absorption in nature is a form of idealism leading to human mastery over nature. Control over the self and the environment renders human beings divine, and results in 'Harmony between microcosm (man) and macrocosm (nature). This reveals humans to be the true gods that they are; "lower nature" is substituted for "higher nature", (ibid.:87).

There is a blurring or masking – an underlying tension – similar to Emerson's that lurks beneath many ideologies within nature religion discourse. The notion that nature is 'really real', the embodiment of Spirit, is pervasive; it is a notion that arises from the idealist tradition, stemming from the work of certain Renaissance magicians, who combined neoplatonism with a Christian interpretation; focusing on an inner gnosis, they saw a spiritual knowledge of nature as part of a mystical union with a larger deity. This is influential today in the veneration of a Goddess who is immanent in the world. Not concerned with control or domination of the natural world, the Goddess stands for incorporation with nature. However, this view fosters a monotheistic and anthropocentric approach that is inherently non-ecological. Countering this idealist position is a more ecological approach. The tension implicit within these different approaches is everywhere present in nature religion.

Plan of the Book

The following chapter gives an overview of the numerous spiritualities that make up nature religion; it also points to some of the underlying historical influences of esotericism, romanticism and environmentalism that have currency in everyday contemporary practice. This is followed in Chapter 3 by a more detailed look at how some practitioners identify with and create relationships and connections with nature. Catching a glimpse through a New Age talk on Deep Ecology at 'Alternatives', a forum for talks on mind, body and spirit held in St James's Church, Piccadilly, London; the experiences and thoughts of a Pagan priestess and Druid; a workshop on the spirit of place held at Atlantis, the well-known occult book shop in London; the work of a New Age healer in Norfolk, East Anglia; radical Pagan protest against environmental destruction; and finally, a shamanic drumming group ritual to contact ancestors, this chapter aims to present an intimate portrayal of some ideas and attitudes to nature; it is inevitably selective – a vignette through some of the multiplicity of approaches.

Chapter 4 looks at ways in which practitioners locate themselves through the themes of place, ancestors and tradition. It compares the work of two shamans: the first, a Romany gypsy *chovihano*, acts as a medium for gypsy ancestors and other spiritual beings. Like other mediums – such as the Victorian Spiritualists (Owen

1989) and the Sora shamans of south-east India (Vitebsky 1993) – he is a channel for the world of spirits. A relationship with the spirits of nature and the land is said to be an integral part of life for many Romany gypsies: in Romany lore *kam*, the sun is father, *shon*, the moon is mother, *puvus*, the earth grandmother, while *ravnos*, the sky, grandfather. The second shaman, a Pagan environmental educator, claims Celtic ancestry but chooses to work with what he sees as a variety of traditions of the land to link people with place. In this Chapter I also use the example of a late Bronze Age timber circle popularly known as 'Seahenge', which emerged from the sea on the north Norfolk coast whilst I was conducting fieldwork in the region, to look at some different attitudes towards what was seen by many to be a sacred monument on a par with Stonehenge. I examine the dissension between local residents, archaeologists, and practitioners of nature spiritualities caused by its appearance.

Dealing with the process of transformation of cognition through magical consciousness, Chapter 5 draws on the philosophical and theological notion of participation, the term coined by philosopher Lucien Lévy-Bruhl and developed by anthropologist Stanley Tambiah to examine consciousness. The main purpose underlying many of the varying practices of nature religion is the transformation of consciousness – this might be to see the world as vital, conscious and interactive – and various examples of this process are given, including relating to spirits in a New Age centre, shamanic journeying using Michael Harner's Core Shamanism technique, and a Romany gypsy healing ritual. Healing involves restoring, or creating, a participatory perception, one that links the person within a wider animated cosmos; it orders and realigns the universe, essentially creating spiritual balance and harmony in the world. According to Richard Katz, with reference to the Kalahari !Kung of South Africa, healing involves a process of transition toward meaning, balance, wholeness and connectedness between individuals and their environments. Healing is more than curing, it seeks to establish health on the physical, psychological, social and spiritual levels, and it integrates the individual, the group, the environment and the cosmos (Katz, 1982:33). !Kung ritual shares many affinities with Romany gypsy ritual as portrayed here.

Specific case studies illustrating how magical consciousness is developed through myth is the focus of Chapter 6. The old European myth of the Wild Hunt is associated with 'soul-ravening' chases, and its origins lie in the belief held by many in the ninth to the fourteenth centuries that during their sleep their spirits were snatched away to ride in a ghostly cavalcade (Hutton, 1991:307). The power of this myth is connected with the urban/rural divide probably created with the rise of the ancient city-state when humans became separated from the natural world, as nature came to represent 'the wild', the chaotic antithesis of ordered society. The mythology of the Wild Hunt draws on notions of a primordial ancient and 'untainted' power as a framework for experiencing magical consciousness.

Utilizing a common folk theme of a god or goddess hunting for souls, this myth illustrates the rhythm of life and death and a certain form of transformation; how practitioners interpret it is the focus of this chapter.

Chapter 7 continues the theme of participation through an examination of the role of fairy stories and nature spirits in creating a sense of being indigenous – of being related to place. David Abram says that language for oral peoples is not a human invention but a 'gift of the land itself'. Language arose not only as a means of attunement between people but also between humans and an animated landscape (1997:236). Does nature religion encourage 'thinking with nature', knowing the land though its stories? Three case studies – of Romany gypsy shamanic workshops, Reclaiming Witch Camp, and the work of a shaman environmental educator – will be discussed in relation to the problematic notions of tradition, authenticity and being indigenous.

As indicated earlier, there is a paradox within nature religion involving a contradiction between a discourse of connectedness and a discourse of esotericism – both are semi-permanent currents within the general 'nature religion' stream – and Chapter 8 raises the thorny question of whether nature spiritualities are ecological. Mostly originating within the Western Hermetic tradition rather than any indigenous practices, nature religion has strong neoplatonic tendencies and these influence contemporary attitudes and practice. There is an implicit monotheism – principally seen in a veneration of the Goddess – and an anthropocentrism, a human-centred focus on the individual in relation to the cosmos. Neither attitude is ecological; this chapter discusses some of the resulting complexities and paradoxes and also raises problematic issues for the academic study of magical consciousness.

The final chapter seeks to locate nature religion within a wider perspective, largely in terms of what it means to those who live in the city. Nature religion is most often practised by city dwellers. Reflecting on nature religion in terms of globalization and postmodernism, this chapter suggests that the holistic world-view of magical consciousness is not necessarily solely a reaction to social fragmentation; it can also be seen as an innate expression of human consciousness that is manifested differently in varying socio-cultural contexts. The persistent underlying theme of this book is that magical consciousness is primarily natural rather than supernatural.

Notes

1. 'Chakras', which refer to the subtle and arcane body in Hindu and Buddhist yogic traditions, and 'ley lines' (developed by Alfred Watkins in the 1920s:

see Chapter 4) are two different but broadly sympathetic esoteric symbolic systems.

2. This view is contested by psychologist Susan Blackmore; she says that the notion of self, as well as consciousness, is an illusion (2002:26–29).

3. Harner claims that people in shamanic cultures do not make such a distinction between different states of consciousness, but that Westerners are unsophisticated from a shamanic point of view, and that in teaching shamanic methods a clear distinction between states of consciousness has to be made ([1980] 1990:48).

4. Alan Watts, the student and theologian of oriental mysticism, was involved with Bateson's research project on the communication of multiple messages (Lipset, 1982:201).

5. Following Bateson ([1972] 2000), Ingold argues that mind and ecology are situated in relations between the brain and the surrounding environment. Bateson saw mind as immanent in the whole system of organism–environment relations, while Ingold goes on to substitute 'life' for 'mind' (2000:16–18; and see Chapter 5).

6. The work is based on a manuscript describing medical remedies from the Anglo-Saxon period, but probably recorded in the tenth century. According to Bates, each remedy had a plant-based concoction to be applied to the patient, a set of rituals associated with the treatment, and an incantation, spell, or charm to be sung as part of the treatment. He used these medical remedies as a basis for building a picture of the world of an Anglo-Saxon sorcerer ([1983] 1996:10).

7. Descartes was against the empirical tradition that saw all genuine knowledge as being based on sense experience and understood by observation and experiment.

8. In the eighteenth century 'the unconscious' came to be seen as something separate from the conscious; it developed an aura of being in opposition to consciousness. It was not until the nineteenth century and Schopenhauer (1788–1860) that what we now call the unconscious became a focus of study. Schopenhauer spoke about the will as an unconscious striving or impulse, anticipating the work of Sigmund Freud and his theory of the unconscious (Morris 1991). It was Freud's pupil Carl Jung who developed a more spiritual interpretation of the unconscious – not as id (an unconscious biologically given process struggling for conscious expression) but as a psycho-spiritual integration (analytical psychology). During the period 1914–1918 Jung experienced a psychological breakdown, and for the rest of his life he sought explanations for what had happened to him, trying to understand the images and symbols that had arisen from his unconscious (Stevens [1990] 1991:7).

9. This dualism between mind and body is not apparent in Hinduism, Buddhism or Taoism where mind and body may be seen as different parts of an interacting whole, not as radically separate.

10. Brian Morris has commented that some scientists repudiate reason entirely as metaphysics, whilst most emphasize a synthesis of reason and experience (personal communication, 19 September 2002).

11. Hermeneutics – deriving from the Greek term *hermeneia* – is the theory and practice of interpretation; it is the basis for a science of the human as distinct from the natural sciences. The concept has been further developed within phenomenology, and usually carries the implication that 'whilst some interpretations are better than others, none can ever be final' (Urmson and Rée, 1991:131).

12. Geoffrey Samuel, as a trained physicist, does not make this connection in terms of physics (personal communication). Ariel Glucklich is in agreement with this position but does note that while the complex mathematical theories of relativity and quantum mechanics have been translated too quickly into sensational justification of occult ideas, this new scientific thinking does provide some tools for the *mental* experience of magical consciousness, but only in conjunction with anthropological and philosophical methods (Glucklich, 1997:72–77).

Nature Religion and Underlying Influences

As Catherine Albanese has astutely noted, tracking the quantum energies of late twentieth-century nature religion will replace experience with 'ideal' construction (1991:155); indeed, the imposition of any conceptual framework will inevitably be selective, emphasizing some aspect while marginalizing or ignoring others. However, this chapter gives an overview of broad categories of nature spiritualities that many practitioners themselves use; it also introduces important underlying influences of esotericism, occultism, romanticism and environmentalism. This material is invaluable for a deeper understanding of the nature religion stream, as conceptualized using Samuel's theoretical framework.

Component Spiritualities

Paganism

Contemporary Paganism is a complex blend of polytheism and animism; it has its roots, like the New Age, in Hermetism. The origins of the term 'pagan' are contested; it was said originally to refer to a 'country dweller' or 'rustic', as opposed to a follower of Christianity, the dominant urban faith; or it was a term for a civilian, a person not enrolled in the Christian army; or a follower of the older religious tradition of the pagus, a local unit of government (Hutton, 1999:4). It has recently been utilized as an umbrella category to describe a religion of nature revival. Paganism today comprises many groups of practitioners of a nature-orientated spirituality, including Witches, some Druids, and Heathens, practitioners of the Northern Tradition, amongst others. Many claim a direct historical relationship, or increasingly, in the light of work which refutes an unbroken pre-Christian pagan tradition, through empathy of spirit with what they see as native European beliefs. Modern witchcraft emerged in 1951 with the repeal of the 1736 Witchcraft Act. This prompted Gerald Gardner to publish *Witchcraft Today* in 1954 in which he claimed to reveal some of the views of a group of English witches. Witchcraft was presented by Gardner to be an ancient system of herbal wisdom and worship that provided a context for the working of practical natural magic. Modern reconstructions of witchcraft have developed from Gardner's writings, and contemporary witches are subdivided into Gardnerians (those who derive their ways of working from Gerald Gardner), Alexandrians (practitioners of Alex Sanders's specific mixture of witchcraft and high magic), feminist witches (which are divided between liberal versions who work with men, and Dianic groups who, in Britain, work only with women), as well as solitary practitioners and 'hedgewitches', those who develop the practices of historical cunning folk – the village wise woman or wise man – such as Marion Green and Rae Beth (Green 1991; Beth 1996).

Witchcraft, as the largest branch of Paganism, is frequently viewed as a 'religion of ecology' with a central conception that there is immanent value in all things, and that this forms a mandate for ecological action and compassion for all life forms. The Pagan Front (later the Pagan Federation) was founded in 1970 to promote freedom of religious expression and 'green spirituality' (Pengelly, Hall and Dowse, 1997:4). For modern Pagans there is allegedly 'no retreat from the world of matter' (Adler, [1979] 1986:372). Pagans say that nature is alive and autonomous; they speak about interconnectedness and communication with all animate and inanimate beings. It is the centrality of nature to Pagan experience and world-view that is said to make it an example of a nature religion (Carpenter, 1996:70). Paganism equates with a relationship to the whole of nature; it places an individual within a wider connecting pattern that is often referred to and visualized as an interconnecting web of wyrd.

The assertion that human beings are a part of nature intimately connected via a web of forces and energies stands in direct contrast to a position of 'master'. Wiccan High Priestess Vivianne Crowley claims that there has been a shift in direction from Gerald Gardner's original stress on witchcraft as fertility religion to an environmental movement. She notes that Gardner, the founder of modern witchcraft, made little mention of nature religion *per se,* being more interested in magical powers and the traditional image of the witch as caster of spells[1] (1998:173), and points out that it was Doreen Valiente, one of Gardner's High Priestesses, who recast the concept of fertility into one that included the mind and the soul: 'There is a spiritual as well as a material fertility, and human life is a desert without it.' Valiente claims that the concern is not so much with literal fertility but with vitality and finding harmony with Nature (Valiente, [1973] 1986:135). For Crowley, the move from an esoteric fertility cult to a more open exoteric movement with 'environmentalism high on the agenda' marks a significant transition whereby Wicca moves 'out of the darkness, the occult world of witchery', to occupy the moral high ground of environmentalism: 'To be at one with nature in one's inner self is no longer enough; radical action to preserve nature is now important' (Crowley, 1998:177–179).

This shift in thinking is reflected in modern Druidry too. Druidism, as well as witchcraft, reflects the concerns of the day and a movement towards nature. The history of attitudes to Druidry, as well as to witchcraft, has been one of 'selective and creative invention' (Hutton, 1996:30). Historian Ronald Hutton notes that 'a large part of the power which the Druids have always exerted over the imagination has lain in the fact that they genuinely existed, but have all the characteristics of legendary beings; for all the real information which we have about them, they might well never have been' (ibid.:31). They have, however, acted as 'potent stimulants to the creative mind', dreamed anew in every age' (ibid.). Ross Nichols, who had assisted Gardner in writing *Witchcraft Today* (Hutton, 1999:244) and was one of the leaders of the Ancient Druid Order, and founder of the Order of Bards, Ovates and Druids, had a neoplatonic view of Druidry: 'Inwards from the origin of all things, the *primum mobile* [the first cause], the coiled Sarph the star-serpent, shown in the Milky Way, is coming from night through the spheres, reaching at last into man and his head, lodging in man's intelligence' ([1975] 1992:269).

Contemporary Druids are more likely to focus on nature, as Philip Shallcrass, joint chief of the British Druid Order, with Emma Restall Orr, explains: 'Druids share with other pagan groups a belief in a power or energy resident in the Earth, or in Nature, often represented as a Mother'; but he adds that individuals are left to decide how they interpret this (1996:75). Emma Restall Orr sees Druidry as an indigenous practice of the British Isles. Being rooted in the land, she sees its foundation in the earth and the ancestors; and it is in the earth that the powers of nature are honoured. Druidry is 'the practice of honouring the life force as it thrives, lives, dies and gives birth again within these lands'. Taking a poetic view of nature, her quest is one of finding inspiration from the land – the divine inspiration or 'awen' must be expressed through the magic of words, music and healing. She says that Druidry is a way of life rather than a religion (1999:6–8).[2] Philip Carr-Gomm, successor to Ross Nichols as chief of the Order of Bards, Ovates and Druids, claims that the reason for the resurgence of interest in Druidry lies in a yearning to 'hear the earth-songs and the star-songs', collectively we have 'turned away from them for centuries, and now we want to turn back – before it is too late' (Carr-Gomm, [1991] 1995:37). To be a Druid today means 'following a path which reverences Nature' (ibid.:71).

The New Age

The 'New Age' has become a diffuse populist term denoting anything from New Age travellers to a particular type of book or music (Sutcliffe, 1998:43). It is primarily a movement which aims to bring about social change by many and diverse means. By its very nature, writes the sociologist of religion Michael York, the 'New Age' is a term of convergence – 'one that is more than the sum of its parts, or at least is not to be equated with any of its parts alone' (1995:172).

The Christian mystic Alice Bailey, who founded the Arcane School and allegedly was the first to coin the term 'New Age' (ibid.:35), was deeply influenced by neoplatonic thinking. She starts her autobiography with the following words:

> From the point of Light within the Mind of God
> Let light stream forth into the minds of men.
> Let Light descend on Earth...

> (Bailey, 1973: viii)

Alice Bailey was said to be a 'prophet' of the movement', and her writings so deeply influenced Eileen Caddy, her husband Peter, and Dorothy MacLean that in 1962 they established Findhorn, a New Age community, on a cold, wind-blown peninsula in northern Scotland as a 'centre of light for the Aquarian Age' (Tompkins and Bird, 1975:317). Findhorn was run on messages and guidance received from God through Eileen Caddy and has become a horticultural mecca for the communication with nature spirits, devic presences, fairies, elves and other such otherworldly beings (see pp.98–102). These ideas had been germinated through the writings and teachings of the Theosophical Society and have been influential in bringing New Age thinking in line with a Christian interpretation of the divine in the form of light communicated by otherworldly beings. Dorothy MacLean communicated with devas, which she described as a pattern of life seeking fulfilment: 'Every plant does have a unique ensouling presence. These messages, however, have not been communicated by individual plants but rather by the overlighting intelligence and spirit – the deva – for each plant species' (MacLean, 1968:78). The devas are the 'architects' of plant forms, while gnomes, fairies, nature spirits and elementals are 'craftsmen' using the blueprints and energy channelled to them by the devas to build up the plant form. MacLean argues that seeing nature in this way transforms how we see the Earth, so that we begin to recognize God in every aspect of the world until 'the world is redeemed, until ultimately the whole planet is redeemed' (ibid.:77). A recent example of this Findhorn New Age neoplatonic vision is William Bloom's *Working with Angels, Fairies and Nature Spirits* (1999) in which he gives practical advice on contacting and working with devas and angels.

The New Age has been described in terms of a new form of consciousness. According to Marilyn Ferguson there was an 'Aquarian Conspiracy' – without a political doctrine or a manifesto – that aimed to bring about a new form of human consciousness. The Aquarian Conspiracy, as advocated by Ferguson, was a new world-view that had arisen as a response to a crisis. In this vision of a different reality, nature's powers were seen as a powerful ally that could bring transformation, not a force to be subdued. Ferguson saw human beings as stewards of inner and outer resources, and fundamentally embedded in nature (1982:30). An expansion of consciousness was required to effect reunion with all living things: 'Just as science demonstrates a web of relationship underlying everything in the universe, a glittering network of events, so the mystical experience of wholeness encompasses all separation' (ibid.: 418). Drawing on Tocqueville, who said that the nations of the world were like travellers in a forest unaware of the destination of others, their paths leading inevitably towards meeting in the centre of the forest, Ferguson claimed that we too, through wars and planetary crisis, have been lost in the forest of our darkest alienation and there too we find our escape: 'We are pressed ever more deeply into the forest, towards an escape more radical than any we had imagined: freedom with – not from – each other; after a history of separation and mistrust, we converge on the clearing' (ibid.:458).

A transformation of society via a wider state of consciousness is called for. We can respond in a positive way to the tragedies of recent history and liberate the future, 'One by one, we can re-choose – to awaken. To leave the prison of our conditioning, to love, to turn homeward. To conspire with and for each other' (ibid.:459).

For New Agers, the earth is entering a new cycle of evolution marked by this new human consciousness. David Spangler, a leading proponent, describes the New Age as a time of abundance and spiritual enlightenment guided by advanced beings, 'perhaps angels or spiritual masters or perhaps emissaries from an extra-terrestrial civilization whose spacecraft were the UFO's [*sic*], they would help to create a new civilization' (Spangler, 1984:18). This new cycle of conscious-ness concerns the invisible and inner dimensions to all life and is, according to William Bloom, made up of different dynamics which constitute four major fields: ecology, new paradigm science, new psychology and spiritual dynamics (Bloom, 1991:xvi). More recently, the popularization of New Age ideas has been given an immeasurable boost by the publication by James Redfield of *The Celestine Prophecy* (1994). Adapting a change of paradigm science within a conspiracy adventure drama within the rainforests of Peru, Redfield introduces nine 'insights' expounded within a Christian panentheistic framework. This pot-boiling spiritual soap teaches the perennial wisdom that all religions are concerned with humanity, creating relationship with a higher source as a means of stopping its abuse of power and of finding a 'positive vision of how we will save this planet, its crea-tures, and its beauty' (ibid.:2).

Western Shamanism

Traditionally a shaman is a person trained to communicate with the spirit world on behalf of his or her people. The word 'shaman' comes from the language of the Evenk, a small Tungus-speaking group of hunters and reindeer herders in

Siberia. The Evenk had an oral culture and termed the mediators between the realm of humans and the spirit world *săman*, a concept normalized by Russian scholars in the eighteenth century into 'shaman' as a term for similar figures encountered in different tribes across Siberia (Price, 2001:3–4; Hutton 2001). It was originally specific to this particular group and, according to the historian of religion Mircea Eliade, when translated means 'the ecstatic one'. The word 'ecstasy' comes from the Greek *ekstasis* and was used to describe any departure from the normal condition of mind or mood. The earliest application of *ekstasis* to mystical experience was in Plotinus as a 'simplification and surrender of the self, an aspiration towards contact which is at once a stillness and a mental effort of adaptation' (Dodds, 1990:72). Eliade's primary definition of shamanism is as a 'technique of ecstasy' ([1964] 1989:4), and in *Shamanism: Archaic Techniques of Ecstasy*, he gives an historical overview of shamanic practices. Originally compiled in the 1940s, it was widely viewed as the authorative work on the subject, but, as Russian ethnographer Vladimir Basilov has shown, it exaggerates the shaman's upperworldly journeys, this demonizes the underworld, frequently opposing celestial to infernal (Basilov 1984, cited in Balzer 1997:xvi; see also Noel, 1997:34), and emphasizes the shaman as an individualized hero figure (Samuel 2004).

The 1970s saw the emergence of contemporary Western shamanism, sometimes called neo-shamanism[3], as a new form of spirituality from the USA. It has been claimed that Eliade's book was the prototype for this movement, but it took Carlos Castaneda's *The Teachings of Don Juan: A Yaqui Way of Knowledge*, published in 1968, and which sold hundreds of thousands of copies, to bring the living experience of an indigenous shamanism to Western culture. This book, and others published by Castaneda on the same theme, is now widely regarded as a hoax in the presentation of fiction as fact; but it did popularize shamanism and led to a fascination with the alternative realities of the shaman. Shamanism is often seen as primordial and authentic. Westerners tend to be fascinated with the exotic world of shamanism and see it as representing that authenticity. Shamanism is claimed to be the original human relationship to nature – humanity's first spirituality.

Shamanism, according to the Western shamanic practitioner Leo Rutherford, is the oldest way in which humanity has sought connection with Creation. Its origins go back to Stone Age times. All of us have evolved from shamanic cultures and so it is not imported: 'it is our roots wherever we live' (1996:1). Rutherford, who first sought healing from the ills of Western culture at Findhorn, discovered shamanism from courses and workshops given by Joan Halifax and Prem Das (Paul Adams), among others, on a Holistic Psychology MA at Antioch University, San Francisco, and he started to 'recover parts of his soul' (ibid.:xii–xiv). Western scientific materialism, says Rutherford, has treated the earth and nature as something to be dominated and exploited, but now, as the unsustainable nature of Western civilization is becoming visible, more people of the industrial world are turning to the shamanism of old cultures for help and guidance in 'finding a way back to a greater balance with nature, with Planet Earth, and with themselves' (ibid.:2). Rutherford, showing his New Age influences, sees the roots of a 'shamanic revival' in the Theosophical Society through the works of Alice Bailey, Freud, Jung, Reich; in transpersonal therapies; in Buddhism and Eastern religions; in the 1960s revolution and the rave scene of the 1990s; and by the opening up by shamans of ancient wisdom (ibid.:13). Rutherford is a shamanic healer and therapist and his approach is eclectic, ranging from South American ayahuasca[4] vision quests to so-called Native American Medicine Wheel teachings.

Native American Medicine Wheel, with its circular notion of power and knowledge, teaches about the balance and relationship of all things; this form of New Age nature religion 'borrows' from Native American spirituality and has became particularly fashionable. The teaching of Sun Bear, who is of Chippewa descent, is based on his vision of the medicine wheel and incorporates elements from various Native American cultures. According to a practical Medicine Wheel workbook published by Sun Bear, Wabun Wind and Crysalis Mulligan (1992), the wheel revolves around a Creator Stone, which is the centre of all life and radiates energy to the rest of the wheel. Seven stones surrounding the Creator form the Center Circle, the foundation of all life, while four Spirit Keeper stones mark the outer circle. Between the four Spirit Keeper stones are the twelve moonstones of the outer circle. From the Spirit Keeper stones radiate certain qualities – of cleansing, renewal, purity, clarity and wisdom, etc. – that are necessary to gain the sacred space of the Creator in the centre. In a Western, usually urban, context, this form of nature religion appears to stand for a regeneration and revitalization of ancient earth-based 'ways of knowing' for those who see themselves as dispossessed or alienated from nature as a spiritual source (see Albanese 1991).

Issues of cultural appropriation, or, in other words, the stealing of an oppressed people's spiritual heritage by the descendants of Western colonialism, are slowly infiltrating popular books and journals aimed at those interested in practising shamanism in the West. This is due, in part, to indigenous activist movements (such as the American Indian Movement, and Survival of American Indians) and also, perhaps obliquely, to anthropological critique reaching more mainstream audiences. Anthropology has been both implicated in aiding colonization – at the emergence of the discipline anthropologists provided information on the colonized – and, more recently, through a political awareness concerned with highlighting the effects of colonial power, the most notable example of the latter, in relation to shamanism, being Michael Taussig's *Shamanism, Colonialism, and the Wild Man* ([1986] 1991).

One anthropologist who has played an enormous role in the development of Western Shamanism is Michael Harner who, in *The Way of the Shaman* ([1980]

1990), a handbook for Western practitioners that concentrates on a method for shamanic journeying to achieve alternative states of consciousness without drugs, gives instructions for finding power animals, restoring power and healing in terms of what he calls Core Shamanism. This is a way of initiating Westerners into an 'ancient state of mind', a way that 'taps so deeply into the human mind, that one's usual cultural belief systems and assumptions about reality are essentially irrelevant' (ibid.: xviii). Shamans are, according to Harner, 'the keepers of a remarkable body of ancient techniques that they use to achieve and maintain well-being and healing for themselves and members of their communities'. He describes shamanism as a great mental and emotional adventure. Through what often seems like a heroic journey, the shaman helps his or her patient to transcend their normal, ordinary definition of reality, 'including the definition of themselves as ill' (ibid.:xvii). Core Shamanism, as a technique for expanding consciousness, will be explored further in Chapter 5.

Today shamanism is being sold as a 'complementary therapy' in workshops and self–help groups. 'Soul retrival' is offered as a practical approach to heal anything from physical accidents to childhood abuse, or rape. There is a significant shift from 'do-it-yourself' style Harner workshops to consulting trained specialists to do it for you.[5] Ross Heaven, in an article in the free publication *girl about town*, explains that the "New Shamans" are here to heal the wound' by either searching the otherworlds for fragments of soul parts that need to be returned and reuniting them with the person, or by acting as guide for their clients to find them for themselves; the outcome is described as a 'clearing of unhealthy ties to negative past events and a re-balancing of energies'.[6]

There is a move to search for Western 'indigenous' versions, and a whole range of shamanisms – from Celtic to Wiccan – are being 'rediscovered'. Weekend workshops and drumming circles, where participants can journey in trance to find their spirit guides, are becoming more and more popular. Shamanistic aspects are incorporated into both New Age (as already demonstrated in Leo Rutherford's work) and Pagan practices. Druid Philip Shallcrass says that Druidry embraces various aspects of Native American traditions (especially the Sweat Lodge) and shamanic practices such as drumming, dancing, chanting, visionary journeying, contact with power animals and the use of power objects such as quartz crystals for healing (1996:72). Circle Sanctuary is a 'nonprofit international Nature Spirituality resource center and legally recognised Shamanic Wiccan church',[7] and Selena Fox, its high priestess, describes her spiritual path as 'Wiccan Shamanism' (York, 1995:115).

Although nature religion does not exist as a distinct and identifiable religious tradition, the philosophies and ideologies that form dominant discourses and practices stem from the Western Hermetic or Mystery tradition. Certain historical and cultural strands of philosophy and ontology have given rise to two specific movements within that tradition: these are esotericism and romanticism; the growth of environmentalism has also influenced practices.

Underlying Influences on Nature Religion

Esotericism and Occultism

According to historian of religion Antoine Faivre, esotericism is a form of thought rather than a specific genre that conjures up the idea of something secret; it is a discipline of the arcane, a restricted realm of knowledge and mystery emanating from a higher level spiritual centre (Faivre, 1994:5–7). Esotericism, as a practice, was a central part of the Western Mystery tradition and it was shaped during the Hermeticism of the Renaissance.[8] The word 'mystery' derives from the Greek *myein*, 'to keep one's mouth shut', meaning a secret revealed to initiates and not to be revealed to others; a truth not understood until revealed; while the term 'mystery religion' has been applied to secret initiatory cults in the Graeco-Roman world that practised rites aimed at effecting a union with a deity or ultimate being as a dimension of existence beyond that experienced through the senses (Ferguson, 1976:125–127). Faivre outlines four fundamental elements[9] to esotericism as a form of thought. Firstly, through the notion of correspondences between all parts of the universe, both seen and unseen, there is a principle of universal interdependence: 'Everything is a sign; everything conceals and exudes mystery; every object hides a secret.' He notes two types of correspondence: those that exist in nature forming a correspondence between the natural world and the invisible departments of the celestial and supercelestial world; and those between Nature as the cosmos or history and revealed texts – such as the Jewish mystical system of Kabbalah – the knowledge of the one aids knowledge of the other. Secondly, Nature is alive in all its parts and must be read like a book. 'Magic' is the knowledge of networks and sympathies or antipathies that link the things of Nature and the operation of bodies of knowledge. Thirdly, imagination is used to 'penetrate the hieroglyphs of Nature'; to put the theory of correspondence into practice by mediating the entities between Nature and the divine world. Lastly, the experience of transmutation or metamorphosis requires that there be no separation between knowledge (gnosis), inner experience, intellectual activity, and the active imagination (Faivre 1994:10–13). How far some aspects of esotericism lead to a non-ecological approach amongst practitioners of nature spiritualities will be examined in Chapter 8.

Occultism refers to a large number of practices – ranging from astrology to alchemy – which are based on the homo-analogical principles of esotericism. Drawing upon hidden or concealed (occult) forces in nature, they are seen to form a dynamic reality – a web of cosmic and divine analogies – manifest through the operation of the active imagination (Faivre, 1989d:3). The human being is envisaged as connected via a number of correspondences to the universe – as microcosm to macrocosm. The basic principle on which occultism rests is that the human being is part of a world that is alive with hidden forces and energies which are understood and conceptualized into various magical traditions. Once the occultist has learnt the connections – the links between his or her internal system and the wider universe – then he or she is able to manipulate these natural cosmic forces according to will. In terms of history, the Renaissance represented a period of great interest in the occult, principally stimulated by Ficino's translation of the *Corpus Hermeticum* and Mirandola's Christianization of the Kabbalah (see Yates, [1964] 1991). This movement shaped Rosicrucianism and Freemasonry, as well as the late nineteenth-century occult revival largely shaped by the Hermetic Order of the Golden Dawn. A surfacing of various underground occult traditions culminated in the 1970s as New Age and various forms of Paganism. It is due to this history that the notion of a magical otherworld had developed in the Western occult tradition. The otherworld, as I discussed in my previous research, developed in opposition to the ordinary everyday realm of human existence (Greenwood, 2000:209–210); it has become reified as secret and exciting, the locus of esoteric gnosis due to its being repressed or denied by rationalist interpretations of the world.

As already mentioned in Chapter 1, the psychology of Carl Jung, which saw the psyche as a part of nature, has been important in terms of helping to overcome the historical and philosophical split between spirit and matter. Jung's work has had a profound influence on the Western occult tradition, particularly though the well-known author and magician Dion Fortune whose writings have taken on board his notions of anima and animus as contra-sexual psychic forces; this has helped a revaluation of 'the feminine' as a repressed psychological principle. According to some Jungians, the Goddess is arising from the depths of the unconscious psyche as a counterbalance to the aggressiveness, technological destructiveness, scientific materialism and spiritual impoverishment that is allegedly representative of the masculine direction of contemporary society (see for example Whitmont, 1987:vii–viii). The focus on the feminine has been further strengthened by the women's movement. What has been termed 'second-wave'[10] feminism started in the 1960s – the time of cultural change, opposition to the Vietnam War, civil rights movements, gay rights movements and student protest.[11] Many feminists sought to reinterpret canonical religious texts and edit out patriarchal elements; others turned to the Goddess, as representative of 'feminine aspects of the sacred', arguing that formal religion had repressed the female aspect of holiness and that it was necessary to seek the missing dimension outside mainstream religious systems. Thus a key element in feminist spirituality is a reorientation towards a veneration of the female, and, as I have argued elsewhere, feminism has had a wide-ranging effect on the Pagan magical subculture as a whole (Greenwood, 2000), and in turn on nature religion.

Romanticism

The Romantic Movement was a product of modernity, a reaction to the Age of Reason. Jean-Jacques Rousseau was considered to be the first Romantic due to the publication of his novel *La nouvelle Héloïse* (1761), and his debate with Jean-Phillipe Rameau concerning French aesthetic taste. Rameau's position was rationalistic and Rousseau opposed it with an argument that is now termed Romanticism (Cranston, 1995:1). The term 'romantic' can have many meanings: in the specific sense as 'the current of cultural and intellectual forces which prevailed after the decline of the Age of Reason' partly as a reaction to the values of that age. It also refers to a certain spirit characterized by freedom from formality and convention whilst pursuing imagination, inwardness and subjectivity (ibid.:38).

As a part of the range of alternative political visions in the nineteenth century, Romanticism drew on Renaissance esoteric theories of correspondences and creative imagination; nature was seen as visible spirit, involving a heightened sensitivity to the natural world combined with a belief in nature's correspondence to the mind (Koerner, 1990:23). Romanticism sparked a renewed interest in *Naturphilosophie* as distinguished from natural philosophy, understood as the pursuit of objective knowledge (defined by Comte, Galileo and Darwin). *Naturphilosphen* such as Liebniz, Hegel and Bergson took an intuitive approach in searching for a reality that underlay data derived from observation; they sought the nature of the relationship that linked God, man and the universe. The *naturphilosophen* saw experimental science as a point of departure in an apprehension of invisible processes of nature; they affirmed a belief in a relationship between man and nature where the mind became spiritualized nature (Faivre, 1989c:31–34).

A political reaction against the Enlightenment, Romanticism was a celebration of reason, progress, notions of a common humanity and universal truth, although some artistic Romantics – such as Goethe, Heine and Shelley – sided with the naturalism and the political philosophy of the Enlightenment.[12] By contrast, it valued the individual, the relative, and the internal, and it explored different levels of consciousness, the supernatural and mythic interpretations of the world. Wild woods, once seen as a threat to the forces of civilization, now offered the 'opportunity of solitude, contemplation and oneness with nature'. The experience of nature became a spiritual act: 'nature was not only beautiful, but was mentally uplifting and morally healing' (Marshall, 1995:268–280). This was particularly well expressed in the poetic works of Wordsworth, Coleridge, Blake, Byron,

Shelley and Keats, among others. Historian Ronald Hutton says Romanticism can be described as 'a tremendous exaltation of the natural and the irrational, those qualities which scientific language had come to identify as 'feminine' (1998:90). Keats linked the moon with female deity in *Endymion III* (11.142–169), a poem written in 1818, and Shelley saw 'Mother Earth' as a goddess in 'Song of Proserpine' 1–5:

> Sacred goddess, Mother Earth,
> Thou from whose immortal bosom
> Gods, and men, and beast, have birth,
> Leaf and blade, and bud and blossom,
> Breathe thine influence most divine.

> (cited in Hutton, 1998:91)

These views added to a romanticized view of nature – of living in an Eden-like harmony – rather than one that confronts the reality of survival. Romanticism was also used to inspire Fascist nationalism and political regeneration (Mosse, 1964; Goodrick-Clarke, 1992; Shama 1996).

For most of history human societies have been composed of hunter-gatherer societies. Agriculture, pastoral nomadism, and urbanism appeared more recently: agriculture and pastoral nomadism 10,000–15,000 years ago, and urbanism 5,000 years ago. All the preceding time our ancestors and other human beings were hunters, fishers and collectors (Hultkrantz, 1982:11–12). Societies with economies based entirely on hunting and gathering have existed since the evolution of the first humans, and it is only in the mid-twentieth century that they have started to disappear (Burch and Ellanna, 1996:1) and become romanticized (along with pastoral nomadism and 'traditional' peasant agriculture). Fascinating Westerners for a long time, and corresponding with an increase in environmental awareness, stereotypes of the 'noble savage' have been developed to offer models of living in harmony with the natural world. This myth has recently been shown to be a political and polemical fabrication of nineteenth-century racist anthropology (Ellingson, 2001).

Shamanism, in particular, is often viewed in romantic fashion, although the West's fascination with shamanism is not new. Gloria Flaherty notes that the curiosity of intellectuals was raised in the fifth century BCE when Herodotus reported the death-defying feats of the Scythian soothsaying poets Aristeas and Abaris. Classical scholars throughout the ages have studied Herodotus, pointing out numerous other 'shamanic' practices of antiquity. They have seen in shamanism the origins of theatre, fairy tales, and of Greek mythology (Flaherty, 1992:3). Flaherty points out that in the eighteenth century there was a 'prodigious supply' of information about the multifarious vestiges of shamanism from all over the world. By this time certain notions of shamanism had become assimilated into the intellectual mainstream. Most eighteenth-century[13] observations of shamanism were written from the point of view of interested yet disbelieving Western Europeans, who subjected shamanism to empirical tests and rational analyses. Flaherty claims there was a tension between rationalism and the 'night-side of nature' which informed the way Western European knowledge was advanced (ibid.:7), and while some tried to demystify shamanism – by the application of rational criteria, by observation, and by the recording of practitioners, analysing them using psychology and linguistics – others sought to record the activities of vanishing peoples amid a fascination with discovering what was seen as the hidden secrets of nature[14] (ibid.:11–22). It is this last aspect of fascination that often seems to dominate contemporary discourses on nature religion (see Hutton 2001).

Environmentalism

Spawned by Victorian nature-lovers and philanthropists and nurtured by amateur naturalists, the history of environmentalism goes back to the nineteenth century when increasing industrialization and urbanization caused changes in perceptions of nature. Increasingly, town dwellers sought to protect nature from destruction. The majority of the population lived in cities and developed the notion of a 'rural idyll' as a counter measure to the work, pollution and pressures of city life (McCormick, 1989). The popular environmental movement started in 1962 with Rachel Carson's *Silent Spring,* an indictment of human arrogance in terms of the larger scheme of things. Carson's view was reinforced by a 1967 paper by medieval historian Lynn White Jun. in which he argued that Christianity, in its Western form, was the most anthropocentric religion the world had ever seen, and bore a huge burden of guilt for ecological problems. In White's view, Western Christianity developed in the direction of seeking to understand God's mind by discovering how his creation operated. By contrast, Eastern Christianity continued to conceive of nature primarily as a 'symbolic system through which God speaks to men: the ant is a sermon to sluggards, rising flames are the symbol of the soul's aspiration'. The solution for White is not the abandonment of religion[15] but an abandonment of anthropocentrism (ibid.:4–6).

Environmentalism is a broad term; there is no clear or consistent definition of its nature or parameters. It might refer to a way of life, a state of mind, an attitude to society, or a political philosophy. Sometimes it is also conflated with ecology (McCormick, 1989:ix). The word 'ecology' comes from the Greek *Oikos* meaning 'house' and *logos* referring to a discourse – a study of plants, animals, or peoples and institutions in relation to environment.[16] The notion of ecology came to shape a nineteenth-century scientific world-view based on historical process. Stemming from Darwin and Haeckel, ecology asserted that human beings are inherently a part of nature; it thus undermined a mechanistic conception inherited from the Enlightenment, as well as transcendent religious ideologies that separated God from his creation. Ecology as a science generated its own ethic: not one of domination (as in mechanistic philosophy and Cartesian dualism) but of respect and kinship with the natural world (Morris, 1996:131–133). Environmentalists draw on notions of ecology by taking an 'eco-system' approach, the view that each form of life has a unique place in the balance of nature being central. 'Deep Ecology',[17] sometimes called 'philosophical ecology' or 'ecosophy',[18] is concerned with biocentric equality and self-realization takes a relational, total-field view (Naess, 1995:3). Arne Naess first characterized a distinction between 'shallow' and 'deep' approaches to environmentalism. Shallow environmentalism is allegedly concerned with preservation and conservation and takes a human-in-environment approach; reformist rather than radical, it focuses on the serviceability of the human habitat for use by people, and it is therefore largely anthropocentric. Naess combined ecological science, the pantheism of Baruch de Spinoza (1632–1677), and Martin Heidegger's (1889–1976) philosophical concept of Being which involved the notion that an entity can 'reveal itself as it really is' in his 'Deep Ecology'. Involving the primacy of self-realization in identification with the non-human world, it concerns a shift from an anthropocentric world-view to an ecocentric or biocentric vision whereby beings are but one component of a complex system: 'the world is no longer our oyster, we share it with oysters' approach.

An alternative to Deep Ecology is 'social ecology',[19] with its emphasis on the social – the environmental crisis is a social crisis. This position is associated with the writings and philosophy of Murray Bookchin (*The Ecology of Freedom*, 1982) who drew on Marxism and anarchist traditions to synthesize a political philosophy of freedom and cooperation. In social ecology the roots of ecological problems can be traced to dislocation in society: imbalance in the natural world is caused by imbalance in the social world. Bookchin is against what he sees as the romantic nature worship – the 'mystical approach'– of Deep Ecology,[20] and he makes cogent critiques of spiritual approaches that must be addressed if nature religion is to be considered ecological; these will be discussed in Chapter 8.

'Eco-feminism' is a 'whole family of often distantly related positions and perspectives' rather than a specific form of environmentalism,[21] but it does give a positive value to the connection of women and nature,[22] and explores the notion that the male domination of women and the domination of nature is interconnected: the environmental crisis is due to the control of women and nature by men. Susan Griffin's *Woman and Nature* (1978) asserted that men set themselves apart from women and nature:

He says that women speak with nature. That she hears voices from under the earth. That wind blows in her ears and trees whisper to her. That the dead sing through her mouth and the cries of infants are clear to her. But for him this dialogue is over. He says he is not part of this world, that he was set on this world as a stranger. He sets himself apart from woman and nature. ([1978] 1984:1)

Carolyn Merchant's *The Death of Nature* ([1980] 1990) saw the root of the current environmental crisis in the scientific world-view that conceived of nature as a machine rather than a living organism. This, she claimed, sanctioned the domination of nature and women. Merchant writes that the world we have lost was organic, based on the idea of nature as a living organism, the prevailing ideological framework in ancient systems of thought. The organismic metaphor was flexible and adaptable and had two controlling images that were projections of human perceptions onto the external world: one of a kindly beneficent female – a nurturing mother – who provided for human needs in an ordered and planned universe; the other was also female but wild and uncontrollable, bringing violence, storms, droughts and general chaos. Merchant argues that during the Scientific Revolution the metaphor of the earth as a nurturing mother was gradually replaced by the idea of nature as disorder, and two new ideas of mechanism and the domination and mastery of nature became core conceptions of the modern world ([1980] 1990: 1–2). This view has led to certain revaluations of 'the feminine', particularly in what is often called 'Goddess religion',[23] and has implications in the consideration of the ecological credentials of nature religion (see Chapter 8).

Thus it can be argued that esotericism and occultism supply the framework for the unseen forces that connect the parts to the whole; romanticism provides the devotional approach to nature; and environmentalism is the context in which nature religion is claimed to be environmental religion. In the next chapter I explore how and why practitioners of nature spiritualities seek to connect with nature.

Notes

1. Crowley notes that Gardner drew on the work of the Egyptologist Margaret Murray, who in turn used the mythological ideas of James Frazer ([1921] 1993). Murray wrote of a pre-Christian pagan cult – which had coexisted with Christianity until it was persecuted during the witch trials of the fifteenth-seventeenth centuries – as a fertility cult which worshipped a dying and resurrecting God (Crowley, 1998:172).
2. *Kindred Spirit*, issue 48, autumn 1999.

3. Some anthropologists seem not to consider Western shamanism 'real' shamanism and thus label it 'neo-shamanism'. It is important, however, to realize that some scholars and practitioners see the term 'neo' as meaning 'new', as in a revival and carrying no such prejudicial connotations. Galina Lindquist, in an anthropological study of Swedish shamanism, calls neo-shamans 'revivers of ancient shamanic traditions' (1997:x). For Lindquist, neo-shamanism is part of the neo-spiritual resurgence represented by neo-Paganism; it is based on Nature worship and claims to revive ancient indigenous traditions (1997:1). Adopting the term 'neo-shamanism' can create a dichotomy between what is perceived to be the genuine traditional original (which can become romanticized and seen in ahistorical and static terms) and, by implication, a later (inferior) version. There is not an unbroken 'shamanic tradition' in Western societies because of their specific histories rooted within different forms of Christianity and also Enlightenment rationalism; they are not 'shamanic' societies, but if shamanism is studied as a human phenomenon the dualism of traditional (non-Western) and non-traditional (Western), and the corresponding associations of authentic and inauthentic, is avoided (see Chapter 8).

4. Ayahuasca is a drink used for producing visionary experiences.

5. An observation made by Geoffrey Samuel in a personal communication, 24 January 2002.

6. *girl about town*, 25 October, 1999.

7. Circle Sanctuary information handout.

8. The word 'esotericism' as an adjective appeared long before the noun, which dates only from the beginning of the nineteenth century. 'Eso' means 'inside', and 'ter' implies opposition, and the word is empty of meaning in itself (Faivre, 1994:4).

9. To these may be added the relative elements of the praxis of concordance – the practice of establishing common denominators between different traditions in the hope of attaining superior gnosis; and the element of transmission: the passing of knowledge from master to disciple (Faivre, 1994:14–15).

10. 'First-wave' feminism is generally taken to mean the movement for women's suffrage in the late nineteenth century and the early twentieth.

11. 'Second-wave' feminism incorporated three different lines of thought. The first was Liberal feminism, sometimes called 'bourgeois feminism', and was associated with feminist causes such as women's suffrage at the turn of the century. The liberal feminist view took the existing structure of society as given, but asserted that certain reforms had to be realized for women to have equality of opportunity with men; the second was radical feminism which started from the assertion that women shared a common sisterhood in oppression by patriarchy. A patriarchy was defined as any society where

power rested in male hands, and the principles of patriarchy were twofold: males dominated females and older males dominated younger; the third was Marxist feminism which was based on a bringing together of Marxist class analysis and feminism and attempted to account for social inequalities due to class and gender. It was concerned with the transformation of social relations of the ownership of means of production and reproduction.

12. I am grateful to Brian Morris for bringing this to my attention (personal communication 19 September 2002).

13. During the course of that century information about shamanism inundated Western Europe influencing Diderot and his *Le neveu de Rameau* in which a performing artist is portrayed as shaman of a higher civilization (Flaherty, 1992:131); Herder examined the universal significance of enthusiasm and inspiration by spirits, noting that all aspects of irrationalism had to be acknowledged openly (ibid.:149); Mozart became known all over the globe as 'the living Orpheus', a mythological figure that the eighteenth century came to imagine as a shaman (ibid.:158).

14. Flaherty says that reports of shamanism appeared at the same time as the rising tide of fear of witchcraft. Difficulties in reportage were overcome through the development of a theologically acceptable paradigm of discourse: as long as the devil was disavowed, questions could be broached (1992:21).

15. White advocated the development of an alternative Christianity where all creatures had equality, as demonstrated by St Francis of Assissi (Fox, 1995:6).

16. 'Ecology' was a term coined by Ernst Haeckel in 1870.

17. This term was first used by Arne Naess in 1973.

18. From the Greek 'eco' – house; 'sophia' wisdom.

19. The term was first used by American ecologist E.A Gutkind in 1954.

20. Deep Ecology does not address social problems – poverty, inequality, racism, sexism, state repression, and neo-colonialism; all of which are linked to environmental issues (Morris, 1996:147–148).

21. A definition offered by Geoffrey Samuel, personal communication.

22. Sherry Ortner, in her well-known paper 'Is Female to Male as Nature is to Culture' (Ortner, in Rosaldo and Lamphere, 1974), argues that women are universally seen as closer to nature, while men are associated with culture. However, ethnographic evidence points to the fact that this may be the case in Western societies but it is not a universal position (see MacCormack and Strathern, [1980] 1990).

23. Feminist philosopher Val Plumwood calls this 'uncritical reversal': putting value on 'the feminine' and 'nature' – both of which are cultural constructs. She highlights the problems associated with reversing the values of the dominant culture (1993:31).

-3-

Connection with Nature

Selena Fox, Wiccan high priestess and founder of Circle Sanctuary in the USA, expresses her relationship to nature in terms of kinship: 'I am Pagan. I am a part of the whole of Nature. The Rocks, the Animals, the Plants, the Elements, and the Stars are my relatives... Planet Earth is my home. I am a part of this large family of Nature, not the master of it...'[1] Selena notes that her earliest experience as a Pagan, although she did not call it 'Paganism' then, happened when she was a young child. She would go out in nature, often her backyard in Arlington, Virginia, and just 'sit quietly with other life forms in nature'. She explains that 'the mystical experiences that I've had throughout my life were full of other dimensions and species' (Hopman and Bond, 1996:236). For shaman Gordon MacLellan, an early encounter opened up a companionship with a toad. He describes how he watched the toad opening its eyes as 'a lump of brown and green transforming, wet mud animating', and realized that Toad had been with him since that first encounter, 'creeping her quiet way deep into the heart of me' (1999:3). For both Selena Fox and Gordon MacLellan nature consists of kin relationships; while for Anne Barrowcliffe, a Pagan priestess and Druid, nature is a way of being in touch with a holistic and natural way of being in the world; 'Humans are part of nature', she says, 'We know this instinctively in every cell of our body, in every breath and every beat of our heart. When we connect deeply with our body and with nature we experience a sense of genuine wholeness which moves us towards greater integration emotionally and spiritually and leads us naturally to act in certain ways towards others and the environment we live in'.[2]

This chapter outlines how some practitioners identify with nature. Historically, there is no pristine Nature 'out there'; nature has meant different things to people at various periods in time. The Enlightenment view of nature as an affirmation of an objective reality was not the same as that of the Romantics who, a century or so later, experienced nature through the feelings that it inspired (Porter, 2001:319). There are a multiplicity of ways in which practitioners of nature religion can adopt an identity with nature – from workshops, talks and seminars to joining a ritual group that holds celebrations at significant points in the year, such as the high-profile Druidic ceremonies that take place at the Summer Solstice at Stonehenge, or at a more low-key local gathering of heathens. Various examples – which all have the aim of connecting with nature in a vital and spiritual way

– will be highlighted here. The first is an account of a talk given by John Seed, an ecologist and New Age philosopher, on Deep Ecology at St James's Church in Piccadilly, London; the second concerns the experience of Anne Barrowcliffe as she experiences nature at Cae Mabon, the elemental centre in the Snowdonian hills; the third is based on a workshop led by the well-known Pagan novelist Diana Paxson at Atlantis, the well-known London bookshop; the fourth is an example of New Age healing; the fifth, an exploration of Pagan direct action; and finally, a reconstruction of a Scandinavian shamanic ritual. Before turning to these examples, however, I shall discuss the issue of identity with nature.

Identification with Nature

Attitudes to nature held by practitioners have been partly shaped by Romanticism. As noted in Chapter 2, the Romanticism movement drew on esoteric corres-pondences linking different aspects of nature – human, natural, celestial and supercelestial worlds – in a universal interdependence whereby all was connected through concealed forces forming a dynamic web. Appearing more as a mood or manner of feeling rather than a clear set of beliefs and ideas, the emphasis was on the individual, the particular and the relative (Marshall, 1995:268). The philosopher Johann Herder (1744–1803) for example, emphasized immediate experience: through feeling it was possible to be at one with the world, an original unity had been ruptured in search of objectivity and knowledge (Solomon and Higgins, 1996:221). In effect, this was a reaction to the Enlightenment and also the Cartesian focus on viewing the mind in terms of reflective thinking and seeing reason as the basis of knowledge. Although Descartes highlighted subjectivity, putting a premium on interiority, introspection and the idea that the mind was an inner realm containing thoughts (an idea not evident in the earliest Greek philosophy), these thoughts were expressly not emotional because emotions were thought to be prejudiced and biased (Solomon and Higgins, 1996:184–185).

Nature had been a key concept of the Enlightenment; initially not necessarily as a radically disenchanted way of seeing the world but, according to historian Eric Porter, as an affirmation of an objective and exalted external reality created by God. Nature was the antithesis of all that was confused and distorted; it linked the divine – as eternal and transcendental – and the human. As '[o]rderly, objective, rational, grand and majestic, Nature enshrined both norms and ideals' (2001:295). Fighting against seeing nature in pantheistic pagan terms, Enlightenment thinkers also saw nature as a resource for the service and contemplation of human beings; it sustained the social order and a 'sense of milieu adapted to the daily needs of the rich man in his castle and the poor man at his gate' (ibid.:299). Everything had its place and purpose in nature. Influenced by Descartes, the 'founder of modern individualism',[3]

Enlightenment philosophers put great trust in the ability to reason in their search for universal truths; it was thought that the secrets of nature could be understood through reason; the order of thought followed universal criteria based on a radical disengagement with the world (Solomon and Higgins, 1996:184,192). The laws of nature governing the globe were 'immutable' and 'progressive' interpreted in the light of a presiding divine design (Porter, 2001:299–302). However, according to Porter, at the heart of this conception lay a paradox whereby Enlightened man wanted to discover unspoilt Nature but at the same time wanted to 'improve' it, aesthetically or agriculturally. By the close of the eighteenth century, utilitarian Nature – Nature improved – was becoming problematized and Romanticism was making it transcendental, holy and subjective; nature became the new religion (ibid.:319).

Thus Romantic expression came to be a religion in a protest against the Enlightenment ideal of disengaged, instrumental reason. Such disengagement, according to philosopher Charles Taylor, carried a profound disenchantment in spiritual outlook. Taylor claims that a fully modern identity belongs to post–Romantic period. The eighteenth century saw a return to nature as moral force: the lives of simple rustic peoples were seen to be closer to virtue than the corrupt existences of city dwellers, and a love of nature was an indicator of profound cultural change (ibid.:302). For Taylor, the meaning of natural phenomena is not defined by the order of nature itself, or by ideas it embodies, but by the effect of the phenomena of nature on humans and the reactions awakened, 'Our attunement with nature no longer consists in a recognition of ontic hierarchy but in being able to release the echo within ourselves' (Taylor, 1989:299). For Taylor, the world of magic represented an imprisoning of the self: the decline of the world-view underlying magic was the obverse of the rise of the new sense of freedom and self-possession. The 'world of magic seems to entail a thraldom, an imprisoning of the self in uncanny external forces, even a ravishing or loss of self'. For contemporary people who are secure in the modern identity or even feel imprisoned within it, 'playing with the occult can provide a pleasant frisson for the contented, or perhaps even seem to offer a way of escape for these who feel oppressed by disenchantment' (ibid.:192).

Taylor's conception of a magical world-view is very different to that held by many practitioners of nature spiritualities for whom magic does not represent an imprisonment of the self in uncanny external forces but an expansion and transformation of a sense of self, as demonstrated by Pagan priestess and Druid Anne's experience quoted earlier (also see pp.45–47). A magical world-view represents a connection to a wider whole. While 'playing with the occult' may provide a 'pleasant frisson' or offer an escape for those 'oppressed by disenchantment', Taylor misses the point as far as practitioners of nature religion are concerned. Their objective is to 'be' in the world in a different way through nature as an indwelling spirit that connects and heals feelings of alienation and loneliness, as well as attaching people to place; it is an attitude that is more akin to the animistic views of many small-scale peoples; the beings in nature become kin, as Selena Fox and Gordon MacLellan have shown.

Another influence on practitioners' identities is Deep Ecology, with its biocentric exhortation to expand notions of selfhood. John Seed, influenced by Naess's psychological approach as well as his views on Deep Ecology, says that the oneness of nature involves a realization that the psyche is a product of the rainforest, 'We evolved for hundreds of millions of years within this moist green womb before emerging a scant five million years ago, blinking, into the light.' (quoted in Devall, 1995:106). Identification with nature comprises an understanding of evolution that takes a person back to the moist green womb of the rainforest, re-linking with the 'biological self' and by-passing the human history of alienation. An ecological identity involves an 'opening to nature', an identification with what is seen as an organic wholeness. The Deep Ecologist Bill Devall says that this is best done initially not with Gaia but with a person's own bioregion in an identification with a specific place rather than a remote and abstract one: 'The more we know a specific place intimately – know its moods, seasons, changes, aspects, native creatures – the more we know our ecological selves' (Devall, 1995:110). The aim is to interweave spirit and matter like 'primal peoples' such as the Native Americans who have a 'broad and deep relationship with place' (ibid.:110; see also Chapters 6 and 7 in the current volume).

The expanding of the self beyond the confines of a narrow ego through the process of identification with larger entities such as forests, bioregions, and the planet as a whole (Drengson and Inoue, 1995:xxii) is termed the 'ecological self'. Naess's idea of 'self-realization' is key to his 'philosophy of oneness'. The 'Self' as known throughout the history of philosophy and in various religions as 'the Universal Self', 'the Absolute', or 'the atman', is problematic because it suggests a spiritual identification, usually with a god or some other divine entity, rather than identification with nature per se. In the Vedanta Hindu tradition, 'atman' means the soul, or spiritual aspect of a person, and it is distinct from the physical body; self-realization or salvation concerns the realization that the soul is Brahman, the supreme Self or world spirit, and that the world is an illusion. As Brian Morris has pointed out, in many religious traditions the soul or spirit is considered to be radically distinct from the body, and the body and the material world are seen as a positive hindrance to self-realization. In some interpretations of the gnostic tradition, the body is viewed as a temporary prison or tomb of the soul, and this has been a precursor of mechanistic philosophy and anthropocentrism, both of which are profoundly anti-ecological. Naess, by contrast, suggests oneness with nature rather than a spiritual being that transcends the natural world (Morris, 1996:151; and see Chapter 8).

Ecophilosopher Warwick Fox sees the need to establish what he terms a 'transpersonal ecology' through a personal identification of commonality with family, friends, pets, homes, football teams, etc. Bias and possessiveness, leading to attachment and proprietorship, are negative aspects of personal identification; however, Fox recognizes that personal identification plays a fundamental role in human development, but it must be situated within a wider context. Also required is an ontological identification that is transpersonal and experienced through consciousness disciplines such as Zen Buddhism so that a 'cosmological consciousness' can be reached whereby all entities are seen as aspects of a single unfolding reality. This incorporates any cosmology that sees the world as a unity in process – such as religions like Taoism, philosophies like those of Spinoza, mythologies, and some scientific cosmologies (Fox 1995:139). A cosmological identity 'means having a lived sense of the overall scheme of things such that one comes to feel a sense of commonality with all other entities...'; this can be developed through the Council of All Beings, for example, as well as practical involvement (ibid.:144–5).

The Council of All Beings is an environmental organization that prepares and allows people to 'hear within themselves the sounds of the earth crying'. Developed in 1985 from discussions between John Seed and Joanna Macy, and inspired by the writings of Naess (Seed *et al.*, 1988:7), the Council of All Beings aims to unblock feelings of despair by allowing people to experience their 'fundamental interconnectedness with all life'. It is not enough to just think about connection, a change must take part on a deeper level – to permeate identity; to place human identity within a wider perspective. This is premised on the awareness that the knowledge that we require is embedded within us and needs to be awakened, 'In our mother's womb, our embryonic bodies recapitulate the evolution of cellular life on Earth.' We can extend ourselves to other creatures, 'to feel the inner body-sense of amphibian, reptile and lower mammal'; these are earlier stages of human life, 'literally part of the ontogenetic development of our neurological system' (ibid.:13). These ideas and practices represent a considerable influence on nature religion. I now turn to a number of specific vignettes showing how individuals participate in nature.

Deep Ecology: Interconnectedness of Nature

John Seed gave a talk at St James's church, a beautiful building designed by Sir Christopher Wren, in Piccadilly, London; it was entitled 'Deep Ecology and the Timeline of Light'. A flyer pinned on to the church door read:

As environmental and social crisis intensify around us, how can we remain effective in our lives. Deep Ecology points to the web of life and describes our connectedness with All That Is. The timeline of Light describes the epic of our evolution and offers a new Creation myth for the 21st century. Together they give a new deeper vision of ourselves and our place in the cosmos. This talk will look at issues around shifting us from numbness and psychological denial into a place of awe and wonder.

In the church, we meditate on 'interconnectedness' for five minutes, and after John Seed has invoked the four elements of air, earth, water and fire we are asked to turn to a person sitting next to us and ask them what interconnectedness means to them. I speak to a woman in her early fifties who had just come back from one of Seed's workshops at Findhorn, the New Age community in Scotland. She tells me that she is attracted to Buddhism, seeing it as a good way to connect with the earth.

'We have ceased to honour the elements in our bodies and our lives', said Seed as he tells us about how he was drawn to direct action through a New Age community in New South Wales, Australia. He was not particularly interested in ecology but heard the trees calling out. In 1984 he was invited to the EarthFirst! action network and his environmental campaigns took off. This included parading a papier-mâché cow outside a Burger King restaurant to protest against the rainforest being cut down to provide land for cattle grazing. He gave a rendition of the chant that he and the other protesters sang:

Lay down your whoppa baby,
lay down your whoppa and your fries
to save the planet baby,
before the planet dies.

The source of the environmental problem, according to Seed, is anthropocentrism and forgetting our interconnectedness with all life. This had created a situation of human beings setting themselves against resources, 'We see the world as being created by an old man with a white beard; we are centre stage.' He contrasted this to indigenous communities who, he claims, see human beings as one strand in a web, 'if one strand is destroyed, it destroys all'. 'Why are we so important that we can tear the world apart?' He proposes a spiritual solution: developing an 'ecological identity'. Deep ecology, he informs us, is a powerful philosophy that transforms understanding, but it is not possible to think out of mess, the structures are deep in the psyche as well as in social institutions, and language conspires with disconnection – 'the environment is out there'. We must feel our way out of the crisis; we must hold our breath and learn that the environment is here within us, in our breath, and in water passing through us.

At this point we were asked to do an exercise of getting to know the hand of someone we do not know. We feel the hand, say hello to it, think back to it as a small child and greet it. We also were asked to think in evolutionary terms: back to this hand as a primate, a reptile, a fin and stars. Seed is here encouraging the expansion of identity – in the manner of Naess's ecological identity – between species, and backwards and forwards in time.

John Seed drew his talk at St James's to an end with an explanation of how he put his ideas into action. As director of the Rainforest Information Centre in New South Wales he works with rainforest organizations such as Rainforest Concern, the Maquipucuna Foundation, and the Endangered Wildlife Trust, and he told us how he and others were working with indigenous peoples, such as those in Equador, helping them protect the forest. His organization had helped local people gain the title to their land and thus legal recognition of ownership, and had then spent nearly a year working with volunteers marking off the area by cutting a 5m wide swathe through the jungle. This was then planted with a living fence of a different tree species. Another conservation method used was buying land to run as tourist resorts. In India they had helped to establish a tree nursery and supplied trees free to any farmer who wanted to plant them, and free permaculture courses for local people. He emphasized the need for working with people on social projects, as this was the only way that the environment would be protected.

Being in Nature: Freedom and Identity

Anne, the Pagan priestess and Druid quoted at the beginning of this chapter, is a member of the eclectic group Mad Shamans.[4] The time she spent at Cae Mabon enabled her to get closer to nature; she said it helped her to express who she really was. Sitting around a fire one evening in a reconstruction Bronze Age thatched roundhouse, the flames illuminating the dark interior, members of Mad Shamans chanted, drummed and danced; this time we were singing a beautiful chant that Anne had composed, as we had on many previous occasions. Linking dancing with fire, wild woods, spring, wind, freedom, sea, sun, and light the chant expresses an elemental and wild connection within nature. The first and second verses are as follows:

> I see you dancing
>   in the fire dancing
> I see you dancing
>   ey ye yo
> I see you dancing
>   my bright one dancing
> I see you dancing
>   ey ye yo

Chorus:
The light of life flows around your body
The light of life within you grows
The light of life flows around your body
The light of life within you glows

I see you dancing
   in the wood dancing
I see you dancing
   ey ye yo
I see you dancing
   my wild one dancing
I see you dancing
   ey ye yo

Anne said that this chant came to her as a way of putting into words and song something of the feelings that arose in her through her Pagan spirituality. The chant was 'born in the Spring, that time of new energy and life'; it is partly about the wild god, 'that presence of the divine that manifests itself through the experience of nature'. It is a 'celebration of that presence and a recognition of that presence as part of ourselves'. Anne says that the 'you' that is referred to is also 'all of us who are open to these feelings, we who are singing this song have the light of life in us as we sing'. Improvised dancing is for Anne a powerful physical and emotional way of opening to the 'flow of energy, of my beautiful wild, open, free nature'. It is also a metaphor for spirituality which is not about a 'fixed, transcendent perfection, but about seeing and feeling spirit as ever-changing and dynamic'.[5]

The beautiful wild, open, and free nature that Anne talks about is sought by many who visit Cae Mabon. It shows how participation with nature may bring an expanded awareness of the deep connection between elements of nature. Imagining the dance (one of the traditional ways of entering a trance state) whilst chanting (another well-established method of altering consciousness) creates correspondence between individual (inner nature) and the environment (outer nature). Anne said that for her Cae Mabon was a place where people could reconnect with living simply in nature, in community with others. Her experience of it was as a place where people could connect and express themselves in many different ways – from ecstatic chant and dance under the stars to silence and stillness. The last time she had been there Anne had been very busy prior to going and spent a lot of time just lying on the ground, often naked in the warm sun:

> I felt I was an empty vessel that was being filled up in some wordless way by being on the earth, soaking in the warmth of the sun, being refreshed by the clear cold stream that flows down from the mountains through the woods, by floating in the sun-warmed water of the deep, dark lake, looking up towards the fantastic majesty of the rocks and mountains rising above the lake.[6]

All is interconnected within such a sacred universe. This experience is magical consciousness, a heightened awareness of an expanded connected wholeness.

Anne considers that many people in the modern world have lost a sense of their own wholeness and connection with nature; they try to fill the void that is left by 'ceaseless consumption and stimulation, which are ultimately unsatisfying and ineffective'. For Anne, nature-centred spirituality is not some 'fluffy irrelevance to the needs of our world, it is its absence that has helped to create the world we live in today'.[7] During moments such as in the roundhouse at Cae Mabon the void is filled, disconnection is breached; the wound is healed, at least temporarily. A disconnected state – the loss of soulful connection with nature – is what the Druid and ecopsychologist Frank MacEwen Owen calls the 'The Common Wound'; it has the corresponding symptoms of alienation, loneliness, and a deep level of pain at being somehow dispossessed, disenfranchised in spirit, or displaced from a sense of 'home' or 'place' (1996:129).

Anne told me that during the last six months she had become involved with the Order of Bards, Ovates and Druids (OBOD), and that she had recently spent a week at their Samhain Camp. She thought that this was 'Druidry in action'. She spoke about how she thought the whole philosophy of Druidry was about honouring nature and the creative inspiration, or Awen, which flows from nature. Anne described how each morning the participants of the camp stood in a circle and took three breaths to connect them with earth, heaven and their centre as they sounded Awen together. The camp was a 'space where everyone was honoured as an expression of the spirit that flows through us all'. One of the most meaningful parts of camp for Anne was the morning talking circle, where a talking stick was passed around the circle and people could share whatever they wished and be listened to with respect and love. Sitting in the circle within the yurt,[8] which we were using for shared space, Anne said how she was struck by how natural it felt: 'Most of our ancestors lived this way, in communities living together close to the earth, sharing inspiration and support. It felt very right':

> The camp centre was a sacred fire, which was kept burning throughout the time of the camp. This was a space to sit, to talk, to chop vegetables, to sing, to tell stories, to look up and see the moon vividly circled by magical haloes. We lived under canvas, never far from the earth, the sun, the wind and the rain. It felt strange to return to my house of bricks and mortar and feel cut off from the elements after living close to them for a week.

Spirits of Place: Everyday Nature

It is not just such high-profile sites, such as Stonehenge and the Rollright Stones, or special places like Cae Mabon, that nature religion practitioners relate to;

sometimes more 'mundane' spirits of place are also sought, including those in the city (see also Chapter 9). Just behind the British Museum in London ten people from varying Pagan backgrounds were meditating to communicate with the spirit of place at Atlantis, the well-known occult bookshop. The group had met to hear Diana Paxson, a well-known Pagan priestess, novelist and ex-environmental educator, speak about Earth Religion in the Northern Tradition. Diana Paxson is the editor of Iduna, journal of the heathen organization called 'The Troth', and steerswoman (president) of the 'High Rede', the governing (executive) body; she is also a consecrated priestess and president of the Fellowship of the Spiral Path, and an elder of the Covenant of the Goddess, an international Wiccan organization. According to her workshop flyer:

> the Great Gods come and go, but all over the world, people have continued to honour the local wights – spirits of hearth and heath, field and forest. In Iceland, they do still. Wights – from Puck and the brownies of Britain to the Roman lares and the Kami of Japan, the 'Genus loci' – inhabit the spiritual ecology of our world. Even in the city we can work with them and reconnect to the world around us and enrich our lives. We will explore these spirits of places with lecture, discussion, ceremony, exercises for getting in touch with them.

Diana, who started magical work in a ceremonial Kabbalistic order, then a women's group, before being introduced to Michael Harner's Core Shamanism, told a small group of approximately eleven of us about her first shamanic journey. Raven had turned up, a pushy spirit animal who spoke to Diana as if she was a 'retarded child'. On the second journey to the Upperworld to find a teacher in human form she asked Raven to take her to her spiritual leader. She came to a place with standing stones. There was a figure with a cloak; a spear was leaning against his side. It was Odin. Diana said that she knew enough to know that she was not making it up. She felt that 'Freya was fine, but Odin was scary'. She said that she needed all the years of experience that she had in order to accept what he was teaching her. She started working with Seidr, which 'translates into witchcraft in Norse', she explained. I will return to examine Seidr later in this chapter.

Diana spoke about making spiritual connection with place. She told us that the modern world has been intentionally deprived of significance and so we had to reconnect to the spirit of place. Most of us had to start in the city where there were spirits, such as wights, in every house and in every store. We do not have a tradition so we should go to folklore and try and move our mindsets so that we become receptive. She said that land spirits in the city tended to be quiet and that the best times to make contact were at dawn, dusk, noon or midnight. To perceive the spirits it was important to find a place within easy reach, and to be quiet – trees and streams were transformative places for land energies. Trees were constantly performing transformative magic by changing carbon dioxide into oxygen. One could visualize a dryad and send it energy; this would start an energy exchange. If people started putting energy in a particular place then the energy would build up and more energy would be attracted to it. Diana said that as a person worked with a little piece of the environment, becoming attuned to its energy shifts and seasonal change, the energy became more attuned.

We meditated on finding the spirit of place at Atlantis. After some time, each participant spoke about what they had experienced. Someone had seen a silhouette of a human figure standing on the bookshelves; while someone else had seen a man, who said he lived at Atlantis, standing on the bookshelf cleaning the books, and who said that he wanted a feather duster. Someone else reported that they had 'got sucked into a daydream'. Another person said that they had seen a little man lying down, clay pipe in hand, who said he would be happy to live in the amethyst by the cash register but didn't really care. This corresponded with another report of a grey figure who was 'laid back' and 'almost indifferent'. Someone else saw a black and knobbly blob, a product of different cultures; it seemed to represent diversity and multiculturalism and respected knowledge and learning. It wanted help and respect and it might help bring people together in a unity. One woman spoke about a 'strong visionary experience' of a dark male figure in a helmet with a long beak that might have been Thoth or Horus. Yet another woman had a visionary experience in which she saw an old-fashioned nineteenth-century coal train filled with golden grain moving through glistening green countryside. Diana said that the spirit was already guarding the shop: 'it's his shop', she said. She had a marble image in her meditation, a small rather grotesque gargoyle Egyptian figure, it allowed us to put offerings on the stone, and told us to put the stone under the desk next to the cash register; it had to be fed beer and honey once a month apparently.

Caroline Wise, one of the co-owners of the shop, said that the participants had picked up things that she already knew. When things had been pretty bad at a period between ownerships of the shop she had seen a black silhouette of a tall thin male. When she arrived early at the shop the back door would open and close but no one was there. She said that the figure was 'on our side; he wasn't with the baddies'. He had been seen independently by someone else and upgraded himself through the ages. He was the guardian of the shop. She had bought a painting by the well-known occult artist Osman Spare and hung it on the back door because it was a good likeness of him. The little man with the clay pipe, she said, was a pixie or an elf that threw the tarot packs when someone behaved badly. Caroline explained that Michael Houseton, the previous owner and founder of Atlantis, had stocked everything occult – not just the respectable, such as Theosophy, but also some magic that was viewed as 'black' at the time. The shop did not promote one religion or practice over another, there was no 'fundamentalism'. Houseton ran an

Order of the Hidden Masters and there was an Egyptian Temple in the basement; it was this latter that explained the references to Egyptian gods that some people had experienced. She explained the reference to the train by the fact that there were railway tunnels underneath the shop but no stations. During the Second World War a train crashed. It was impossible to get the people out during the bombing, and so this train was perhaps the train going to the Summerland, the Pagan land of the dead.

Healing Nature

When I was conducting fieldwork in Norfolk and staying in a small north Norfolk town, I happened to walk into a shop that sold wooden furniture and New Age/Pagan artefacts – such as green man plaques. I got talking to Julia, a woman in her early fifties who was sitting behind the counter; she told me she was a healer and a born-again Christian and that she taught healing, relaxation classes and hypnotherapy (although she avoids using that word after Paul Mckenna popularized it: 'it puts people off', she said[9]). Julia told me about a book that she was writing on an old typewriter on the counter. It was an autobiographical novel about a woman meeting a Romany gypsy. Julia had come from a well-off family, with 'diamonds, the lot', and had married a butcher; but she had given up everything to be with her half-gypsy partner who was nineteen years her junior. We talked about her partner, who was gypsy on his father's side, and who had made many of the wooden chests and tables for sale in the shop.

On another occasion I sat down on one of the blanket chests; Julia sat on another and told me about how she healed. She said that when she was going to do a healing she always wore white and called on the universal energy, which she called 'God'. When she is healing, Julia keeps one hand on the person's body as she feels their energy aura with the other hand. Starting with the head, she works downwards, feeling where energy is out of balance, where areas are too hot (here she moves energy away), and where they are too cold (here she draws energy to the place). She opens up the patient's energy pathways – she referred to their *kundalini*, and she tunes into their meridian lines. When she has finished she grounds the energy in the patient's feet, perhaps holding them for fifteen minutes, before starting to talk and counsel the person. Julia told me that her patients always felt energized and fantastic afterwards. She said it is a wonderful experience; it is like being in a school play: 'I get butterflies in my stomach as I feel the energy working through my chakras opening them up.' She can feel the energy coming over her like 'cobwebs of love', caressing her arms, making the hairs stick on end as it comes through her. As she tunes into the energy she feels ecstatic; she calls the energy the 'Holy Spirit', and it flows through her and out of her hands: she has to send it into someone. She focuses on the person to be healed and builds up a spirit relationship with them.

I asked her how she saw the energy that she tapped into. She said it was all colours and she could see it pouring out of her hands, 'Look at your hands against a dark background or a white background, with eyes partly focused; it's like a heat haze shimmer on a tarmac road', she said. I asked if this energy was God. She replied: 'It doesn't matter what you call it: Allah, or whatever. It's everywhere and comes down. All paths are the same.' Was it in nature? 'Yes, absolutely', she said. Julia told me how she laid down in a field; she could feel the earth beneath her and the warm sun on her face. She and her partner had just moved to a small village outside a town in north Norfolk and she could walk outside into open fields: 'All the money in the world is not the same as that experience', she told me. Was God nature? 'Yes, he is in nature, but we also relate to a higher spirit being – we evolve upwards, we become more spiritual. We are flesh and spirit, but we aim to become more spiritual, "Praise, the Lord", she said. Julia's form of New Age Christianity was very eclectic – the Holy Spirit works through the Hindu chakra system of *kundalini* and meridian lines – and focused on her relationship with what she saw as a universal energy coming down from a higher spirit.

Julia's healing work using universal energy is similar to the idea that we can expand consciousness to 'quantum realms'. Leslie Kenton, a Core Shamanism teacher, writes that a move into quantum realms – the seat of creative powers, intuition, dreams and spiritual experiences – involves learning to collaborate with non-physical energies or spirits by the 'natural alignment of personality' with the soul so that the 'inside and the outside sing the same song' (1999:3). The distortion of living in a sea of mundane consciousness – the environment that lacks an awareness of the interconnectedness of all life – can be cleared through practices such as detoxifying the body, meditation and shamanic work that brings a person closer to their soul (ibid.:11–12).[10] A quantum leap journey involves transcending conditioning to express the self fully in the expansion of consciousness. Kenton sees shamanism as a direct method for such an expansion of consciousness; it gives direct access to revelations and spiritual experiences unmediated by restricting world-views or organized religion, one that is apparently pre-religious, pre-political, and pre-philosophical; it is a 'highly democratic methodology'. Shamanism is a highly practical and easily learned technology for accessing quantum realms of zones of consciousness, variously called the transcendent, mystical, non-ordinary reality, the sacred, the otherworld etc. (ibid.:25–29). Shamanic skills are no longer the province of a few gifted people; they now belong to all.[11] Nature is a 'great carrier of sacred power'; it is in our bodies and our being, and is communication, through DNA, with plants and animals – 'knowing is built into our being' (ibid.:67). We can reconnect with nature as healing energy by coming into contact with our own internal sacred space, and by 'making friends with nature' around us (ibid.:75).

Radical Pagan Protest: Protecting Nature

In the late 1980s the Pagan magazine *Moonshine* was instrumental in setting up the networking organization Paganlink, and published a booklet called *Awakening the Dragon: Practical Paganism, Political Ritual and Active Ecology* in which a call was made to the Pagan community to act positively to end the wanton destruction of the earth. It contained a political ritual for people to gather together at the same time each month to 'raise the dragon', directing the magical imagery towards the sword Excalibur, a symbol of truth, love and honour. The dragon represented the power and the wrath of the land to challenge what they called 'bedroom paganism'; it also encouraged people to empower themselves through action in the days of the Conservative government of Margaret Thatcher. Dragon outlined a list of absolutes around which a Pagan ought to live – such as taking the bus rather than driving, and fitting double-glazing, etc. Paganism and action were seen to be inseparable; non-action was a sign of impotence. Andy Letcher, an environmental protester and Druidic bard, observes that the Pagan response to *Moonshine*'s gauntlet has taken many forms: from sending 'strong thoughts' to the Minister for the Environment, earth-healing rituals, picking up litter and recycling, to physically obstructing bulldozers in direct environmental action. He also sees much of what he calls 'virtual Paganism', a Paganism cut off from the environmental movement, an issue to which I will return in Chapter 8.

The dragon became a symbol of Pagan environmentalism (see pp.54–55) and an environmental group of the same name was set up by Adrian Harris on 22 July 1990. Dragon claims to use 'magick' and ritual to 'bind and protect, to stop ecological destruction and channel positive energy to those who are also fighting for the rights of the earth' (promotional leaflet). Dragon runs practical sessions focusing on conservation work, training workshops, and fundraising; these are clearly focused on the environment. Adrian Ivakhiv, in his study of New Age pilgrims at Glastonbury and Sedona, notes the syncretistic and creative ways in which dragons have been symbolized as earth energy and with the 'sacred feminine' in contemporary mythologies. Ivakhiv draws on the work of historian Ronald Hutton in which the flying reptilian monsters of Scandinavian and Germanic myth become transformed into 'vessels of great spiritual power'. Hutton points out that although the contemporary symbol of the dragon is based upon Scandinavian, Germanic, Chinese and Babylonian myth, these ancient peoples would not have recognized it for it is a modern mythology, and corresponds with Lévi-Strauss's ([1962] 1968) notion of *bricolage* (Hutton 1993:125–26: Ivakhiv, 2001:35). The dragon is a good example of a symbol used in magical thinking; it represents interconnectedness on many different levels. In this sense it is better understood as comprising a part of a language of magical consciousness rather than through history. The symbol of the dragon unites Pagans. Indeed, Adrian Harris defines

Paganism as a way of relating to the world that encourages a reconnection with a unity of everything:

> The wholeness I have spoken of, that oneness of everything which we experience in moments of spiritual knowing, is what I call the sacred, and Pagan ritual is both a path to the sacred and a way of honouring it. In our rituals we reconnect with ourselves, healing the rift between body and mind through ecstatic dance, chanting and the drama of ritualized myth. We lose our ego-centred selves and achieve that somatic knowing of the unity of everything (Harris 1996:153).

Adrian outlined his position regarding spirituality and environmental action at an interfaith seminar on *Songs of the Sacred Landscape*.[12] He said that within contemporary Paganism there is a catch phrase – 'Think global, act local' – and that it was impossible to explore the global without examining the local in our personal lives. He said that his background was Anglican Christian, that he had studied philosophy at university and become an atheist, but that he had been guided back to a spiritual path through Wicca because it was earth–centred and had a strong feminine influence. He thought that spirituality was like an ecosystem – it was diverse but united in relationship. Wicca was difficult to define but it existed in a dynamic relationship with its surroundings – each element was like a species in ecology: the ancient earth held the roots and Wicca was young growth and a part of the earth's diversity. He felt that the Wiccan Wheel of the Year, as the eight celebratory festivals, wove people's lives into the pattern of the universe through nature (see pp.62–63).

Claiming that environmental activists were often driven by their power of anger, Adrian said it was important to feel the roots of passion. The element of fire, as passion, 'made things happen'. Power represented 'to be able', the fire within: the power to change the world for the better. People had lost touch with this and felt disempowered, but change only comes from change within individuals by 'rekindling flame from myth – from its true source'. Adrian saw myths as eternal truths that bound the secular with the spirituality of the people as 'a different truth every time we hear them'. He thought that we need modern myths because 'advertising, chemical pollution and consumerist lies make the soul die and we lose connection with the earth'. Wicca helps remind us of the 'power of true myth and ritual brings it to life – ancient wisdom speaks again'. The healing of the planet must involve the healing of the self, of restoring self-worth as spiritual beings: as 'spirit grows so does inner power'. The function of ritual was to help people understand their spiritual strength. The spiritual was brought to bear on the political. For example, at Twyford Down 'many paths were involved in the protest against the planned motorway development,[13] and the inspiration was drawn from inspiration and respect for nature and the 'instinctive belief that the earth is sacred'.

Radical Paganism is said to be half 'spiky' and half 'fluffy' – a mixture of direct confrontation with authority over road-building and the planned development of countryside, and an alternative lifestyle framed by a romanticized and mythologized Pagan past.

> Imagine a bomb up the bum of suburbia. But the bomb is made of organic flour, wrapped in ivy, painted in funky colours and thrown by pixies; half punk, half pagan. The spirit of the direct action protest movement is like this, half 'spiky', half 'fluffy' – half politically hard, half warmly, humanly, soft. The movement boils with life lived to the brink, to the full, its emotions intense, raw and extreme. (Griffiths, 1998:9)

When in 1992 two protesters pitched a camp on a hill at Twyford Down, near Winchester, as a statement against the Conservative government's road-building programme, a whole direct action movement was galvanized. The Minister for Transport had announced 'the biggest road-building programme since the Romans', this being road-building an ideological keystone for a government which 'regarded public transport (and the social interaction, unionism and limited contractual opportunities that accompanied it) as anathema and car use (with its private ownership, individualism and juicy road-building contracts for party donors) as the stairway to heaven' (Monbiot, 1998:8). A new 'tribe' of protesters was formed at Twyford Down. Calling themselves the Donga Tribe (from the Matabele word 'Dongas' which means 'trackways') because they camped on the Iron Age trackways, they consisted of a group of 15–20 young people who lived for most of 1992 on Twyford Down to try to stop the land being destroyed for the M3 motorway (Plows, 2001:3; Worthington, 2004:199–200). Alex Plows, a member of the tribe, described how it was through Paganism that she became radically politicized, and how she came to see all life as sacred. Alex sees all things as interconnected; she is aware of how exploitation at a social-economic level works: 'I seek out connections between road building in this country and the displacement of indigenous people in Colombia and around the world by oil companies. Political, economic, social, environmental, and spiritual are linked. I care and I campaign' (Plows, 2001:4). Alex sees Twyford Down as a sacred site with mythological and spiritual connections; she feels she was pulled there as part of a spiritual warrior quest: '[m]any of us at Twyford felt a past life connection, and in living onsite together, sensing cycles, getting wood and water, exploring physical connections, it felt like the wheel came full circle' (ibid.). She explains how the group would protect the site through weaving night-time spells, using chants, incantations and ritual, and through protection spells made during drumming and chanting sessions. Through ritual, energy was gained from the earth:

> If our motives are pure then we can be so powerful with the Earth spirits' help. Sometimes we would stop work for the day by running onto the site dressed in a wicker and cloth

dragon and sitting on the machines. Or we would meet the bulldozers with chants, our faces smeared with chalk from the Down, carrying sage sticks and hazel pentacles. (Plows, 2001:4)

However, the occupation of the site ended on what came to be known as 'Yellow Wednesday'. The Dongas had been living on the land throughout the autumn of 1992. When the bulldozers came up the hill the tribe had always managed to turn them back – the camp was protected by a ditch (dug in the shape of a dragon), runes, and a hawthorn hedge. This changed on 9 December when the yellow-jacketed security guards arrived.

The roads were eventually built at Twyford Down, but the anti-road protesters won the ideological argument and a culture of Pagan protest has remained. Historian Andy Worthington points to protests against the construction of a toll bridge between the Isle of Skye and the Scottish mainland; a proposed bypass near Newcastle; a link road for the M11 through East London; a bypass on the outskirts of Bath that would destroy Solsbury Hill, an Iron Age hill-fort; the M65 Blackburn bypass; and the Criminal Justice Bill, among others (Worthington, 2004:201–202).

I visited another protest site in Kent. West Wood, part of Lyminge Forest, an ancient woodland near Canterbury in Kent, England, has become another focus for direct action. Under threat from development by the Rank Group, which had been given permission to purchase a thousand acres to turn it into a holiday centre, it has become the home of a number of groups of protesters. In March 1997 they moved into the wood and have built numerous defences such as tree houses and underground tunnels. In 1999 there were around 20–30 people living permanently in the woods, with others coming and going. Part of the defence system is magic. In the words of Pagan protester Jani Farell-Roberts:

> There is a seedbed for magic in this country, a place where young people remember what their grandparents taught them, where the Craft grows as it always has: deep among the trees; in the heather; in the moonlight. This is not the seedbed of the town, of the urban coven or grove, where sacred traditions are treasured amid suburbia. It is the seedbed of the protest camp, of those who leave their cities and their houses because they feel they are called to protect the wild. (Farell-Roberts and Motherwort, 1997:24)

This is a romantic portrayal of magic that links Paganism into an allegedly hereditary witchcraft tradition or 'Craft'; it is a call 'to protect the wild' which echoes a confrontation with wild nature in a 'Wild Hunt Challenge' explored in Chapter 6. The Lyminge protester Motherwort (Huxley, 1979:5) describes how her co-protester Jani summons magical energy symbolized by the dragon, a creature representing the animating spirit of the natural world and representative of transformation:

Jani is telling us about the dragon energy that she has woven through the wood, singing and dancing, invoking the primal power of the Earth Goddess, wakening her. The night is with us, the trees surround us, the energy is high because we are so close to the wind and fire and stars. No need to imagine a magical space – this is one!

We begin to hum, whispering, *come dragon, come dragon, come, come come, we your daughters, we your sons*, a deep, drumming refrain. A tune springs up from nowhere and we are singing. The pulsing energy of Lyminge is thick with dragon energy now. The low pines are filled with circling mist. As we reach a crescendo we are shaking with the red energy of the earth. The dragon is here and we will turn them back; we are too strong for them ... we are here, in love with Lyminge, dancing in the moonlight. The earth is strong! We are strong! We will win. (Farell-Roberts and Motherwort, 1997:27).

In August 1998 I visited Lyminge for an open summer camp for visitors organized by Jani Farell-Roberts to see the protest camp and experience what it was like in a woodland fortress. Following signs through the wood, I arrived at the camp to an *ad hoc* breakfast discussion about an altercation the previous evening. Jani's Pagan group had held a ritual on a burial mound, and this had upset some non-Pagan protesters who had attacked two of the Pagan group, one being bitten quite badly on the arm and another attacked by the throat. There were various protest groups scattered around the wood and each had different views and approaches to the land that they were protecting. A ritual was held to one side away from the central campfire. The spirit guardians of the four quarters of the circle were greeted, each person present brought some contribution to the circle – this might be a thought, wish, or reflection. Adrian Harris, the founder of the Dragon environmental group, went around the circle with a Tibetan bowl; the group started humming to its reverberations. There was no overt organizational structure to the event, and things appeared to happen spontaneously. Mid-morning a large group of people started chopping organic vegetables for a stew, the ingredients of which were put in a large cauldron on the fire to cook; people tended the fire and wandered off to collect firewood. During this time I spoke to one man in his mid-sixties who told me, in Pagan romantic tradition, that his grandmother had taught him witchcraft in the New Forest. When he was a boy she had made him lie naked in streams with just his face above the water. This, he said, was a classic way of altering consciousness, and 'you don't feel cold until afterwards'.

After lunch the feminist witch and author Starhawk, and her partner David, arrived to lend support to the camp. Starhawk, or Star as she likes to be known, is well known for her protest activities and was then involved in protecting Headwaters Forest in northern California; she has also has been at the forefront of the anti-capitalist, anti-World Trade Organization demonstrations in Seattle (see pp.158–159). Their arrival was a studied and very low-key event, and people wandered off busily engaged in activities. Woody and Karin returned from a walk in the woods and suggested that everyone should go and talk to the fairies. Woody said that he had just spoken to the fairies; they had said that they were more than happy to talk to everyone. He described them as between eighteen inches and two feet high, and as 'warriors' wearing brown. In the event it was decided that the camp should break up into small discussion groups to talk about the experience of magic first.

One member of the discussion group that I joined took me off to see the tree houses and the underground tunnels deep in the wood. Seeing these came as a bit of a shock as I realized the hard realities of living in a protest camp – the conditions were primitive, verging on the squalid, to say the least. There was little that could be romanticized here. There were makeshift tents made out of ex-army type dark-brown canvas and rudimentary cooking and washing facilities. The tunnels were reinforced with all manner of odd bits of furniture, branches of trees and pieces of wood and metal and screened by high fences that also consisted of anything that had been close at hand. *En route* we bumped into Starhawk's partner David who was also looking around, Starhawk having been taken off to speak to the fairies,[14] and who allegedly sensed a great urgency, almost panic, to have wild places protected before human beings destroyed them all.

Andy Worthington says that such spiritual response was a political impulse arising from the notion that the earth, as a Great Mother, is sacred. This concept, for some, has filtered through from the ecological Paganism of the anti-nuclear protests of the 1980s, especially from the Women at Greenham Common; but for others it is a 'visceral response to what they perceived as nothing short of the rape of the land' (Worthing, 2004:203).

Past Nature: Encounters with Ancestors

Drumming groups, where participants can practise shamanic techniques, are a by-product of the growth and popularity of Michael Harner's Core Shamanism. I joined one such group formed through workshops conducted with Jonathan Horowitz (who had initially trained with Michael Harner) in London and attended regularly, once a month, for over a year. On one occasion in October 1998 the group conducted a *seidr*, a shamanic technique from the Nordic tradition. *Seidr* is a ritual practice whereby one person, or a number of people, journey on behalf of the community who sing to provide the power to send them into the spirit world. The word comes from the Old Norse *sidr* and comprises a complex of beliefs and practices; in its broadest sense it is a technique for gaining knowledge about the future or trying to change the options for events to come. Comprising a multitude of practices performed to attempt to intervene in the events of the future, it is a process for gaining knowledge from 'outside the balanced structure and order' (Raudvere, 2002:109–112). According to anthropologist Jenny Blain, in the Old

Icelandic literature there are people identified as working with spirits – they have many names such as 'seidkona' or 'seidwoman' and 'seidmadr' or 'seidman' – and they practise *seidr* (2000:24). The model for the oracular *seidr* performed today by Pagans comes from the Saga of Erik the Red[15] in which a Greenland seeress is consulted to determine why a community is having problems (for an account of contemporary interpretations of northern European shamanic practices see Lindquist, 1997; Blain 2002b).

For those journeying, the drumming group constructed a platform from tables and covered them with blankets. Chairs were placed on top, and then everyone sat in a circle at the bottom of the construction. We passed around a 'talking stick' so that everyone had their say in the discussion of which questions we would ask of the spirits. We all had to agree on the question that would be asked. A number of questions were suggested: How could we improve personal communication with ancestors? How could we contact past lives and ancestral lines? What we could do to help natural resources? Someone said that 30 per cent of the world's resources had been lost in the last thirty years, and that the ozone hole was now bigger that the size of Europe. This was seen to be due to having lost touch with Mother Earth. Eventually, it was decided that the 'seers' should journey to ask advice about how to heal our relationships with ancestors. From the discussion amongst the Core Shamanism practitioners it was obvious that many of us had uncertainty about who our ancestors were; many expressed confusion or problems of disconnection with their immediate ancestors or family (see Chapter 4). One woman said that she was trying to establish relationships with her deceased grandparents and wanted help for establishing individual connection. Another woman said that she had relationships with three of her dead grandparents, and was hoping that the *seidr* would help her make connection with the fourth. Yet another older woman, who was a healer, said that she had wanted our intention to be on healing the planet, but she eventually conceded that if our own connections with our ancestors were not made we had no hope of healing dolphins, or anything else.

Three people volunteered to journey on behalf of the group. They climbed the platform and sat on the three chairs, back to back, forming an outward facing circle. As they went into trance they rocked slightly, leaning forward. They held staffs and flowers, letting the latter drop to indicate that they were back from their journey. The rest of the group formed a circle around the platform, and with staffs in hand sung the 'seers' on their journeys. The singers were told to 'let the universe sing through you' and chanted a '*seidr* song': moon open/power open/spirit open/come through us now. We raised the power by singing for about twenty minutes until the last 'seer' had dropped their flower. The first to report back was a man who said that he had started off in a church, then gone down a straight road, down a waterfall and found himself in a circle. Each element, water, fire, air and earth spirit was encased in a drum. He went into the drum and came out as light. He saw that the planets had energy and that this affected the earth. He saw how changes in the planet occurred. The second 'seer' went down a tunnel. At the bottom of the tunnel she found the god Cernunnos surrounded by animals; he was giving them a drink. 'Why didn't more come to drink?' she asked. She looked into a cauldron and saw threads of the moon shining therein: anyone who wished could take them. Then the moon met the sun; this was a place to connect. She said that she shot back (to ordinary reality) 'like a lift'. The final 'seer' said that the ancestors took her and she found a power animal that she had never had before. It told her that the ancestors are all around, all around, always with us, and that every time a person felt love it meant that the ancestors were there. We could connect with them through song, power, music, anything. Ancestors are flowers, trees, animals, they love dancing, and a good way to connect with them is at full moon at a natural spot. Sit by a tree and the magic of a tree comes to you, and this could be when the ancestors come. The spirit of the tree danced around everyone to help us connect with our own ancestors, 'she touched everyone here'.

This chapter has comprised a series of glimpses into some of the ways in which practitioners seek to engage with nature; the next chapter will examine three key issues: those concerning place, ancestors and tradition.

Notes

1. In a Circle Sanctuary handout.
2. Personal communication, 27 October 2002.
3. Augustine anticipated Descartes: 'To focus on my own thinking activity is to bring to attention not only the order of things in the cosmos which I seek to *find* but also the order which I *make* as I struggle to plumb the depths of memory and discern my true being' (quoted in Taylor, 1989:141).
4. This was the group that I had my Snowdonian experiences with, as recounted at the beginning of the Preface.
5. Personal communication, 27 October 2002
6. Personal communication, 27 October 2002.
7. Personal communication, 27 October 2002.
8. A yurt is a type of nomadic tent originating in Asia.
9. Julia told me that in her hypnotherapy sessions people are always in charge of themselves, unlike Paul McKenna, who she alleges will do one thing and say another to trick people into performing on stage.

10. Leslie Kenton's book is a practical manual for achieving 'quantum consciousness' and she gives a meditation for reconnecting with the world of nature by conversing with a plant (1999:77–78).

11. Kenton says that we must pay respect to tribal cultures, give thanks for having preserved living shamanic skills, then we must turn to these skills – which belong to all of humanity – to give power for life (1999:46).

12. Held in Lewes, East Sussex, on 25–27 October 1996

13. When asked if the campaigns worked, Adrian replied that at Twyford Down the road was built but that the anti-road campaign was successful because it had increased public awareness; the movement also contributed to the ending of the government's road-building programme.

14. There is a long association between witches and fairies in folklore. European folk tales tell of worlds inhabited by little people called by various names such as elves, pixies, boggarts, or goblins. The land of faery is a magical place and there are many cases of humans being abducted into its mysterious realms (Arrowsmith and Moorse, 1977). In folk beliefs it is often difficult to make distinctions between witches and fairies, and ideas about both have merged at certain periods and changed through time. Eliade has written about a group of Romanian healers who cured diseases caused by the fairies. Organized into cults, these healers met in night gatherings ruled over by the Doamna Zînelor, a Romanian version of Diana or Aradia, both leaders of Wild Hunts (1975:149–72). Aradia, possibly a corruption of Herodias, was the medieval name for the Queen of Witches, a daughter of the goddess Diana who was said to represent the moon, while her brother, Lucifer, 'the Lightbringer', represented the sun (Walker, 1983:54). Ginzburg has argued that beliefs such as these form part of an old and deep-rooted Mediterranean and east European complex of shamanistic beliefs, later being diabolized by the Christian Inquisition (1992a). Thus fairies are connected with both witches and the mythology of the Wild Hunt in folklore (see Chapters 6 and 7).

15. The seeress Thorbjörg is asked by a farmer named Thorkel if she will prophesy for a small Greenland community who have fallen on hard times:

> It was Thorbjörg's custom to spend the winter visiting, one after the other, farms to which she had been invited, mostly by people curious to learn of their own future or what was in store for the coming year. Since Thorkel was the leading farmer there, people felt it was up to him to try to find out when the hard times that had been oppressing them would let up. (Thorsson, 1997:658)

−4−

'Calling to be Remembered': Place, Ancestors, and Tradition

Before the sun has left the sky, one minute,
One dear minute, before the journeying night,
To call to mind the things that are forgotten
Now in the dust of ages lost from sight.

Like foam of a wave on a lonely seacoast breaking,
Like the wind's song where there's no ear to mind,
I know they're calling, calling to us vainly –
Old unremembered things of humankind.[1]

'Like foam of a wave on a lonely seacoast breaking, Like the wind's song where there's no ear to mind' – these old unremembered things of humankind are calling but we have lost our ways of relating to the earth, as this evocative poem that I found pinned to a barn wall at Cae Mabon in Wales eloquently describes. The central issue for many practitioners of nature spiritualities is one of finding again the 'forgotten ancient past' held within lost traditions located in the land. Archaeologist Richard Bradley notes that 'Natural places have an archaeology because they acquired a significance in the *minds* of people in the past' (2000:35); historian Simon Schama observes that they acquire a significance for those in the present: 'Landscapes are culture before they are nature; constructs of the imagination projected onto wood and water and rock' (1996:61); and anthropologist Barbara Bender points out that nature is culturally constructed through the mind and the imagination, combining experience and understanding in the manner in which we engage in the world (Bender and Winer, 2001:4). The human mind, as David Abram has argued, is provoked by the tensions and participations between body and animate earth; it relates to a 'place-specific intelligence' shared by all beings of an area (1997:262). For practitioners of nature religion the land is alive with spirits of place, spirits of ancestors, deities and otherworldly beings such as fairies or dwarves.

A central issue here is one of 'tradition'. Ever since Hobsbawn and Ranger (1983) pointed out that the term is used to confer a sense of authority and legitimacy to certain – often relatively new rather than 'timeless' – practices, tradition has been associated with notions of power and authenticity. In terms of tradition, the authentic, as historian Philip Deloria astutely notes, is a culturally constructed category created in opposition to a perceived state of inauthenticity. The authentic serves as a way to imagine and idealize the real, the traditional and the organic in opposition to the less satisfying qualities of everyday life (1998:101). The spiritual paths that comprise nature religion do not have a continuity of 'indigenous' tradition, or of identifiable sacred scriptures like Buddhism, Christianity or Islam, for that matter. The countercultural Western esoteric tradition is one that is mainly located within either a Christianized framework – for example, high magic – or, in opposition to it, as in modern witchcraft (see Greenwood 2000), and views held by practitioners are shaped by mythologies which are not necessarily primarily located in nature as I shall argue in Chapter 8. However, attitudes to land and relationships with ancestors are important to how practitioners engage with nature. Ancestors, who might inhabit a certain landscape, are often seen as a benevolent source of collective wisdom and tradition; they bring order and healing, putting a person back in touch with their own inner nature as well as the environment. Relating to the past helps people locate themselves in the present and gives authority to their spiritual practices.

The discussion in this chapter centres on the three key themes of place, ancestors, and tradition, and I will examine these themes in two ways. The first part of the chapter is focused on the work and world-views of two Western shamans: Patrick 'Jasper' Lee, who, along with his partner Lizzie May-Gotts, has developed Romany gypsy shamanism workshops for non-gypsies, and Gordon MacLellan, a Pagan environmental educator who works with a variety of traditions of the land in schools, workshops for practitioners of nature religion, and conservation organizations. The second chapter section examines varying interpretations of the past raised through the re-emergence of a 4,000–year-old late Neolithic timber circle in the early summer of 1998, which became popularly known as 'Seahenge',[2] at Holme-next-the-Sea, north-west Norfolk. An exploration of the meaning of Seahenge will reveal many different ways that practitioners view the land: from a New Age belief that there are planetary intelligences trying to convey neoplatonic metaphysical messages through the timber circle, like crop circles, to Native American Medicine Wheel entrances to the underworld, to the view that the monument was a sea altar in a sun ley alignment with Stonehenge in Wiltshire.

Tradition and Place

Practitioners frequently relate to nature through a solar calendar cycle of eight festivals. In the Northern Hemisphere they are Samhain/Samhuinn (31 October to 2 November), Yule/Winter Solstice/Alban Arthuan (Light of Arthur) (longest night, 20–21 December), Imbolc/Oimelc (2 February), Spring Equinox (equal day and night, 20–21 March), Beltane (1 May), Summer Solstice/Alban Heruin (21/22 June), Lammas/Lughnasadh (1 August), Autumnal Equinox/Alban Elued (21 September).[3] These festivals structure practitioners' relationships with nature in a cyclical round of regeneration and renewal based on individual experience (see Greenwood 2000 for examples). Although rituals do shape many people's experiences, some – mainly shamanic practitioners – prefer to work without a ritual structure. Jo Crow started practising witchcraft in a Dianic coven (which recognized only the Goddess, but was not separatist); she has since concentrated on shamanism. She saw witchcraft as connecting with the seasons in a structured way through the eight festivals. The witchcraft circle was contained in a safe place – 'like a capsule'. Using watchtowers, guardians, etc. created a separateness which by this detachment 'necessarily excluded part of the cosmos – to draw a circle would cut something out'. However, Jo said that her biggest experiences were not to do with sitting in a circle but in walking in nature. On one occasion a bee had landed on her hand and she 'started a love affair with it'. She felt elated. She added that thunderstorms made her shiver, and 'to stop and do a ritual would take that away'. Jo felt that she had to move away as she 'didn't do well with sets of rules' and that 'witchcraft didn't quite reach the deepest parts of me that were yearning'. She added that 'there were times when I did rituals and wondered why I was doing them as they didn't move me, they didn't work'. Jo moved to shamanism as 'a way of opening up to everything that was there'. She told me about an experience that she had had at a Winter Solstice witchcraft ritual when she had visited New Grange, a Neolithic burial chamber in Ireland, in trance and had experienced 'her who weeps over bones'. Jo felt that this was a 'very ancient energy' of grief and pain that became life had a different feel to the rest of the ritual and that everyone could feel it; this was 'powerful, direct and deep'. It was an unexpected experience that had 'moved every hair on her body'.

Tradition forms a central part of a particular spiritual practice; perhaps most importantly tradition grounds the present in the past, giving it legitimacy. Traditions make claims to the past in ways that many archaeologists might see as outlandish; some accuse practitioners of inventing a fanciful (and false) prehistory. This is problematic, as archaeologist Robert Wallis has pointed out, because the accusation of invention of tradition infers that there is an ultimately knowable historic past (Wallis 2001:226). The notion of tradition has political implications, particularly concerning issues revolving around the appropriation of tradition. Anthropologist Piers Vitebsky points out that what he terms New Age neo-shamans, in their attempt to revive what they see as ancient wisdom, are often inspired by cultures that are avowedly foreign. They adopt a culture, but specific elements are stripped off – such as clan cults and ancestor worship – as these are so local they are not easily transportable. Relocation takes place on a global scale and with global claims that what they are practising is a new sort of community-based religion (2003:287–288). The adopted culture's local nature is co-opted in transplanted form and it becomes a metaphor for the appropriator's more diffused sense of locality. Relocalized it creates a kind of global indigenosity. Vitebsky claims that the original culture's holistic nature is shattered for social, political and epistemological reasons but retained as a cardinal value. He argues that the holistic ideal is unattainable and that indigenous knowledge is replaced by 'globality' as a weaker concept at the level of global decision-making (ibid.:292–296). Aspects of Vitebsky's argument hold true – the appropriation of Native American culture in particular. Sun Bear, who is half Native American and half European, is founder of the Bear Tribe Medicine Society whose camps are attended by non-Native Americans (Albanese, 1991:156). Sun Bear has been accused of marketing Native American heritage to the highest bidder. He is not recognized as a leader among his own Chippewa people and is pretending to be something he is not, according to Rich Williams, a Cheyenne/Lakota who works at the University of Colorado. The Circle of Elders of the Indigenous Nations of North America requested that the American Indian Movement (AIM) undertake to end the activities of Sun Bear and other 'plastic medicine men' (Churchill, 2003: 326–327).

However, the appropriation of other cultures does not form the whole story as much of the underlying influence behind nature religion comes from the Western esoteric tradition. While there are some movements within nature religion that do 'play Indian', as I have already outlined, it is a gross over-simplification to accuse all practitioners of Western shamanism of appropriating other cultures; there is an interest in learning about and reviving north-western European magical culture before the full imposition of Christianity (see, for example, Bates 2002).

To give a more in-depth account of attitudes to tradition, place and ancestors I now turn to the work of gypsy shaman Jasper Lee.

Gypsy Shamanism

The experience of the Core Shamanic *seidr* described in Chapter 3 made me reflect on the issue of ancestors in nature religion, and I had the opportunity to discuss this at length with the Romany gypsy Patrick 'Jasper' Lee. I first met Jasper, who is a gypsy shaman or *chovihano* (the female version is a *chovihuni*), and Lizzie May-Gotts, his *patrinyengri* (Romany herbalist assistant and 'liaison person' with the spirits), at an academic conference on shamanism at the University of Newcastle in 1998. Jasper was wandering around the conference holding a small container, which afterwards I learnt contained a worm to be used for a demonstration healing ritual (see following chapter). Some time later, I met them again at a party at a mutual friend's flat and had the opportunity to speak to them. A correspondence developed between Jasper and I during which I expressed my confusion and difficulties regarding ancestors.

During the course of the exchange of lengthy letters I told Jasper about my unease concerning the whole issue of ancestors. My anthropological training has made me very aware of what Western imperialism and colonialism has done to the rest of the world, especially to what are often referred to as 'shamanic societies'. As a white Westerner, whose culture has appropriated the spiritual heritage, as well as the land and the lives, of non-Western peoples (the Native Americans and Australian Aborigines being the most publicized examples) I have an acute awareness of the destruction. Coupled with the fact that I had no direct personal ties to any of my immediate ancestors, and because of my cultural history, I could not see them as a source of wisdom or truth that I would want to espouse. I expressed my feelings in a letter to Jasper and he replied, saying that he understood my feelings about the question of ancestors but that part of his training as a *chovihano* was to learn how to let things go no matter what they were – rather like letting the wind blow through you and you still being there, unharmed'. This was sometimes a very difficult thing to do, but he said that *chovihanos* have always had to learn this. Jasper said that he shared my concerns about keeping an awareness of racism and other forms of oppression but that it was possible to let it all go too.[4]

In my response, I expressed interest in what Jasper had said about his training of letting things go. I said that I could understand the psychological importance of this, but was concerned with 'owning' responsibility for being part of an oppressive culture (by virtue of being of white European descent and *gauja or* non-gypsy). I was aware of differences between the gypsies and mainstream Western cultures, but I could relate very easily emotionally and spiritually to the Romany culture of which Jasper was talking. I therefore decided to take Jasper's advice, while not forgetting about the political dimension of the difference, and experiment with trying to contact ancestors through my own journeying (or spirit travellin' as the gypsies used to call it). On one such journey I was told by the spirits that I should be a part of a special ritual that Jasper and Lizzie were going to celebrate in Totnes, Devon, at the eclipse of the sun by the moon – the Sacred Marriage of Kam and Shon – in August 1999. When I wrote to Jasper explaining my journey and asking to join in the ritual he invited me to stay on afterwards for a couple of days for a healing session (see following chapter).

Jasper explained how he thought that the loss of ancestors was due to a bad spell put on Western Europe:

Yes, dark clouds, pain, and the absence of ancestors: they all go hand in hand in these modern times; they are perhaps an inevitable result of our modern times, and it can be very uncomfortable, and indeed a difficult puzzle to solve. It's always good to remember, of course, that it isn't your fault. It's the bad spell that was put over western Europe hundreds of years ago, a spell that took the land's natural power away. (Cast by self-centred sorcerers, so my Ancestor says). I believe it's a spell that all our more ancient ancestors knew would happen. And the spirit of western Europe had to burrow deep underground to hide. I believe the older-style sorcerers will help her escape – hopefully I am one! However, western Europe still lies sleeping, because she has had to hide for so long. And she won't surface again, truly, until the time is right [see Chapter 7]. We sorcerers who have more insight mustn't in fact encourage her to come up until the time is right, because we have to protect that sacred power, at all costs...

It's all still sleeping, and only just beginning to stir. The spell is like you and I and all creatures are small leaves caught up in the force of a great vicious whirlwind, being twirled unavoidably round and round; it's an immensely hard spell to break. So it's a constant task for me, working out how we can weaken the force of the bad spell, and help this great vortex of more natural energy to surface once again... We have all been enchanted. Call it oppression, a bad spell, or what you will, but yes, it has happened, and it constantly causes much damage. But it is possible to change it. All spells can be broken. And we can also help by letting the illusion of the thing go... Because it *is* an illusion, one we've been pressured to live with for generations...[5]

Jasper invokes the ancestors (*puri foki*) and he has inherited his great-grandfather's ancestor, communicating regularly with him since he was 'knee-high'. This spirit being is called 'Puro', but he is more commonly referred to as 'the Ancestor'. Having two main guises, the Ancestor is either a younger, ruthless and testing being of about 35 to 40 years old, or an older and more tolerant 'Merlin figure'. He often wears a green eighteenth-century costume with long boots and a battered top hat draped with multi-coloured material. From time to time the Ancestor might also appear as a young boy. According to Jasper, his appearance 'all depended on what he wanted to put over'. Jasper is also helped by a spirit being called 'Tom', whom he first saw in a library when he was five years old looking at picture books. Tom is one of the *biti foki* (the little folk, or fairies), a guardian of the forest, and 'woe betides anyone who picked flowers without asking, or who did not give an offering of beer, wine, or milk'. Jasper had been warned about Tom by the ancestors as he apparently 'talked you to death', but Tom also took a part in healing work.

Lizzie says that she is in particular communication with the *biti foki* 'Picolo', who wears a tall pointed hat with a huge brim, breeches and a tailcoat; he is a particularly friendly fairy spirit guide for her. Lizzie's role as *patrinyengri* is to support the *chovihano* in his healing work by going into a light trance and observing his body language. She also asks the herbs – particularly rosemary, parsley, and sage – to help in the process. Part of her job is to make potions from herbs such as 'flying ointment' (traditionally made from goose, hedgehog or pig fat with hemlock and various herbs which are, according to Lizzie, 'best kept secret to preserve the magic') and mugwort teas to clear the head and facilitate psychic visions.

I was invited to one of Jasper and Lizzie's introductory workshops. On this occasion Jasper conducted a guided journey where we were invited in our imaginations to get into a boat, float down a river, open our senses to the otherworld, and bring back something for luck. Jasper went into a trance, went around the group making sure that everyone was all right, and tried to 'clear the mists' so that people could see more clearly. Afterwards he explained how he had 'flown down the river' to meet the Ancestor, who had told him if anyone was having trouble. The Ancestor remained there standing with him and, according to Jasper, had expressed the desire to speak to us all. He spoke of the 'old magic' that had been left alone; it was 'strong magic'. Much magic, he said, has been watered down because people do not respect it, but if used in the right way it could be strong. This magic was like the energy in a vortex which had been pushed down under the earth in the western part of Europe, and that there was no great separation between the ordinary world and the other world because of this vortex. The Ancestor offered blessings to everyone, and said that everyone's ancestors were sending the same. Jasper said: 'He's quite excited; he's shaking me because the magic has lain dormant for a long time!'

Romany Tradition

Jasper makes much of the ancient gypsy shamanic tradition of handing down family knowledge. Saying that shamanism was practised by ancient Romany people in Britain and Europe for hundreds of years, he claims that it is a deeply enriching and healing craft that has 'power, passion, light-heartedness and strong elements of magic and sorcery: much of it the very stuff of our childhood fairy tales'. The craft is practised 'in accordance with ancient natural laws and the Earth's natural cycles', according to an article written in *Patrin*, the newsletter of the Romany Life Foundation (Spring 1999, no. 1). Using the notion of tradition, Jasper and his partner Lizzie recreate a Romany animistic world-view that they say can bring non-gypsies closer to an inspirited sense of nature. They run shamanic training programmes, and for all those who complete the five parts there is an opportunity to join the *Devlesko Boler*, a 'sacred circle' of initiates and elders who make decisions on spiritual welfare, and who 'continue to practise Romani rituals and traditions in the original old way'.[6]

Jasper told me that he grew up in a family of psychics in Kent, his grandmother and mother could journey and 'see things'; they also accepted that they might have knowledge gained from previous lifetimes. Claiming to have been trained in ancient Romany traditions by his great-grandfather, a practising *chovihano*, Jasper says that when he was born his great-grandfather knew he was to be the next *chovihano* because his hand was twisted; this was a sign, and he was always treated as special. However, Jasper has broken with his family because he felt that the knowledge of the *chovihano* was going to be lost; he talks about the ways of the *chovihano* with some pain because he says he is making sacred traditions public; some gypsies say this will invite bad luck. He says that there are some in his family, particularly his parents, who are not happy about his openness about gypsy traditions. Sometimes, waking in the middle of the night with enormous doubts, he has thought: 'What am I doing? I'm breaking the old golden rule of preserving for us what is sacred only to us' (1999b:31). Nevertheless, Jasper has chosen to make what he says are secret traditions, with origins that date to ancient tribal values of Western Europe, available to non-gypsies.

Romany shamanism was practised in Western Europe long before the decorative gypsy wagon and long before the romantic idea of the gypsies was born in the latter half of the nineteenth century. We are talking here about ancient tribal values, living in the woodlands and on the heathlands of Britain and Europe over the last 700 years, still nomadic in this century and still in their thousands in this country just a hundred years ago, according to an article in *Patrin* (Spring 1999, no. 1). Jasper is recreating 'indigenosity' as a sense of feeling connected to place, through the adaptation of gypsy tradition for non-gypsies by invoking ideas about animism as a way of relating to nature, thus 'rekindling links with the Europe of the past',[7] and by identifying with Native Americans. He wrote to me about how he had been emotionally moved by a film shown in a Native American museum: 'It was very much like my own story, with the tribe being wiped out, and the little boy became the storyteller and was left a legacy, sort of thing. Of course, I burst into tears in the theater... It was a moving film and I related to it so much'.[8]

For Jasper, being indigenous does not concern having roots in the land – he freely admits that the gypsies originally came from northern India – but of learning to talk to trees as well as tables and kettles, and fairies or *bitti foki* as well as stuffed toys (a great favourite was hedgehogs [*hotchiwitchis*] and worms). In the case of trees, Jasper had a series of 'Old Man' oak trees: he pointed one out to me outside Lizzie's parents' home in Kent, another in Totnes, Devon (where we did some otherworldly journeys just before the Eclipse), and a younger one down the road from their new house in Sussex. In each case, Jasper journeyed with the tree, developed conversations with it, and gained insight from the experience. As far as the soft toys were concerned, there were a whole family of *hotchiwitchis* and a couple of worms that sat on the bookcase in the living room; they were introduced to newcomers and engaged in rituals – on one occasion in Totnes we conducted a 'worm wedding' where the worms 'jumped' over a broomstick – and were generally perceived to be a part of proceedings; at some stage or another, most people were presented with their own *hotchiwitchi* by Jasper and Lizzie.

Jasper's shamanism is heavily dependent on gypsy tradition; however, just what constitutes Romany tradition is open to debate. The gypsies were a diverse wandering people of Hindu origin from North India who were exposed to a multitude of influences in their travels from Afghanistan, Persia, Syria and Egypt to the Balkans and Greece before arriving in Europe in the fourteenth century.[9] Gypsies have always been marginal to the mainstream society in which they have found themselves, and their identity has been formed in opposition as a response to exclusion and exploitation as scapegoats and immigrants. Nevertheless, they have tended to accept the religions in which they have lived: there are Catholic, Protestant and Muslim gypsies; this shows great eclecticism in religious belief and practice. The Gypsy Evangelical Church is a mass pan-gypsy organization that transcends tribal subdivisions (Fraser, 1999:313–316).

Gypsies have also been seen as preserving an older religion associated with magic, fortune-telling, sorcery and witchcraft. George Borrow, an early twentieth-century traveller and writer on gypsies for the Bible Society, notes that English gypsy men were dealers in horses, spending their spare time mending tin and copper utensils of the peasantry, while the women told fortunes: 'Dabbling in sorcery is in some degree the province of the female Gypsy. She affects to tell the future, and to prepare philtres by means of which love can be awakened in any individual towards any particular object' ([1914] 1935:20). The gypsies were attractive to a Victorian culture fascinated by romance. Charles Godfrey Leland (1824–1903), first president of the Gypsy Lore Society, did much to popularize the view that gypsies were priests of a practical peasant religion of the 'old faith' of witchcraft – a shamanism which 'seems to come from the same Tartar–Altaic source which was found of yore among the Indian hill-tribes' ([1891] 1995:xxix). Leland starts the first chapter of his book *Gypsy Sorcery and Fortune Telling* (1891) as follows:

> As their peculiar perfume is the chief association with spices, so sorcery is allied in every memory to gypsies. And as it has not escaped many poets that there is something more strangely sweet and mysterious in the scent of cloves than that of flowers, so the attribute of inherited magic power adds to the romance of these picturesque wanderers. Both the spices and the Romany come from the Far East – the fatherland of divination and enchantment (Leland, [1891] 1995:1).

Gypsies have represented a form of otherness to mainstream society; consequently, they have held a particular interest. According to George Borrow they awaken feelings 'hard to describe' ([1914] 1935:11). Anthropologist Michael Stewart, in his study of Hungarian gypsies,[10] sums up the fascination, 'Gypsies are a part of our world and yet are distinct from the rest of us. They live in the world we know, yet they seem to offer an alternative way to be in our world' (1997:12). Stewart claims that the gypsies' difference reminds us of our ordinariness and that there is always ambivalence about our feelings towards them. This is due to a combination of attractiveness and threat: 'The woman who offers to bless you in the subway with a gift of heather might be the same lady of folklore who steals your children' (ibid.). The fact that gypsies have Indian origins gives them an exotic fascination, and it is this lure that makes the path of the Romany shaman attractive to many people.

Ancestral Rebirth

Taking up my invitation to join the Romany eclipse ritual, I travelled down to Totnes in Devon, south-west England, on the Monday before the event. I was met at the station by Jasper who talked excitedly about the forthcoming proceedings as we walked up the steep hill to their flat. In the evening there is a small ritual for the 'elders', those 'the ancestors had chosen to be there'. Jasper, Lizzie and four others of us, plus toy *hotchiwitchis* (hedgehogs) and worms,[11] formed a circle around a white candle placed on a green tin tray which held the contents of Jasper's small shaman's bag: a white feather, a piece of the 'Old Man' (a special oak tree with which he journeys), and a piece of jasper. Salt was sprinkled over us for purification. We each took a Tarot card for insight into what the occasion would bring into our lives. Jasper went into a trance and the spirit of Kam (the sun) came through him. Kam, speaking 'for himself and Shon' (the moon), told us that we were welcome. The clouds were parting and the sun and moon, our father and mother – our ancestors – were welcoming us. We were all alienated, and they were so grateful to see us. He told us that we were going to be tested; we were going to go beyond a known or unknown boundary. However, Kam reminded us that he and Shon were our parents, that they loved us as children, and that they were beings like us – they were here with us and not distant in the sky to be measured or observed. They moved in a world similar to ours and they were like us. At this point Jasper started crying and there was much emotion. We were all given new names – mine was Bitti Kam (Little Sun) and Lizzie's was Bitti Shon (Little Moon).[12] After a while, Jasper came out of his trance and people recounted their experiences, looked at their Tarot cards and discussed their significance.

On the following day Jasper told us how, according to legend, the Romany gypsies were born of the sun and the moon during an eclipse. The sky was grandfather and the earth grandmother to the sun and the moon, as well as mist, fire and wind. The sun and the moon mated and the gypsies were born of this incestuous marriage between brother and sister. He explained that the eclipse would facilitate our rebirth through this primal myth. He told us that we were going to get into the spirit of the sun and the moon, to take on their characters – we would be 'sucked up in a beam, being one with the experience'. We had to watch and listen (*dik* and *shoon*) and omens would come. Nature would provide lessons, and we would form new relationships with nature.

Jasper lit the candle in the middle of the circle and salt was sprinkled around each person. Jasper went into trance:

> You are going to be brought to the boundaries; you must step across and be adventurous. None of you have anything to lose, so be courageous. Tear up the rule-book many of you have been walking about with for so long. We can achieve a great deal for ourselves if we look in the mirror. The person looking back can teach. The ability to look back and learn from this person will be our challenge. We have the protection of the ancestors; you are with the *chovihano* and will come to no harm. You are safe and cared for by the ancestral family. Don't worry – this is a time to let go, and to find the person you really are, to get to like that person, become best friends.

In the afternoon we walked along by the side of the river Dart that flows through Totnes, to a spot just beyond the 'Old Man' oak tree. We sat in a circle and practised a chant – *Mulee, nomeriben, Kam ta Shon, Camoben* – which we were going to sing during the eclipse. Jasper sang a song about the romance between the Kam and Shon – *choo mande, choo mo pirreno* (kiss me, kiss me my sweetheart). Afterwards Jasper spoke about how Kam catches up with Shon and they come together to mate; our chant was to encourage the whole process. Jasper played his tambourine as we went on another journey – lying in a circle by the side of the river – to help us get into a dream state. He told us that the countryside around – the cows, trees, and the river – was there to help. The sun was a small boy in the morning, a young man at the eclipse when he mates with the moon, and he dies at night before being reborn the next morning.

Back in Jasper and Lizzie's flat that evening there was another trance session. This time Jasper's Ancestor came through, and so did Shon, the spirit of the moon:

> I travel along the beams to make contact with you. I am the spirit of the moon, Shon. You do not hear me…
>
> [We do hear you]
>
> Ah. I travel a long way to find you. My brother and husband visited you yesterday and now it is my turn. I speak to you with the aid of many spirits and the *bitte foki* to help my spirit communication with you. They gather to keep those out who shouldn't be here, those who tease and have fun. They are sent out of the way so I can be with you.
>
> I influence you in many ways, my brother and husband is a silly old fool, but I am more confident… I may seem small in the sky but I know the ways of men and women, and I see what is to happen. Perhaps I am more courageous. My husband and brother mourns the past, he worries about the way things go and how happy things used to be. He doesn't play with people the way I do, he takes them the way they are. I know you often think of the moon with a smiling face, but I'm not always like that. I'm not as jolly as he is. We are not far from you. We are here, with your beating hearts. When

you look up in the sky you make contact, we look down and think you are far away, but you're not.

Ah, it's going to be such a lovely time and I'm pleased you are going to be with us. Many questions, but that amuses me. My brother and husband will tell me off but I think it's wonderful that you're learning your way. I have a sense of humour too. I am just Shon who will help you to dream, call on my spirit to carry you off. Can you trust me? Understand how I operate, take a gamble.

I have to leave you. Thank the *bitte foki* for giving me voice; thank the *chovihano* for otherwise I couldn't let you know how normal this is. I embrace you all. Please come to us. We are old, we are your mother and father. This universe is shrinking; we're coming back together as a family. At one time we were all a family. Your *chovihano* will give you the story of that. The *chovihano* has been sent a long way while I speak to you. I look forward to kissing your cheeks. *Kushto Bok* (good luck).

The spirit of the moon withdrew and in her place came Jasper's spirit helper, the *bitte foki* Tom, who spoke in a high voice:

We look at the flowers we put on your heads and through them into your brains.

I expected tea and cakes, and a tablecloth… My family has trouble fitting into our home in the tree.

What's inside our brains? Worms, all wriggling, then words jumping up and down … now there's flowers on your heads.

When Tom had departed, Kam returned for 'a few short words':

I will return to give you just a few short words. I come with the help of the *chovihano*. I am the spirit of the sun and I would like to give just a short message to say that this time is very special to me – to have a great communication between my children and me is something I cannot describe. I make my way to you via the *chovihano*. He turns himself into a beam and I can fly along it to reach you. I fly to you as a golden bird. There are many stories about me flying around so I can change myself into a human being acting as a human being, just for a short time.

Use your powerful minds to shape shift to a road, a channel or a path to meet me, your golden father. I am greatly honoured and I will sweep you up when I and your mother come together. We will be as one family together. This means so much to me. We are in your hearts. We are your family. The sun makes shadows. You may perhaps not be able to look at me, but look at me with your minds and I will help you. I am your father and I will not forget you. Thank you. *Kushto bok* (good luck).

The following day we dressed in brightly coloured 'sun' and 'moon' clothing, went to a secluded spot, sat in a circle and performed our ritual whilst the eclipse was taking place. It was a very moving ceremony for all concerned. I felt that there was a compression of time, place and past, and that all was interconnected at that specific extended and elongated moment. We were told that transformations in our lives would occur. This ritual was primarily aimed at healing alienation at an important moment in Romany mythology – the point when the gypsy race was born. It marked a significant point in Jasper opening up allegedly traditional Romany practices and folklore to non-gypsies in the spirit of healing the earth from the bad spell put on it. The participants of the ritual were introduced to their ancestral family and in the process had to face a test 'to go beyond a known, or unknown boundary', a rebirth into a new relationship with nature.

I now turn to the work of Gordon MacLellan, a Pagan environmental worker and shaman, for a different approach to working with the land.

Gordon MacLellan: the Blend of all that is Britain

Many practitioners, as demonstrated by the Romany gypsy example above, strongly identify with a particular tradition as a spiritual path; some claim to be Celtic shamans or practise Celtic shamanism, others adopt a Heathen cosmology and seek to recreate northern European magico-religious practices as they imagine them. By contrast, Gordon MacLellan focuses on being inspired by the dream of the land and celebration rather than any specific tradition such as that of a 'Celtic shaman':

No. We have no direct, inherited tradition.
No. We do not belong to a single, identifiable community.
No. We are not necessarily Celtic.
No. We do not even have elders and definite ancestor connections.
Yes. We live in the land called Albion, we are inspired by its Dream and we work with the people that live in these islands now.[13]

There are threads of connection to the past, links with ancestors, and traces of ideas to pick up and use, but we 'act *now* for the people who are around us *now*, not in some long-gone *then* or some hoped for *still to come*': 'We belong to the moment whose air we breathe as we work. And if that action draws on an old tradition so be it, but it is just as likely to call for a change in that older pattern or for the shaping of a new one.' (MacLellan, n.d.b:2).

Gordon describes shamanism as 'an ancient spiritual path that explores a way of living in harmony with the world around us'. 'Shamans perceive a world where everything is alive, where spirit – that sense of self and personality that we find in ourselves can be focused to some measure in every other inhabitant of the world.' This harmony is not passive but an active and dynamic relationship with the living world that recognizes the relationship between all that exists (1999:1–2). Shamans work with spirit people: 'A shaman knows that the spirit people are around us all the time, busy about their own lives, ignoring us, helping us or irritated by us.' Gordon has a 'family' of spirits who work with him as a 'cooperative':

> the bonds that hold us are based on mutual respect and love and maintained by our work and our celebrations. It is perhaps easiest to look at it all as a set of friendships: we are together and like good friendships we have our times when we work well together and times we do not but, overall, we are 'the family', we stay together, we help, protect and empower each other and the collective is stronger than any of its individual components (MacLellan, 1999:5).

Bonds are formed through spirits from a range of traditions, drawing on many mythologies; they are not exclusive. Britain, according to Gordon, can be a strange land to live in – it is the magical home of the Druids and of King Arthur, amongst others. But perhaps more importantly, Gordon sees the land dreaming and humans being part of that dream who are 'both nothing and valuable at the same time' (ibid.:3). The spirit world is the Otherworld; this is not particularly Celtic but is simply itself and consists of a past and a present. The land in its dreaming remembers, and a human being may encounter the accumulated residents of this land:

> There we encountered the accumulated residents of this land. There I meet with spirits who 'technically' arrived with the Vikings in their longships, or find Saxon Wayland in his smithy or meet the Faeries who pick and choose and have used human stories to shape themselves over all the long years of human presence here. There are distinctly Celtic presences and even older people who say they have always been here, stones taking shape and voice and watching all of us living and dying... And the wolves we lost from the everyday world a couple of hundred years ago, they are still hunting in the wood of the Otherworld for the land still remembers them (MacLellan, 1999:3).

Harking back to a Celtic Golden Age is, for Gordon, an escape from addressing the 'blend of all that is Britain'. The role of the shaman is to create celebration – to find the paths to encourage people to relate to the world they live in, 'People still want to make connections: with themselves with each other and to mark the changing world around them'. He says that old customs survive, are revived, or new ones are created or evolve (ibid.:4).

Involved with a number of conservation organizations, including English Nature and the Sacred Land Project, Gordon has worked in South Africa where he has been involved in teaching environment awareness projects to teachers, wardens, and people working in national parks and botanical gardens on an open access year-long environmental training course.[14] He has recently returned from working with environmental educators at Chicago Zoo. The Sacred Land Project is a non-denominational organization that enables local groups to put together resources, expertise and publicity profiles to initiate projects on sites of special religious significance. I met up with Gordon at a Sacred Land Project meeting in Beckenham, Kent, England. It was held at a church that had been rebuilt after a fire. The Project had assisted in the creation of a meditation garden located behind the altar and surrounded by the fire-damaged walls, which had been left as a symbol of renewal and creative spirit arising out of the destruction. Archbishops of the Church of England, Hindus and Pagans chatted together over cups of tea and biscuits. Most of the work of the Project is concerned with Christian sacred sites, but it has also helped to landscape the grounds around a Hindu temple in the West Midlands, and a Tibetan Buddhist peace garden in a converted Victorian courthouse in Lambeth, London.

Gordon was born in Redhill, Surrey, but grew up in Cumbernauld, a new town on the outskirts of Glasgow framed by the Kilsyth Hills. He took me on a tour of the area before we went on to Kilmartin Glen in mid-Argyll, Scotland, the place where he feels most linked to his ancestors. We walked from his childhood home to his old school – a modern comprehensive of 2,000 pupils – past the small wood (with a stream flowing through, now filled with rubbish) where he had done his first magical work; past a long tunnel (built for the drainage of a bank, but now filled in) where he and other children had played. He remembered the smell and the sound it had made. We walked past the rival school (a Catholic comprehensive) and back to his parents' house. Gordon is a charismatic and dramatic figure who 'cuts a dash', often wearing a long flowing frock-coat, scarf, and trousers which lace-up at the ankles; his hair is long, tied back in a pony tail and cropped short on the top and frequently brightly dyed; he wears skull earrings. As we walked back to his parents' house he was noticed. Groups of children stopped talking as he walked by; he often winks at them if they stare.

The trip to Scotland inevitably prompted a discussion on ancestors and tradition. We visited Kilmartin and sat in the Nether Largie South, Ri Cruin and Bruach an Druimein cairns absorbing the place. The landscape is rich in remains of a past in artefacts, buried settlements and signs of past relationship between the land and its people (Butter 1999). For Gordon it has many layers of meaning; he can also find some of his family buried in the churchyard. Gordon is Scottish and identifies as 'Celtic' but is against ethnicity as a sense of possession of the land. He is also against the claim that certain people, by virtue of their ethnicity, claim to be able to speak for the land. For him the land has universality: it can speak through anyone.[15]

Gordon is also a founder member and central organizer of the eclectic group of shamanic practitioners called 'Mad Shamans'; these are a group of friends who view themselves as a family and meet a couple of times a year to share space and celebrate, but not as a formal magical working group with a specific focus such as a witchcraft coven (see Preface and pp.45–46). Mad Shamans are selective in choosing their members, and unashamedly so – a person has to fit in. One of the features of Mad Shamans is that it provides a forum for discussing shamanic issues and, according to Gordon, there are 'long involved, convoluted discussions about all sorts of things – the nature of community, anger, vengeance and the glee of a good curse; teaching/apprenticing/mentoring ... almost anything seems grist to the mill – and when we step on a conversational path it just opens further and further ahead of us – endless variations and possibilities that might work/happen/be happening...' What does this mean for tradition? Is the endless range of possibilities discussed by Mad Shamans an effect of not working in an established tradition? Gordon reflected:

> Does an established tradition close down the options – 'we do things this way' or whatever might remove the need to be aware of alternatives. Access to that immense range of possibilities I think should be one of the strengths of the 'alternative' worlds/ communities – or at least to the pagan one but people seem so eager to create their own 'traditions' with all the narrowing of options that brings without maybe bringing the strength of options proved by the testing of time that would hopefully come with a tradition that has grown with a people over the years. But all the possibilities we are offered – or are open to us can trap us too – too many options and we maybe snap into displacement activities...[16]

This raises issues of the restrictions associated with a certain tradition, but also the lack of security of 'no tradition' and too many options that may have a negative effect. Further to our discussions of these issues in Scotland, Gordon sent me a copy of an article by Frank Henderson MacEowen, 'a shamanist in the traditions of his Scottish Highland ancestors'. Critical of Michael Harner's Core Shamanism, MacEowen writes that shamanism is an ancient religion not a set of techniques; it is about 'restoring souls, not extracting the soul out of the practice', and one of the ways that souls are restored is through the 'enactment of traditional shamanic rituals that reaffirm the person's place in his or her family, clan, community, and culture' (2001:17). Core Shamanism has been criticized for having no tradition and for focusing on shamanic methods of journeying or soul retrieval rather than specific cultural practices, as already indicated with reference to Piers Vitebsky's work on p.4; see also pp.209 and 211). Nevertheless, MacEowen admits that Core Shamanism may open doorways for finding one's own tradition. Giving the example of his friend, the author Tom Cowan, he describes how Cowan studied with Harner's Foundation for Shamanic Studies and that this experience opened the door to his own Celtic ancestor spirits and traditions. Once he had crossed the threshold, he 'found himself in the spiritscape of his own primal Celtic ways and druidic knowledge'; this led him to deepen his practice through 'intensive cultural studies and spiritual pilgrimages to ancestral haunts in Ireland and Scotland'. MacEowen sees shamanism as an ancestral faith that is effective in the healing of family issues because, according to him, we all carry dysfunctional ancestral patterns within ourselves and our families, and so shamanism is a useful way to explore ethnic and religious heritage in order to heal ancestral wounding and soul loss (ibid.:18).

In Gordon's eclectic view of the land's dreaming there is room for many approaches; he works to bring people and place together to relate to the land spiritually. Gordon does not offer people one tradition, as Jasper seeks to do in his creation of a romanticized and inevitably selective vision of the past – 'the old ways'. Anthropologically, there is no surviving tradition passing on from his great-grandfather, and it is likely that Jasper has realized the financial potential for selling Romany gypsy shamanism in courses and workshops, but that does not detract from the potential of such practices in establishing new connections with the natural world for practitioners of nature religion. The skill of recreation has always been a skill of shamans in so-called traditional shamanic societies – it has had to be. By definition a shaman is someone who can bridge the gap between the everyday and spiritual realms; he or she is a 'troubleshooter', resolving problems ranging from healing a sick person, sorting out community tensions, to finding the whereabouts of food to eat. This demands a certain amount of creative and imaginative flair. Jasper was not brought up as a travelling gypsy, his family had settled in Kent and maybe much of the culture associated with living closely with the land had been lost. Certainly, I got little indication that Jasper was closely connected with the natural landscape. When we went out for a walk in a local wood in Sussex on one occasion he made no observations to me about flora and fauna, as a naturalist or someone intimately connected with nature might. Rather, he and Lizzie were more preoccupied with looking for 'fairy holes' at the bottom of trees. In addition, when I asked him whether a particular tree was a hornbeam, he had no idea if it was or not. We also lost our way and I got the feeling that neither he nor Lizzie felt at home in the wood. Jasper's nature seems to be largely the nature of the imagination and the otherworld, one that does not closely correspond with the nature of the living environment. On the other hand, there is much of value in what he teaches. On a personal level, the healing ritual that I underwent with Jasper and Lizzie to reconnect me with my ancestors (described in the next chapter) was very powerful; it had the effect of opening up my connections with ancestors, and of helping me to let go of painful past memories. Perhaps Gordon is right when he says that the land in its dreaming remembers and that human beings may encounter many presences through this dreaming; maybe 'tradition' is more specifically about the human need to define boundaries for social and/or political reasons.

Differing Interpretations of the Past

Coming from a culture of discontinuity with the land, most practitioners have their own interpretation based on experiences of places and how they feel about them; they develop a specific symbolic and mythological language as revealed through 'inner nature' (a subject that I shall explore in more depth in Chapter 7). Indeed, Alan Richardson, in his book *Spirits of the Stones*, claims that it is important not to treat mysterious sites as 'dull remnants of a dead culture' but as vital places within the psyche that can be accessed by anyone, and that the realm of the megaliths is 'not so much a geographical location with historical overlays and archaeological remnants, as a very deep stratum of consciousness inside us all' (2001:3). Richardson thinks that there is no need to travel to sacred ancient sites because these are symbolic gateways to levels of consciousness and universal energies within the mind that can be reached by travelling within; this is similar to the meditation on the Kabbalistic Tree of Life glyph and demonstrates one of the varying attitudes in contemporary magical practice (see Greenwood 2000 for a discussion on learning the Kabbalah). Despite showing a certain dislocation from place, there are important hermeneutic aspects to Richardson's work concerning the creation of mythic meaning and its associated language of magical consciousness. This is shown in his recording of occultist William Gray's experiences of channelling the spirit of an ancestor at the Rollright Stones in Oxfordshire. This ancestress was a small old crone who was 'skin-clad', wore an amulet necklace and carried a skull rattle. Grey thought the crone was channelling the powers of the Otherworld, acting as a guide between the living and the dead (Richardson, 2001:108). With no direct tradition Gray created his own from his own experience, as do many practitioners. This direct experience is particularly well demonstrated by some attitudes to Seahenge.

Seahenge, a Bronze Age timber circle found at Holme-next-the-Sea on the north Norfolk coast, was built at the same time as the sarsen stones were being erected at Stonehenge, and many of the local residents of Holme felt that it had special significance as well as special energies. The circle had emerged from the shifting sands of the desolate coastline and its excavation revealed conflicting world-views held by archaeologists, practitioners of nature spiritualities, and local residents concerning perceptions of prehistory and relationships with nature. During the months before its removal, Seahenge became the focus of a battle between the archaeologists working on the site and Pagans. The former wanted to remove the circle to protect it from the ravages of the sea to conduct archaeological investigation; the latter, those of a more spiritual persuasion, saw Seahenge as akin to Stonehenge as part of a sacred landscape that should be left to nature – even if that meant its eventual destruction by the sea.

Initially English Heritage had proposed recording the circle and then allowing it to be eroded by the sea, viewing it was too expensive to preserve. However, they later decided to excavate it following a campaign by local people, Pagans (such as Clare Prout from the mostly Pagan organization Save Our Sacred Sites) and archaeologists who wanted the circle excavated, preserved and then displayed (Wallis, 2001:221). This prompted another campaign by those who did not want the circle removed. Feeling that none of those involved in the decision-making process about what was to happen to the timber circle at Holme had taken account of its spiritual and religious aspects, Sam Jones, a local painter and spiritual healer, started a protest group 'The Friends of Seahenge' against the proposed excavation and removal of the circle by English Heritage. She approached the Council of British Druid Orders (COBDO) – an organization of fifteen Druid orders formed in 1988 to approach government bodies primarily to create access to all at Stonehenge – for support. Rollo Maughfling, Archdruid of Stonehenge and Glastonbury, and a representative of COBDO, became involved in the campaign to save Seahenge, as did other Pagans such as Buster Nolan, Hazel and Des Crow. The practitioners of nature religion at Holme seemed to have many interpretations of Seahenge, but a common feeling seemed to be one of empathy or harmony, seeing it in any one or a combination of ways: as an entrance to the Otherworld, as another manifestation of a deity and akin to crop circles, or as being part of a energy or ley line of the earth. The last two reflect various ideas from 'earth mysteries',[17] a term for spiritual interpretations and understandings of the earth that gained popularity in Britain in the mid-1970s. Each time the protesters saw the circle it was a deeply spiritual event for them; it appeared that the circle has the ability to change perception. According to Hazel: 'My reaction upon first seeing the circle was surprise at how small it was, but then on entering, how vast it feels and how powerful.' Champion comments that the circle could easily be lost amid the wide, north Norfolk sky and windswept landscape, yet 'once you were standing in it, it felt like the centre of the world' (Champion, 2000:47). This was a feeling echoed by televison presenter Tony Robinson when he stood in the centre of a Seahenge replica made by the Channel Four Time Team archaeological programme shown in December 1999.

In an East Anglian magazine for mind, body and spirit, *Eastern Light*, New-Ager Michael Green suggests that there is a link between Seahenge and crop circles. Many New Age practitioners and ufologists thought that crop circles – large-scale designs made in cereal fields – were the work of intelligences trying to communicate with earth (Devereux, 2000:45–47). Over the last ten years, Green claims, the non-human makers of crop circles have used ancient imagery to convey a metaphysical message. Pointing to one of the earliest, the image of Gaia appearing in 1990, to symbolize 'the role of our Planetary Intelligence as the Earth Mother of all living things', he makes comparisons with the concept of the

World Tree, whose 'symbols appeared in 1998 as crop formations'. Green quotes the historian of religion Mircea Eliade ([1954] 1972) to link the Siberian shamanic use of trees as an archaic symbol of the World Tree:

> Indeed, so old are these ideas that they passed with the earliest settlers into North America across the land bridge known as 'Beringia' some time before 30,000BC...
>
> Amongst the Sioux Indians, the central wooden tree support of the sacred lodge symbolises *Wahan Tanka*, the Great Spirit, who is the centre of everything. The enclosing wall posts of the lodge represent the movements of the moon. As that visionary shaman, Black Elk put it, 'The moon comes and goes, but the sun [as symbolized by the central tree] is forever' (*Eastern Light*, No. 23, n.d.:13).

Associating these ideas with the movements of the Indo-Aryan peoples, Green makes connections to Vedic concepts of ancient India. Quoting Vedic scholar Jeanine Miller (1985), who states that the thousand-branched tree of life whose 'roots, high above, are deeply embedded in heaven and whose branches come down to our earthly realm, brings the divine life to all', he also sees the same concept in the teaching of Tibetan Djwhal Khul, as channelled by the New Age prophet Alice Bailey (1955): 'a tree with root above and flowers below... Deep in the tree, between the root and flowers, the Eye of God is seen, the Eye that knows, the Eye that sees, the directing Eye.' For Green the symbolism of the inverted tree represents the manifestation of deity: 'drawing on the resources of the unmanifest, the Eternal One, from above, and whose fruit (nectar) is the myriad forms of cosmic life in the universe below – a beautiful concept as relevant now as it was for prehistoric man' (*Eastern Light*, No. 23, n.d.:13). A neoplatonic interpretation of the Eternal One manifesting projected onto early humanity and all humanity. Linking the crop formation that 'appeared' at Alton Priors on 9 July 1998 – whose visual symbolism was also a celestial tree – to Seahenge, Green thinks that both reveal 'a seven-fold message', 'The septenary emanation of Deity in manifestation, the Seven Spirits before the Throne of God, the Seven Archangels, is now being revealed in all its beauty and power at this time of crisis for humanity' (ibid.:14; see pp.178–180).

Another interpretation is that of Buster, a Pagan and a tree surgeon who was involved in many demonstrations at Seahenge. Concerned that trees were dying, he created an inverted tree medicine wheel made from a salvaged yew tree to demonstrate that the tree roots had been destroyed by fungus and insects due to pollution and lack of water. The medicine wheel was, according to Buster's partner Yantra,[18] a copy of the ones used by Native Americans who had a 'strong relationship to their environment'.[19] When Buster heard about Seahenge he could not believe it as he had not heard about anyone else putting an upturned tree in the centre of the circle before, and he took it as a sign to take action. Buster took out an injunction – which had the support of Prince Charles – against English Heritage to stop the excavation. Buster saw the upturned tree as the entrance to the Otherworld, as the first three verses of his poem *Upside Down*, demonstrate:

When you go out walking in countryside or town
Everything you're looking at, is really upside down,
Feet glued to the planet
As you're strolling through the trees
You're hanging there suspended,
In a sea of moving weeds.

The birds are all a'swimming
In currents in the sky,
Below them, on the bottom
The clouds move gently by.

And down, down, in the distance
The stars begin to shine
Let go and you're falling...
into endless, endless time...

This poem expresses the 'otherness' of the Otherworld – the falling into endless time appears to represent the change in perception required to enter into another way of seeing the world – the Otherworld is an inversion of this one.

Although not inverted, the tree is a connecting point with other realms in Scandinavian mythology. The god Odin made a voluntary sacrifice by hanging upside down on the World Tree Yggdrassil to obtain hidden knowledge. According to Hilda Ellis Davidson, the World Tree is a symbol of universality, it was said to spread its limbs over every land; it formed a link between the gods, mankind, the giants, and dead, and it was visualized as 'a kind of ladder stretching up to heaven and downwards to the underworld'. The conception of a pathway linking different worlds is one that she says is familiar in the beliefs of shamanistic religions. It is 'developed with rich abundance of detail in the mythologies of the peoples of north-eastern Europe, northern and central Asia, and even further afield, in the regions where shamans are trained to cultivate the mantic trance, and claim to have the power to send their spirits out of the body for long journeys to the other world'. The tree that links the different regions plays an essential part (1964:191–192). The World Tree thus formed a link with the gods, humanity, otherworldly beings such as giants, and the dead. One of Odin's aspects is as a god of the dead, and he is associated with the dead (see Chapter 6 on the Wild Hunt). Hilda Ellis Davidson notes that in the *Edda* poem *Baldrs Draumar* Odin rode down the long road to the underworld on his horse Sleipnir and braved the dog guardian of the threshold in order to consult a dead seeress (ibid.:143).

Francis Pryor, a director of archaeology at Flag Fen,[20] holds views that would appear to concur with the interpretation that the inverted tree represented a meeting point between different realms when he says that the people who built the timber circle may have envisaged a parallel world inhabited by their ancestors. The upturned oak, he thinks, may have represented an inversion of the world, as death is an inversion of life. The circle, situated at the boundary of the land and the sea may have marked a place and state of transition. David Miles, chief archaeologist at English Heritage thought that the upturned tree trunk could have been used as an excarnation altar on which the bodies of the dead were laid to be picked clean by scavenging birds. The bones may then have been removed and preserved separately or cremated (Champion, 2000:81–82). It has been suggested that there was a two-phase funerary practice during the Neolithic: the first part consisted of excarnation or exposure of the body; the second concerned the gathering of bones, breaking them – perhaps to release spirit – and burning, before collective burial and interment in the burial barrow or tomb (Castleden, 1998:185).

A third interpretation pointed to the importance of ley lines. Rollo Maughfling, the Archdruid of Glastonbury and Stonehenge, spoke at a special meeting, held at the University of East Anglia to discuss Seahenge on 11 March 2000, about how it had been important to fight to save Seahenge from desecration. Claiming that Seahenge was a sun centre in alignment with others in Britain, he said that the first point of light enters Britain on the shore of East Anglia; this then shines down to Stonehenge along the ley lines of many important monuments. Maughfling is drawing on the idea that a 'ley' is an alignment of ancient places across the country, and, in this case, that there is a sun alignment connecting Stonehenge with Seahenge. As noted earlier, Alfred Watkins, an amateur archaeologist, is responsible for introducing the idea into 'earth mysteries'; but his ideas have not been accepted by mainstream archaeology.

According to Hamish Miller and Paul Broadhurst, two writers on earth mysteries, Watkins's discovery of ley lines was based on a revelation and a vision 'by some process independent of the rational mind'. What Watkins saw was a network of lines linking 'ancient sites; earthen mounds and encampments, old stones, churches built on pre-Christian sites, holy wells, moats and ponds, crossroads'. Alignments of these 'remnants of antiquity' covered the land and radiated out to include 'mountainous peaks and hills where beacons had once been lit'. Watkins thought that a web of intersecting lines was 'woven over the face of the Earth, laid out by some remote prehistoric culture and preserved for thousands of years by the natural evolution of sacred sites' (Miller and Broadhurst, 1998:21). This vision revealed a web of intersecting lines – a prehistoric sacred map. The linking together of cosmological features as sacred sites has been very influential in earth mysteries, and is seen to be a revelation of ancient earth secrets.

It is obvious that to try and move Seahenge would be tantamount to sacrilege in this view. Rollo Maughfling said that putting the monument in a museum away from its original location would destroy it; a special site like Seahenge could only be studied within its environment and its removal constituted vandalism to be compared with the Roman invasion. Adding that national monuments gave an understanding of early Celtic communities, Maughfling said that Seahenge might have been a Druid oak grove. He pointed out that Seahenge was irreplaceable as a place of Druid worship today and that it was a 'sea altar'. The revival of the sanctity of the living earth was the only resolution for planet earth, he claimed.

Each interpretation is an attempt to create a revitalizing narrative to the past, in the process landscape is given new meaning (Vitebsky, 2003:287); this is the process of participation in nature.

Conflicting Views

The confrontation between the scientific 'objective' archaeological discourses and spiritual views regarding Seahenge was essentially about differences regarding participation with the land. Participation 'opens a window onto the enormous and pregnant, but clouded issue, of *science* versus *religion*', says Stanley Tambiah (1991:86). For practitioners of nature religion, and indeed many local residents, what was important was Seahenge's connection with place: it was important that it should remain *in situ*. If it was removed a connection to the Otherworld, relationships with ancestors, the past, and the spirits of the land would be broken. It would become just 'old bits of rotting wood', as one Pagan commented, even if authentically reconstructed and relocated. More importantly, Seahenge has become a contemporary symbol of everything that is important for many people today; that is, harmony with the earth and the naturalness of nature as opposed to a Promethean view of science.

Although claiming connection with their spiritual ancestors, practitioners of nature religion view the past from the present and they tend to look back with rose-tinted spectacles. It is impossible to know how people in the Bronze Age or the Neolithic would have viewed life.[21] The nature of Neolithic society is a controversial subject partly because it has been imagined and represented in various ways. For example, in 1740 William Stukeley saw Neolithic Stonehenge as evidence of a stratified society with druids, archdruids, kings, princes and nobles. However, by 1935 Stuart Piggott interpreted the archaeological evidence to portray a more peaceful and idyllic scene (Castleden, 1998:204). It is inevitable that interpretations of the past vary; there is always a political dimension to how history is recorded and who records it. Relationships with landscape are complex and perhaps it is inevitable, given the Western history of control and domination of nature, that practitioners' relationships reflect this varied legacy. Notwithstanding, practitioners of nature religion generally tend to favour a romantic perspective, viewing mainstream science with scepticism, if not outright hostility. Where a scientific world-view is accepted it is likely to be re-envisioned as 'new paradigm science' associated with systems theory and networks, as popularized by Fritjof Capra (1996). The effect is the tendency for those interested in spiritual attitudes to nature to be hostile to scientific archaeological investigation.

This was made clear during the excavation of Seahenge – the archaeologists and the protesters appeared to form two opposing camps,[22] although this belies the fact that there is an ongoing communication between various nature religion groups such as ASLAN (the Ancient Sacred Landscape Network), Dragon Environmental Network, and the Pagan Federation, and archaeologists and anthropologists. At any rate, any meaningful communication, if there was one, had broken down at Holme. I spoke with representatives of both sides and found that each camp saw the other as 'the enemy'. One archaeologist told me that he believed that 'the Druids' – as the practitioners of nature religion had become collectively known – had cursed the archaeologists. He did not take this lightly and appeared to be greatly concerned, telling me that the things the Druids had been saying had really started to get to him: 'they were so hostile', and had threatened to 'knock his head off' he said. The Druids had told him that the monument was used for sacrifice and that the archaeologists would be sacrificed; they had also predicted that if the circle were moved all manner of disasters would befall both the archaeologists and the country, 'for the millennium, the eclipse, and everything'. The archaeologist said that the Druids were more interested in publicity than anything else, and concluded by saying that he could write a novel about his experiences. Sam Jones, who saw the circle as a symbol of a calm natural and harmonious feminine energy and felt that it should be left where it was, thought that only nature could decide its fate. She saw science as a threat: 'I seek to honour nature and spirit above science and feel that science has led us astray and threatens our existence' (Champion, 2000:46). After the circle had been removed, a one-day meeting was organized by members of the School of World Art Studies and Museology at the University of East Anglia to debate issues raised,[23] as the situation had become so bad.

The conflict between the Druids and the archaeologists centred on the way that a wedge from the central inverted tree stump had been removed with a chain saw by a tree surgeon for radio carbon tests at Queen's University, Belfast, and tree-ring analysis by the Dendrochronology Laboratory at the University of Sheffield.[24] The Druids saw this as an act of vandalism and symbolic of the insensitive approach of science.[25] The archaeologists were viewed negatively during the removal 'as manifestations of imperialism' and as 'an uncaring discipline, typical of a dominant elitist society' (Ucko, 1990:xv, quoted in Wallis, 2001:222). According to archaeologist Robert Wallis, these events exemplify the increasing tension between site custodians and opposing groups, including local people and neo-shamans. Wallis argues that the neo-shamans and their peers are not addressed seriously in site management stategies, and that Seahenge is typical of the increasingly activist positions that neo-shamans are assuming in relation to archaeological sites (Wallis, 2001:221).

This chapter has sought to raise some of the issues related to place, ancestors and tradition in nature religion. The following chapter will address the question of magical consciousness, the *experience* that comes through participation with a wider spiritual reality.

Notes

1. *The Peacemakers*, Gower, 1997 (translated by Tony Couran).
2. 'Holme Timber Circle' has little to offer the imagination. 'Seahenge' was neither a henge nor built by the sea, but the term was full of mystery, feeling and atmosphere (Champion, 2000:105).
3. In the Southern Hemisphere these dates are reversed; for example, Samhain is celebrated at the time of Beltane in the Northern Hemisphere (see Hume, 1997).
4. Personal communication, 5 March 1999.
5. Personal communication, 6 April 1999.
6. *Patrin*, Winter 1999, No. 4.
7. In his editorial of the newsletter of the Romani Life Foundation (RLF) he notes that the RLF is 'looking forward to a *kushti* future as we continue to grow in numbers with Romani Gypsy shamanism developing a firm place on the map of indigenous cultures. As many of you will know it has taken a while for my culture to be recognized as an indigenous culture in its own right. We are still educating people all the time. But as many discover, the romani *drom* [path] relates specifically to Europeans and is therefore refreshingly close to home, whether we live in Britain, USA, Canada, Australia, or elsewhere, (Spring 2000, No. 5).
8. Personal communication, 12 April 2000.
9. Angus Fraser says that maybe it is a forlorn hope to prove the origins of the gypsies. By tracing the development of the Romany language he shows how Romany language and its speakers have been exposed to a multitude of historical demographic and socio-linguistic influence over centuries (1999:10).

10. The experience of gypsies in Western Europe is different to those in Eastern Europe, due to pressure to assimilate under communism in the latter.
11. Jasper told us that gypsies always carried toys, and they became advisers. He said it seemed crazy, but the gypsy world was animistic; everything was seen to have spirit. 'In Romany cultures everything is teeming with life, you are never alone, they advise you, teach you, and join in to have fun!'
12. These new names conferred new relationships. At the celebration party after the ritual Lizzie and I teamed up as a 'dynamic partnership', expressed through a dance we performed together.
13. www.phhine.ndirect.co.uk
14. Gordon told me that the course provided people of all colours and ages to get involved in an area where such mixing does not normally occur.
15. Personal communication, 19 September 2000.
16. Personal communication, 3 May 2000.
17. Paul Devereux claims that the term first appeared in 1974 as a headline of an article in *The Whole Earth Catolog* in an attempt to summarize aspects of a new wave of ancient mysteries writing. He says that this was a time when archaeology was in turmoil over new dating systems and theories. The term 'earth mysteries' was used by the journal *The Ley Hunter* in 1976 and it then became popular in Britain, but not in North America, where the term 'ancient mysteries' is more frequently used (2000:6).
18. At the meeting held at the University of East Anglia I spoke to Yantra, Buster's partner.
19. There is no evidence suggesting that medicine wheels were used by ancient Native Americans. They are more likely to be a New Age synthesis of many Native American traditions formulated by Sun Bear, who is the son of a Chippewa (Ojibwa) father and a European (German/Norwegian) mother (see Albanese, 1991:156–163).
20. Flag Fen is a Bronze Age village site, discovered in 1982. It was constructed as a palisade, the size of Wembley Stadium, in the middle of the Fens.
21. Rodney Castleden has pointed out that studies of burials in Yorkshire show that there was a simple egalitarian society until about 3500 BCE. After this time he thinks there was increasing differentiation, until in the late Neolithic of 2500–2000 BC a simple four-tier society had evolved, in ascending order of importance there were: children, women and adolescents, men and bigmen (1998:208).
22. However, I spoke to one senior archaeologist not involved with Seahenge who told me that he thought the situation in Norfolk had been very badly handled. It was not typical, he said, and he thought that the views of the archaeologists there did not represent current archaeological thinking, which was much more sensitive to alternative spiritual interpretations of space.

23. The meeting was organized by Robin Skeates, a lecturer in Material Culture and Museum Studies, and Anthony Hyams, a combined Anthropology, Archaeology and Art History student, and was held at the university on 11 March 2000. The discussion focused on the different perspectives on Seahenge and raised issues of who had the right to own, manage and interpret the material remains of the past.
24. *Eastern Daily Press*, 2 December 1999. I am grateful to Molly Rich for bringing this to my attention.
25. The size of the wedge, and the manner in which it was removed, was later regretted by Richard Morris, chair of the English Heritage Ancient Monuments Advisory Committee at a one-day meeting held at the University of East Anglia to discuss Seahenge on 11 March 2000.

–5–

Magical Consciousness

Magical consciousness, as an aspect of human cognition, may be equated with what Lévy-Bruhl has termed 'the law of participation'. Lévy-Bruhl saw participation as a psychic unity, a fundamental state of mind, that included individuals, society, and the living as well as the dead; he described it is a type of thinking that created relationships between things through unseen forces and influences (Tambiah, 1991:86–87,105–110; Evans-Pritchard, [1965] 1990:83). Magical consciousness is based on analogical rather than logical thought, and involves the association of ideas, symbols, and meaningful coincidences. Described variously as 'altered states of consciousness' (ASCs), shamanic states of consciousness (SSC), or non-ordinary reality, magical consciousness is usually brought about through the application of one or more techniques, such as dancing or drumming (or a combination of these); it may occur in or out of a ritual setting. Primarily concerning a shift in consciousness to an expanded awareness, it may involve the invocation of spirit beings.

Bateson's work on the primacy of the unconscious in the non-verbal arts is used as a starting point for a discussion of magical consciousness in this chapter. Bateson sought to understand the 'code' for partly unconscious messages. In so doing, he made observations about how the mind thinks abductively using metaphor, symbols and connections (see p.8). He admits that abductive thinking – as the lateral extension of abstract components of description – is 'a little uncanny'; but all types of knowledge form the basis of abduction, including 'Metaphor, dream, parable, allegory, the whole of art, the whole of science, the whole of religion, the whole of poetry, totemism..., the organization of facts in comparative anatomy'. He claims that 'all of these are instances or aggregates of instances of abduction, within the human mental sphere' (Bateson, 1985:153). Abductive thinking using metaphor and symbols that speak to the unconscious and an otherworld of spirits is the language of magic.

How do practitioners come to experience magical consciousness? Using selected examples, I describe the transformational aspects necessary to expand consciousness. The first concerns one woman's feelings of 'unconditional love' and a connection with the natural world that occurred during visits to Findhorn, the New Age centre in Scotland. The second demonstrates how Michael Harner's Core Shamanism can be a framework for Westerners to experience a holistic state of consciousness, one that generally avoids the 'stealing' of indigenous cultures (Vizenor, 1995; Churchill, 2003) or of 'playing Indian' (Deloria, 1998). I use two experiences based on Harner's drumming methodology – my first shamanic journey and one undertaken by one of my students in which we both, on separate occasions, transformed into animals – to illustrate how holistic (i.e connected) patterns of thought are formed. The third is a case study of a Romany healing ritual conducted to cure my 'soul loss'. Magical practices are seen to be intimately concerned with healing; they are often viewed as a 'route to wholeness', uniting mind and body, self and nature, and thus overcoming social isolation and fragmentation (see Greenwood, 2000:121–125). As ethnologist Holger Kalweit has noted in his book *Shamans, Healers and Medicine Men*, healing means 'physical and psychic transformation on all levels' (1992:1). The ritual described here locates the anthropologist, as a non-Romany (*gauja* [feminine], *gaujo* [masculine]), within a holistic Romany culture created for workshop practitioners; in the process individual consciousness is expanded (and healed).

Focusing on magical consciousness as a pan-human faculty of mind has implications for the ways in which nature spiritualities are studied. Some social scientists seek to create significant differences between Western and non-Western approaches to magical practices. In a paper comparing indigenous shamanism in tribal India and Arctic Siberia, anthropologist Piers Vitebsky claims that Western New Age neo-shamanic movements appropriate indigenous knowledge, and they lose its holistic cosmology in the process (Vitebsky, 2003:295–296). In a similar vein, religious studies writer Paul Johnson, in a critique of Harner's Core Shamanism, argues that shamanism has been universalized and individualized as a therapy technique. Core Shamanism, he claims, has created a new ritual form based on universal non-contingent status and therapy; this reflects a particular kind of fragmentation and diversity found in modern societies – 'an explosion of a single coherent world-view into multiple fragments'. Neo-shamanists apparently 'battle' against the disembeddedness of radical modernity through their reliance on indigenous sources (Johnson, 2003:347). Like Vitebsky, Johnson, whilst noting that traditional societies are always in the process of re-creation, compares traditional shamanism with modern Western versions – and the latter is invariably considered unfavourably. Both authors, therefore, claim some distinction between 'proper' shamanism and Western variations, the latter apparently having no capacity for developing holistic cosmologies.

By borrowing shamanic techniques the original cosmology may indeed be lost, but I argue that practitioners of nature spiritualities create new meanings, relationships and connections through participation; these help formulate different holistic world-views (see endnote 3, p.35). Consequently, my approach is different to that of Vitebsky and Johnson. Focusing on the process of participation as human cognition, I examine how thinking magically is developed through the practice of various nature spiritualities. Indeed, if magical consciousness is viewed as an awareness of holistic interconnections and cosmologies, then the dualism between so-called traditional indigenous and modern Western ways of thinking is largely dissolved and different understandings of this material are possible (I examine the implications for this approach with reference to other studies of shamanism in Chapter 8).

Participation in Nature

Anthropologist Roy Willis claims that all human cultures simultaneously recognize a duality in world-view or cosmology while also recognizing an underlying commonality or continuity (1994:7). He draws on philosopher Lucien Lévy-Bruhl:

> As far as we are permitted to go back into observable primitive societies ... man has had the revelation that reality is such as he sees it and at the same time there exists another reality, or better said, that the reality given to him is *at one and the same time what it is and other than what it is*. (Lévy-Bruhl, 1975:103. Cited in Willis, 1994:8. Willis's emphasis)

Willis applies Lévy-Bruhl's generalization to all human cosmologies – 'primitive' and 'modern' – to demonstrate oppositional complementarity and the logical contradiction between principles of separation and continuity. The continuing mediation between two juxtaposed domains or aspects of a unitary reality Willis calls the 'transorganismic dyad' of self-and-other as modes of being peculiar to *Homo sapiens* (Willis, 1994:12–13).[1]

Lévy-Bruhl was the first to suggest that human beings had two coexisting forms of consciousness: rational-logical and mystical; he went against the Enlightenment premise that the predominant mode of thinking was rationalistic. Lévy-Bruhl adopted a phenomenological interpretation of 'primitive' experience. For him, primitive mentality was pre-logical and was formed by collective representations (not by innate structures of the mind); it was an alternative system of thought to what was seen as the modern logical mentality.[2] Lévy-Bruhl argued against Frazer's evolutionary ideas: primitive mentality did not represent an earlier evolutionary stage but was founded on the 'law of participation', a type of unity where there was no demarcation between nature and the supernatural and which had its own coherence and rationality. Mystic unity was based on participation and on an association between persons and things that in Western thought would be logically distinct; it created a fundamentally different relationship between the individual and society, based on the notion that *mana* or energy suffuses the individual and his/her body and the whole environment. In addition, the social world included the dead who reincarnated into the living ([1910] 1966). Lévy-Bruhl explained, in *Les Fonctions mentales dans les sociétiés inférieures*, that he used the term 'mystical' for lack of a better one and 'not with allusion to the religious mysticism of our own societies, which is something altogether different, but in the strictly defined sense where "mystical" is used for the belief in forces, in influences, and in actions imperceptible to the senses, though none the less real' (cited in Evans-Pritchard, [1965] 1990:83).

Accused of making too strong a contrast between primitive and civilized societies, Lévy-Bruhl's later work postulated two universal coexisting mentalities in humans – the mystical mentality and the rational-logical mentality. The mystical experience was characterized by emotion induced by the presence of invisible powers and contact with non-ordinary reality. As Evans-Pritchard concluded in his discussion of Lévy-Bruhl's work, it is not so much a question of primitive versus civilized mentality as the relation of two types of thought to each other in any society, whether primitive or civilized; it is 'a problem of levels of thought and experience' (Evans-Pritchard, [1965] 1990:91).

Taking up this theme, Tambiah suggests that it is possible to separate two orientations to the cosmos – two orderings of reality that women and men everywhere are capable of experiencing. The first is causality, which emphasizes atomistic individualism and distance – Lévy-Bruhl's rational-logical thought – while the second is participation, an orientation to the world which places that person in the world fully as a totality and where action is often expressed through myth and ritual (1991:105–110); this is what Lévy-Bruhl called mystical thought.[3] To illustrate participation, Tambiah draws on the anthropologist Maurice Leenhardt's work in Melanesia (1982). Melanesian life, according to Leenhardt, was a dynamic totalistic weaving of nature, society, myth and technology in which the Melanesian village was the centre of a mythic landscape. Mountains, rocks, trees and animals were endowed with the power of an ancestor god and totemic life (Tambiah, 1991:106).

Thus, participation, as an orientation to the world that is holistic and 'mystical', is the basis of magical consciousness. Magical thinking forms part of a whole collection of knowledges in the process of consciousness; it creates connections between phenomena and events through forces and influences unseen but real. Magical thinking is also analogical thinking and it has, in William James's terminology, a noetic quality – it forms the basis of a state of knowledge ([1902] 1977:367). Indeed, anthropologist Geoffrey Samuel argues that human thought, including the most rational, takes place within a framework of analogy – through pictures, images and concepts – and that analogical thinking guides the purposes of rationality. Visionary states, according to Samuel, are not irrational or pre-scientific or non-scientific, they are examples of analogical thought (1990:109). Echoing Aristotle's metaphysics of a scientific study of Being, Samuel sees analogical thought as part of many ways of knowing, where knowledge is not something contained in the mind but a 'patterning of mind and body as a totality'. This includes commonsense, informal and non-scientific knowledge implicit in daily activities – from how our brains operate to factual knowledge of getting to work and tracking animals, as well as of modes of operating within traditional societies that have been hard to incorporate effectively within Western rationalistic theory. Such knowledge becomes formal when it 'crystallizes out' attaining stability in law, bureaucratic organization, and in scientific theories (1990:3–7).

Analogical thinking is akin to what Jung called 'synchronicity'; by this he meant the 'meaningful coincidence' of outer and inner events that are not causally connected (von Franz [1964] 1978:226–227). Based on the idea that an inner unconscious knowledge links a physical event with a psychic condition, meaning often being symbolically indicated through dreams (Jacobi [1964] 1978:357–358), synchronicity is not dissimilar to James Frazer's notion of 'sympathetic magic', the psychological association of ideas, thoughts acting on each other at a distance through an invisible ether-like medium (Frazer, [1921] 1993:12).

Part of many ways of knowing, analogical thought is an aspect of consciousness; it is shaped through relationships with spirits. Gordon MacLellan, the shaman whose work was discussed in the previous chapter (and which is further described in Chapter 7), elucidates how a relationship with spirits might operate when he talks about his family of spirits. As previously noted, Gordon works with a group of spirits; he is the only one who is human. Some have been with him for thirty years, others for twenty years; a few are more recent, while some 'just come visiting'. There is a core of about five. On most days he will make time to be with them, to meditate or dance, by slipping out of this world into the spirit world. Gordon sees his spirit family as a presence that is always there but at some times more consciously; they work better together than they work alone, they are 'bound by love' (2001:259). Gordon explains how trance dance is a medium where human and spirit meet: 'a dancer becomes a focal point where spirits, energy and people all meet. A dancer may move through the patterns of energy that he sees around him or may tell stories in his dancing or, possessed, dance the passion of the spirits he works with'.[4] The dancer becomes the mediator of the spirit world. Gordon sees his relationship to certain spirits in terms of friendship, in the 'plethora of possibilities' that come from seeing the world as alive: 'the pattern of friendship reverberates in the non-human world too. There are spirits of animals, spirits of plants, spirits of stones... There are spirits from myth and folklore, and there are the bigger spirits who are gods' (MacLellan, 2001:258).

I was able to see the meeting between human and spirits when Gordon organized a Sacred Trance Dance as a spring celebration. This was a special event; he says he does not usually dance in public. However, on this occasion the spirits had told him to perform in front of people, and so he had arranged a special sacred dance where he would dance the spirits that he worked with. He invited friends, fellow Pagans and shamanic practitioners, but also those who were unfamiliar with the 'spiritual' shamanic side of his work such as colleagues in environmental education and those involved in interfaith sacred land projects. Fifteen people met in a beautiful black and white wooden village hall in Didsbury, Manchester, to celebrate the coming of spring. The first part of the evening was organized so that everyone had a chance to make music and dance, but gradually the attention focused on Gordon's relationships with his spirit family. This was an occasion when the spirits were to be made known as they danced through him. Gordon, face painted and wearing a fringed leather robe, slowly entered a trance state (see cover image of this volume). As the drumming increased, it was evident to me that there was a participatory communication between Gordon and the spirits in process, the other-than-human was coming through into the human form. At times there seemed to be a non-verbal discussion going on as Gordon's body appeared to act out questions and answers in a swirling profusion of expressive movements.[5]

Examining Participation

It is very difficult to describe the spirit communication involved in Gordon's dance; this is because the relationship is mostly incommunicable in words. Gregory Bateson argues that this is because the written language is the wrong code for its expression. Dancing conveys something that is inaccessible to speech; it is a primary process more easily understood through metaphor. In his attempt at mapping a theory of the non-verbal arts – poetry, works of art, dancing, religion – Bateson quotes the dancer Isadora Duncan who, when asked to explain the meaning of her dance, said 'If I could tell you what it meant, there would be no point in dancing it' – if the message could be communicated in words why dance it? Bateson suggests that what artists such as Isadora Duncan may be trying to communicate is a particular sort of partly unconscious message, and that this message might be about the 'interface between conscious and unconscious' ([1972] 2000:137–138).

Inverting Freudian notions of primary and secondary processes – whereby conscious reason is seen as normal and self-explanatory, while the unconscious is repressed as well being seen as mysterious and distorted through dreams – he argues that unconscious components are continuously present in multiple forms. In everyday relationships we continuously exchange messages about unconscious materials, and he argues that it is important to exchange metamessages by which we tell each other what order and species of unconsciousness (or consciousness) attaches to our messages. Discourses about relationships are commonly accompanied by a mass of semi-voluntary kinesic and autonomic signals that provide more trustworthy comment on the conscious verbal message, which may be deceitful. Art becomes an exercise in communicating about the species of unconscious-ness – a particular sort of partly unconscious communication about the interface between consciousness and unconsciousness ([1972] 2000:137–138). Bateson asserts that the conscious mind has poor access to the unconscious, which is coded and organized differently to conscious thought with its structured language. When access to the unconscious is achieved by way of art, dreams, poetry, religion and intoxication, etc., there is still a 'formidable problem of translation' because much of the primary process – which is more archaic in an evolutionary sense than the conscious operation of language (ibid.:141) – is metaphoric and is not focused on specific things or persons but is centred on relationships (ibid.:139).

In trying to understand the form of psychic integration coded within a work of art, for example, Bateson points out that the aim is to find the meaning of a particular code chosen. For example, it is not in order to translate art into mythology (an aspect of art that can be most easily reduced to words) and then examine the mythology because that would negate the problem of trying to understand the code of the art. Understanding a code is done by an 'approximate synonym of pattern, redundancy, information, and "restraint", within a paradigm'; in other words, looking for the pattern. For example, from a tree visible above ground it is possible to guess at the existence of roots below ground – '[t]he top provides information about the bottom'. Alternatively, it is possible to guess at the position of parts of the circumference of a circle from a drawn arc. We need to have a conceptual system, which will force us to see the 'message' in the art object as both itself internally patterned and also as itself as part of a larger patterned universe (Bateson, [1972] 2000:129–130).

Bateson's view that dancing might be about the communication of a partly unconscious message goes some way to explaining Gordon's dance; certainly Bateson is right when he says that dancing conveys something inaccessible to speech. However, explanations in terms of conscious and unconscious messages do not go far enough. It is necessary to expand the framework of analysis and Bateson does this using Cybernetics[6] as a new approach. In terms of Gordon's dance, it appeared that a two-way communication was going on between Gordon and members of his spirit family:

> When I dance, my innermost self becomes still and the movement of the dance sets me free, I become all the spirits that I work with. I see with all their eyes, we enjoy the physical form of the dance. I feel a world that thinks and its presence humbles me and sets me free. (MacLellan, 1996:147)

The dance is an invocation. This could be explained in terms of Gordon expanding his consciousness to unconscious (spirit) aspects: he gives the spirits space to express themselves. Or is it that he 'lets them in'? Gordon's innermost self becomes still; he is the spirits. In a sense, he 'hands over' his body to become a vehicle for the spirits. Gordon himself explains that shamanic control is about control of the self, not control over other things (like a magician conjuring up things to do his will, for example). He says he 'may move over and let something else move in for a while, but that's my choice'. His spirit family is very tightly woven together, but within that he is still 'Gordon the Toad' (2001:264).

Gordon's relationship with his spirit family is similar to the one that Jasper Lee, the gypsy shaman introduced in the previous chapter, has with his spirit Ancestor. After a healing ritual, during which the Ancestor 'came through' and spoke using Jasper's body, I asked Jasper about how it felt. He replied:

> I go up out of my head. I seem to go to the left ... [I go] through the ceiling, through the roof. I'm aware of spirits gathering and look for the Ancestor who joins himself with me. Then I stretch myself like dough. That goes on and on and then I can be used for whatever is needed. I cease to be human and become dough... It feels nice to be protected by the Ancestor. I'm not unconscious of what's going on but it's in the distance.

Jasper explained that when he came back into human form the transition made him jerk and jump in a 'series of changing patterns in a timeless universe'. He indicates that he is conscious of what is happening but, for him, it is more a question of spirit communication – of 'bringing through' a non-corporeal consciousness.

This demonstrates the expansive nature of magical consciousness; it is a different awareness of a holistic interconnected pattern of energies and forces. An experienced shaman may 'tune in' to any element, or strand, within this pattern and 'go with' whatever it brings – as in a shamanic journey – or, alternatively, 'let through' or 'give voice' to a specific spirit being. The process involves a participation between the shaman and his or her world of spirits. This may include conscious and unconscious elements: much shamanic work involves working with symbols and metaphor; these are sometimes seen as 'gateways' into alternative realities. The whole procedure may also depend on the intent of the shaman. Both Gordon and Jasper had the intention of invoking spirits: Gordon had arranged a special trance dance to introduce the spirits that he worked with, while Jasper ordinarily invokes his Ancestor for healing rituals. The whole experience is seen to be an opening, an expansion, into other realms of consciousness and other conscious beings. Magical consciousness is not confined to the individual and the personal; it is inclusive of other consciousnesses. How these consciousnesses are viewed is dependent on spiritual path or tradition. This raises the thorny question of whether the spirits have a separate reality. The dilemma raised is whether the spirits are 'real' or whether they are a part of Gordon's and Jasper's imaginations, part of their specific psychologies and individual minds. The question may be answered by an exploration of what is termed 'mind'.

Historically, since Descartes associated mind with individual human reasoning, mind has been located in the brain. However, Bateson views mind as a part of nature; he constructed a picture of how the world is joined together in its mental aspects as a vast matrix of interlocking message material (Bateson, 1985:29–30). For Bateson, mind works inwardly and outwardly in its environment (ibid.:234). Mind is a processor of information; but it does not work through creating patterns of difference, nor is it anchored in the workings of the human brain, as in Lévi-Strauss's view. Mind, for Bateson, is immanent within the whole system of relationships within which humans are enmeshed. Bateson takes an ecological perspective on the mind; he recognizes two ecologies: one of material and energy exchanges, and the other as an ecology of ideas – an 'ecology of mind', or the process of thinking using mental maps formed through ideation and abduction.

Although Bateson sees the mind as empty – as a 'no-thing' that exists only in its ideas – his notion of abductive thinking (the process of recognizing different patterns through metaphor etc.) links the body and the ecosystem within a meta pattern. Looking for the patterns that connect, Bateson asks: 'What pattern connects the crab to the lobster and the orchid to the primrose, and all the four of them to me? And me to you? And all the six of us to the amoeba in one direction and to the backward schizophrenic in another?' (1985:16–17). Connections, he argues, occur between three stages: first-order connections compare the parts of any creatura with other parts of the same individual; second-order connections involve comparing crabs with lobsters to find similar relations between parts; and third-order connections compare crabs and lobsters with orchids and primroses, and so on. Connections are also made in terms of the mind, or minds, sharing stories 'whether ours or those of redwood forests and sea anemones'. It is through the mind that connections are made. The pattern created is a 'dance of interacting parts (only secondarily pegged down by physical limits)' (ibid.:22–23).[7] For Bateson the individual mind is immanent in the body and also in pathways and messages outside the body. And there is a larger Mind of which the individual mind is only a sub-system. This larger Mind 'is comparable to God and is perhaps what some people mean by "God" but it is still immanent in the total interconnected social system and planetary ecology' (Bateson, 2000:467).

Gordon's dance is about participating in such an interconnected system as an inspirited pattern – a web of wyrd – whereby the act of dancing enables spirits, energy and people to meet in a world that is alive. Jasper participates in a 'series of changing patterns in a timeless universe' in order to communicate and bring through a spirit being in the form of his Ancestor for a healing ritual. From this process of participation new connections are made, relationships are renewed or created, and a new pattern emerges. Understanding this must be within the terms of the dance or spirit communication itself. This is the 'right' code for its meaning and message; it by-passes the issue of whether the spirits are real or not and gives insight into how practitioners of nature spiritualities not only create conceptual systems or 'mental maps' but also, more importantly, how they come to see and live their lives. In order to demonstrate magical consciousness I now turn to some examples.

Transformation of Consciousness

There are many consciousness-changing techniques employed in nature religion – such as dancing, drumming, chanting, sex, and the use of psychotropic substances. It would take a study in itself to examine the multitude of varying ways employed to alter perception to experience participation. I have discussed this – as well as magic and the otherworld as a source of knowledge, and the witchcraft invocation of deities – elsewhere (Greenwood, 2000:30–32, 95–102). The importance of the shift in consciousness to participate in otherworldly reality is worth emphasizing here. It is particularly well described by Carol, who was a feminist witch and is now a shaman. She sees the Otherworld as:

> [a] land of everything out there and in here too [pointing to herself]. It is a whisper away; it is a shift in consciousness to see the bigger picture and the threads that weave through everything that has ever existed. It is multidimensional, a heartbeat away... You can also shift consciousness to see the spirit in this room, the life force and auras, they speak to you through smell, pressure on your body, through vision, not only eye vision but many different visions. The spirit residing in me merges the otherworld with this world (Greenwood, 2000:27).

The shift in consciousness enables a different perception to 'see the bigger picture' and the 'threads that weave through everything that has ever existed'. These are the threads of connectedness that link the individual into the wider pattern of life, as Ruth's experience at Findhorn makes clear.

Findhorn: Opening Up to Different Possibilities

Ruth, who is sixty and a manager of a team of social workers in London, described to me the experience she had of Findhorn in 1980 when she learnt to relate to plants through their spirits. Ruth told me that when she was working in the garden doing some planting out she was advised how to plant and how to attune and 'bless' the plant afterwards. At first Ruth was sceptical but then she realized that each plant that she blessed seemed to respond to her 'with a very slight bracing of itself'. She ponders that it could have been her imagination, but can still remember her feeling of wonder at such a thing. Ruth describes how she was shown a special part of the garden, a wild area that was left for nature spirits. When she was walking in the vegetable garden with the group one day, the Findhorn gardener suddenly came up to her and asked if anything was wrong as he could see something in her aura. This surprised Ruth as she had received a message the previous evening that a work colleague had died very suddenly. The gardener showed her a special part of the garden where the nature spirits lived. He said that all gardens should have an area left fairly untended so that nature could encourage the spirits to inhabit that area.

This space was left after Robert Ogilvie Crombie (Roc), after attending a course led by prominent New Age spokesperson George Trevelyan in 1966, had what he described as an 'identification' with the Greek god Pan. The god stepped behind him and then walked into him so that 'we became one and I saw the surroundings through his eyes. At the same time, part of me – the recording, observing part – stood aside.' Crombie said that Pan stepped into him: 'the woods became alive with myriads of beings – elementals, nymphs, dryads, fauns, elves, gnomes, fairies – far too numerous to catalogue' (Higton, 1990:92–93).

One of the nature spirits spoke to Crombie about ecology saying that humans upset the balance of nature, and polluted the living earth so that it would not heal. It reprimanded him, saying: 'You pollute everything beneath you and everything above you. Everywhere you go is fouled and destroyed. Are you so stupid that you cannot realize you are destroying yourself?' (ibid.:93–94). Pan went on to tell Crombie, who was in contact with Findhorn, that a wild area should be left for nature spirits in the Findhorn garden. From this experience with Pan, Crombie arranged for some space to be reserved for the spirits at Findhorn, explaining to people that nature spirits were happy to help humans if they were asked; however, they 'must never be taken for granted and should be given love and thanks for the work they do' (ibid.:94).

Talking to the nature spirits felt right to Ruth and she started to see plants and trees in a different way. She describes how one afternoon the group at Findhorn went for a trip into the Scottish hills. The scenery was 'beautiful, magical, with large trees, streams and waterfalls', and they walked amongst the woods, 'breathing in the natural beauty, looking deep into the waterfalls, at times stopping just to gaze at the scene'. They began to touch plants and hug trees, sometimes holding hands and attuning to a particular tree. It was an 'enchanting experience'.

Ruth told me that the long continuous process of opening up started after her marriage broke up. She said that she thought that crisis such as this could be cathartic, it had opened her up to compassion: 'As you heal you begin to notice others, and you develop compassion.' This took Ruth into the caring profession:

Looking back to twenty-five years ago, I was just coming out of a recovery process from a crisis brought about by the break-up of my marriage… During my first job as an unqualified social worker, I took part in some encounter group work at the local community health centre. From there, I decided to go on a residential experiential group work course over five days. There we did lots of different therapeutic group work, including guided fantasy. I found myself opening out on many levels and making a deeper connection with people on my return to the community.

Ruth also found that her views about mystical experiences started to change, and, quite by accident, she also started to consult a clairvoyant. 'I found a degree of acceptance within myself which had not been there before', despite questioning where the clairvoyant was getting her information from. Although she was sceptical, Ruth shifted her view, thinking that maybe things did happen in the way the clairvoyant said: 'My consciousness seemed to be "opening up" to different possibilities.' Ruth was also attending a group in intuitive massage and meditation at this time. The group became quite close and there was a strong emphasis on understanding body–mind connections. More visualization work took place on this course. A trip to Findhorn seemed to be a natural progression, and an opportunity to go to Scotland arose at the completion of her two-year social work training course. And so it was that Ruth found herself in the New Age community.

Ruth described how there was an emphasis on connection at Findhorn: from the preparation of food, cooking, general maintenance and cleaning to working in the garden. Everything was treated with respect – a broom or hoover had to be treated as special; people were encouraged to connect to each other by holding hands, dancing in circles, and meditations. As the week went by, Ruth gradually fitted in with the routine. Before eating the delicious vegetarian food, they would have a short time for 'attunement' whereby all would sit quietly and tune into the present moment with each other. The atmosphere was very peaceful and joyful, but without any obvious religious overtones. We were advised to appreciate and respect everything at Findhorn, everything had meaning and therefore deserved to be treated with respect – from 'the furniture to the tools we used to clean and work with'. Everything was interdependent.

Another aspect of Findhorn that Ruth found important was the emphasis on 'unconditional love' and the belief that every 'real need' would be met. It was explained that Findhorn had evolved in this way. The experience of Findhorn opened Ruth up to another way of seeing the world. She felt that her sensitivity to nature was dramatically changed, and she felt attuned to plants, flowers, trees as never before: 'I would not consider cutting a flower from a hedgerow, whereas previously I would have had no hesitation in doing this.' Ruth said that she really believed that there could be nature spirits looking after the welfare of the environment and that we should let them get on with their work; she found she was connected to the natural world in a much more fundamental way than previously.

Findhorn had had a transformative effect and Ruth felt connected. Ruth believes that the emphasis placed on 'unconditional love' at Findhorn led to a further development in her life. Earlier in the year the clairvoyant told Ruth that she would meet a black man who would be significant. Ruth thought this was unlikely to happen where she lived at the time, but two weeks later she was astonished to see an African man in her local pub. Eventually, Ruth got into conversation with him and a relationship began. Whilst at Findhorn, Ruth became more aware that she had to face the challenge of discrimination by some people who did not approve of relationships between people of different racial groups. Ruth says that Findhorn opened her up to unconditional love: 'You've got to connect up with everything – people, humanity, everything. You've got to embrace it.' Within a matter of weeks Ruth became pregnant and saw this as part of the process of connecting with nature through unconditional love. When she talked to friends about her experience, some scoffed saying that it sounded 'airy fairy', but Ruth felt that something very, very significant had happened to her.

Ruth's experience is a good example of magical consciousness – an opening up to an expanded awareness and the deep changes of transformation that the experience may bring. Ruth was made aware, or became aware again, of the connections between herself and nature, as well as her connection with other human beings, despite racial discrimination. As she said, her consciousness seemed to be 'opening up to different possibilities'.

Ruth returned to Findhorn in the summer of 2003 to participate in a week's workshop called 'Theatre of the Earth'. Although seeing herself as a novice in dramatic art, Ruth soon discovered that the workshop was about a very different type of performance. The participants spent most mornings visiting natural sites in the area, such as caves, the river, the beach, a lake and woods. They were asked to commune in various ways with nature, i.e. observing, singing, dancing, copying, and making notes of personal experiences. Ruth had several deep experiences and found, as the week progressed, that she was 'merging more and more with nature':

> Once, sitting on stones by the riverside, it dawned on me that everything around me was interacting, the river, the stones, the trees, wind, birds … and I began to realize that I had to do something myself in order to feel part of the movement all around me. I got up and twirled round on slippery stones – feeling a bit of a fool – but suddenly something shifted and I became sharply aware that everything was in motion. A whole flock of birds alighted into the nearest tree and I realized I was seeing more clearly, feeling more deeply. Later in the week, I had a particularly moving experience when performing a dance for a very large tree!

As the week progressed Ruth became aware that she was in some kind of process. The group was told by the workshop leader that they were going to perform with and for nature. On the morning of the performance all participants dressed in costumes and went to the nearby sand dunes. Ruth had selected a traditional African dress, blue and white with two scarves of similar colours. She tied one around her head and the other she eventually tied to the end of a long twig. Her face had been painted by another woman in the group. Ruth explained what happened:

> On the way to the dunes, I wasn't sure what role I was going to play in the performance. As the very colourful group walked slowly along the path towards the dunes and the sea, I could sense myself becoming more and more merged with the natural surroundings. The sky was a brilliant shade of blue with a few white clouds, matching my dress and my scarves, one of which was blowing in the breeze on the end of the twig. On the way, I was thinking about my part in this performance – who I was going to be – dressed in this strange attire. By the time we reached the dunes, I had decided that in this performance I was an African Sky Spirit visiting Findhorn. I had no difficulty in getting into the role and participating in the dramatic performance. It is hard to describe what was happening, maybe something like taking part in a musical piece with lots of improvisation and changes of rhythm – but no conductor!

On later reflection of the experience, one thing that struck Ruth was the connection between her first and second trips to Findhorn. When she left Findhorn in 1980 she was dealing with her inner process on issues of race. A life-changing event occurred to her after leaving Findhorn the first time: the conception and birth of a half-African daughter. Ruth comments that what surprised her about her second visit to Findhorn was the connection with the African Sky Spirit and how everything had just fallen into place for her on the day of the performance. The experience that Ruth recounts shows how *magical consciousness* can have very real effects on people's lives.

I now turn to some more examples of the process of transformation of consciousness, starting with my own account of a particularly powerful experience, one that had a profound effect on me whilst I was conducting fieldwork amongst London magicians in 1993. Being a fairly typical shamanic journey, it offers insight into the process of the changing perception of participation with other beings through metamorphosis. It occurred at a conference on Performance, Ritual, and Shamanism organized by the Centre for Performance Research in Cardiff. The workshop was led by Dan Noel – who had been trained by Michael Harner, and who was the subsequent author of *The Soul of Shamanism* (1997) – and it illustrated the multi-dimensional aspects of magical knowledge that I was grappling with in my research at the time.

Shape-shifting: Snow Owl

A group of about twenty of us lay on the floor preparing to go on a journey to the Underworld to find our spirit guide, our 'totem animal'. We had been given a short talk by Dan Noel on ways of gaining access to the Underworld. Noel had suggested that we find a 'way in' through a hole in the ground, a cave, waterfall, pond or crack in a tree. He had also instructed us on the appropriate etiquette if we met any Underworldly creature: we had to let it approach three times to be sure that it wanted to become associated with us, and to make sure that it was truly an Underworld guide.

I was keen to 'have an experience', to find out what people had been talking about when they had attended shamanic workshops. I was thinking about my entrance. I thought a hole/crack in a tree might be appropriate because I was also an apprentice high magician at the time working on the Kabbalistic 'Tree of Life' glyph. However, this did not work. I was trying too hard. I had willed myself into the crack. Then I realized that maybe I had to wait. I went to the edge of what I felt was the Underworld and tried to jump down into the darkness – but nothing happened, I was consciously willing it too much. I eventually resigned myself to not being able to 'travel' on this particular occasion (we were warned that this might happen). Then the flash of a dream came to me (in the language of magic, my unconscious mind took over from my conscious). I had dreamt, some time previously, that I was climbing down a deep tunnel into the middle of the earth – I had found my entrance:

I went down the tunnel – it was tight and dark (like in the dream), it was a labyrinth of connecting warren-like tunnels which became tighter and darker and darker. I felt the pressure of the earth on me and all around me. I couldn't breathe and I was paralysed by fear – too frightened to go on and too frightened to stop (this feeling brought up memories of vertigo I had experienced as a child). However, I knew that I had to go on. As I crawled on it got tighter and tighter – I lost my skin, it was stripped off me, and as soon as it was off, like a snake's, I felt myself come to an opening in the tunnel, a round space. Had my muscles and fat gone as well as my skin? No! Just my skin – I felt freer and found myself swimming in water in the round opening. It was black water – like oil. I found myself swimming with a dolphin or something like that. Was it my spirit guide? No! I felt the need to go on. This time the tunnel was narrow but I could swim and it seemed to be a straight line. Anyway, it was easier. As I swam I felt the rest of me disintegrate and slip away, until I reached another space – an opening. I stopped and looked down on myself. I was a pile of bones. My bones were being picked over by a large black crow. Did this crow have a message for me? I felt quite attuned to it – it was OK. As I approached it looking for its meaning, to my surprise it turned into a large white owl, a large white snow owl. This was a surprise as I wasn't expecting it [my spirit guide] to emerge quite so strongly. At this point my stomach started trembling which gradually increased to quite a strong juddering. I felt I could quite easily be overtaken by this force. I became at one with the white owl, she let me nestle in her warm feathers and we tried to fly. My juddering increased – we hopped around my bones, flying for a few wingbeats until we took off into the sky. My body felt attuned and in rhythm, and my breathing settled down. We swooped around and I felt at one with my large white owl. I realized that she was very significant to me.

After this realization (that I had found and been taken by my totem animal, and that this had particular meaning for me at that present time), I wanted to reflect on the experience. It was almost too much, and I needed to get away from her to adjust. I waited for the drumming beat to change, the signal that we were returning – and I re-entered the everyday world.

I wrote at the time that this clearly illustrated the body and 'out of body'experience of travelling to the otherworld. At one and the same time I knew I was lying on the floor of the workshop, I was aware of my breathing and the physical effects of my body juddering. At the same time 'I' had disintegrated, part of what I was had gone as I became aware of new dimensions of myself – I imagined what it was like to fly, and the owl symbol did have very real significance for me. I came to understand an aspect of my experience in different terms. The journey into my unconscious mind and the symbols that I retrieved had significance when brought back to my consciousness.

Lévi-Strauss makes this same point in a comparison of shamanistic techniques with psychoanalysis in his analysis of the Cuna Indian shaman assisting a woman during a difficult birth. The cure, for Lévi-Strauss, consists of making explicit a situation originally existing on the emotional level. By rendering it acceptable to the mind, pains in the body are controlled. The sick woman believes in the myth and belongs to a society which believes in it. 'The tutelary spirits and malevolent spirits, the supernatural monsters and magical animals, are all part of a coherent system on which the native conception of the universe is founded' (1979:323). Similarly, I had been given a Western shamanic map of 'going down into the Underworld' as a framework that structured my unconscious mind. I looked for 'messages' in the form of animals. I had been given the map and all I had to do, in theory, was to suspend my rational conscious mind to follow it.

Magical consciousness works through an inner imaginative transformative process, by association, seeming co-incidence and through experience of many different levels of awareness, which are interpreted by symbols. As the anthropologist Victor Turner argued, symbols have a multi vocality conferring meaning in the social and the psychological realms (1967). Symbols are powerful agents of explanation in the otherworld. A white owl which 'came to me' on my first journey may represent a powerful force linking this world and the otherworld. Whenever I saw a white owl the association with the otherworld and all its symbolic connections were renewed. The owl symbolized darkness (she had 'emerged' from a large black crow, and her whiteness symbolized light in darkness), hunting by night, finding information. She is a symbol of moving 'between the worlds', of shifting boundaries and changing levels of consciousness. The owl is 'a symbol of a holistic world where nothing is static. But above all she may be a teacher. If I travel to the otherworld with a specific question or problem she will help me gain information, which I may bring through to structure and inform my everyday life.

I have since come to understand this experience in terms of the changing process of magical consciousness. Having a deeper understanding of this experience, I now see it as an initiation into participation. While I would not want to suggest that an otherworldly encounter such as this gained in a workshop is similar to a shaman's initiation, it does echo in some respects a traditional schema of suffering, death and resurrection (Eliade, [1964] 1989:33). The journey brought me face to face with my personal fears – of not being able to breathe (I was asthmatic as a child) and of the distortions of the senses and disorientation due to vertigo. I also experienced what it was like to undergo dismemberment and death of the self in an 'out of body' experience as I looked down on myself as a pile of bones. As I have later come to appreciate, the change from black crow to snow owl is significant. Representing an important aspect of transformation, a common theme in magical consciousness, it shows how nothing is static in otherworldly reality. Nothing is fixed in terms of boundaries or shape; metamorphosis is common – such as the movement from crow to owl – and this is frequently referred to as 'shape-shifting'. Shape-shifting is a central part of the process of moving from an awareness of individual ego to participation in the multi-dimensional world of the spirit. It involves a paradox, as one Pagan explained to me: 'As I become more me, I become less me.' By this she meant that as she became more conscious of her own potentiality to experience other dimensions – other consciousnesses – she was made more acutely aware of her own place in the wider scheme of things. The experience of going out of herself gave her more insight into herself.

'I ate the frog'

This aspect was illustrated by a journey that one of my students experienced as part of the university course I was teaching on altered states of consciousness.[8] I had drummed about ten students on an Underworld trance journey, and having come back to everyday reality they were discussing their experiences. One student reported that she had become a snake and had eaten a frog:

> I finally arrived at this particular alley in the wood, my favourite that we called 'les racines' as the roots of the trees there come out of the soil and are very twirly and

beautiful. I got through these to the 'underworld', spontaneously as a snake. Once inside it felt quite dark and humid. As a snake I was gliding along this underground tree-bark tunnel where a little stream was running quietly, and I could still feel the drumming reverberating. It seemed to be quite a long time moving and seeing the world from the perspective of a snake. The tunnel gradually became half open revealing tropical forest surroundings. At one point I could see human legs ... a couple of men trying to catch me, but I bit a leg and escaped back into the tunnel.

A bit further I was stopped by the sight of a friendly frog looking at me. I ate the frog ... she was inviting me to do so (nothing was said but it was understood) then once I shed my skin, I became the frog but as a transformed amalgam, I was a tall frog-like creature, feeling strong and incredibly agile. I could see my body: muscles, green smooth rubbery skin, and my hands had very long fingers with sticky 'suction-tips', like frogs do. I began exploring the forest, moving fast and feeling very light. I climbed quickly up this massive tree to the top and looked at the beautiful jungle from above, I could see very far, all the tree tops and the insects, butterflies flying around ... as I came down I carried on wandering around, until I noticed tiny humans walking (as a regular city crowd seen from above) on the forest floor. I grabbed a couple and ate them and carried on exploring. Soon I felt the drumming change and went back to where I arrived but this time went through the forest pond where giant lily pads were. Through the water I swam until I came out of the sea ... (in Brighton!).

In the process she had become the frog, and she said that eating the frog had felt a friendly thing to do. The other students laughed at this, saying that it did not appear very friendly (the man sitting to her right jokingly moved away from her). The woman was unsure what the eating meant and I suggested that it might represent an act of transformation. In otherworldly reality, eating is not necessarily associated with death *per se*, but with the symbolic death of one state and the birth of another, as is commonly demonstrated in small-scale societies' initiation rituals[9] as studied by anthropologists (for example, Turner [1967] 1972, [1974] 1975 Strang, 1997:241; and see Chapter 7).

Participation is sociocentric, holistic, expressing continuity in space and time with a sense of encompassing cosmic oneness, but it also involves the process of transformation as metamorphosis from one state or being – such as a snake – into another – a frog. Tambiah suggests, as already indicated, that participation occurs when 'persons, groups, animals, places, and natural phenomena are in a relation of contiguity'; this is a place of existential immediacy where there are 'shared affinities' (1991:107–109). In other words, a different relationship is experienced, one which has been described by Victor Turner as *communitas*, a non-structural or spontaneous relationship which develops among individuals in passage between social statuses such as those undergoing initiation ritual. Turner describes the state of communitas as non-hierarchical; it possesses a common substratum which is 'beyond all categories of manifestation, transcending divisible time and space, beyond words, where persons, objects, and relationships are endlessly transformed into one another' ([1974] 1975:22).

Practitioners of nature spiritualities may experience such new relationships; perhaps the most obvious is through the communitas that can develop during Pagan direct action – protesters construct an alternative community by living together and by creating their own mythology. The very act of living in a protest camp may induce feelings of solidarity and shared purpose, and an alternative culture is created. According to Jodie, a Pagan environmental protester, environmental protest involves 'putting yourself on the edge of society to bring an awareness of issues, as a chosen mission'; it also involves objecting to nature being used as an object – nature is respected and has inherent divinity. For her, Paganism involved a re-emergence of Romanticism, Hermetism and 'making it up as you go along – we have to make our own culture'. She said that site life was like living in a bubble to construct a different form of consciousness whereby a person felt a part of nature: 'when you live in a tree it becomes part of you, a house, Yggdrassil'. Such protest is an initiation. 'You have to face things within' – it involves getting to know people, overcoming a fear of heights, a fear of police, and also a fear of being rejected by mainstream society. She said that people come from hurt perspectives but that site life opens the mind to other ways of living, through the creation of myth and through communal visions due to the ingestion of psychotropic mushrooms. This process of changing perception to create communitas utilizes other cultures because, as she says, 'Westerners haven't had much culture' in the sense of a culture that seeks relationship with nature rather than one that seeks domination and control.

An alternative way of experiencing participation is through a type of nature spirituality that is located within a specific tradition. One such example is Romany shamanism developed for non-Romanies. In this practice healing must occur before the would-be practitioner can truly experience the Romany world-view. Healing involves the establishment of a spiritual community: in the past there was spiritual community, unity, and harmony with the earth, and it is to this practice that I now turn.

Healing and Magical Consciousness

In *Magic, Witchcraft, and the Otherworld* I argued that healing was central to notions of magical transformation. Behind the swirling and glittery mists of popular conceptions of magic and mystery is the notion that communication with otherworldly realities is a healing and balancing process; the otherworld is a source of healing (Greenwood, 2000:117). During the process of a healing ritual conducted by the Romany shaman Jasper Lee and his partner Lizzie May-Gotts, who acted as his herbalist assistant or *patrinyengri*, I discovered that healing concerns a process of identifying the spirits of sickness which cause soul loss, and that the establishment of health involves a spiritual connection to the ancestors in a reaffirmation of cohesion between the everyday world and the otherworldly realm of the dead.

In Romany tradition the dead are a benevolent source of collected wisdom and tradition; they are not potentially dangerous. They are not like the !Kung ancestors who try to carry the sick off to their realm during a healing ritual; neither are they angry gods to be appeased. Romany ancestors are unlike Korean restless ancestors and ghosts that bring affliction, illness, financial loss and domestic strife (Kendall, 1988:8); or Sinhalese ghosts (preta) who also have a malign effect on the living and bring misfortune, disease and sickness to the living. The latter have had an extreme attachment or craving for worldly things when they lived as human beings, and have failed to proceed to one of the Buddhist heavens, or to be reborn in another existence (Kapferer, [1983] 1991:22–23). Neither do the Romany ancestors bring sickness to the rebellious, as Lugbara ancestors are alleged to do. Lugbara lineage consists of both the living and the dead; the dead exercise lineage authority as well as the living, as John Middleton was told:

> It is good that an elder invokes his ghost against his disobedient 'sons', who do not follow his words. A man stands in place of his (dead) father, and if a wife or child does him ill he will cry to that father and trouble will seize that child. This is good. (Middleton, [1970] 1972:492).

By contrast, the Romany ancestors offer security and order in a fragmented and changing world that is out of touch with grandmother Earth. Rather than being the source of potential illness, they are the means by which healing is effected. As the fountainhead of Romany tradition, the ancestors are an expression of 'the old ways'. Healing concerns creating relationship with the dead via the mediations of the *chovihano*, who acts as a 'gateway' to the ancestors. There is no radical separation between the living and the dead – the dead are the essence of life and are a part of the living everyday world.

Romany Healing: 'A Good Piece of Drama'

The first Romany shamanic healing ritual that I experienced was held in a well-appointed flat overlooking Hampstead Heath, North London. In this particular ritual a small group of people interested in Romany tradition experienced healing first-hand. About ten of us – a mixture of academics, healers of other traditions, and those generally interested in shamanism – sat around a single candle; a white goose feather and a black crow feather were placed either side to represent light and dark. Alongside was a bowl of water, a bay leaf and some garlic. Salt for protection was sprinkled over us as Jasper explained the fundamentals of gypsy healing before the ritual commenced. We were told that Romany healing was a light-hearted affair, and that although in the past rituals were conducted with the utmost respect to the spirits there used to be much talking, joking, and beer-swigging at healing rituals. We were also informed that gypsies were free with their emotions and that on such occasions they often ran high. In the past there would have been two circles – an inner one of people to be healed and an outer one to hold and contain the helpful spirits, and also to offer protection against those spirits with malevolent intention. The aim of the healing was to name the spirits of the illness, personalize them, and 'send them packing'. The *chovihano* has 'to pretend that I'm as bad as the spirit of sickness is; con it, enchant it'. He asks it how it is, and tells it that it is very wise, talking to it as if it is a thing of power. He jokes, laughs, and pretends to be on the same side as the spirit of sickness as he encourages it to move into his body. When the spirit has left its host and entered the body of the *chovihano* his aim is to 'lay the boot in' to get 'on top' of the sickness with the aid of the *patrinyengri*, whose role is one of accomplice. She plays a part in the drama by colluding with him in tricking the spirits by befriending them, asking them what they are feeling, and advising them to leave if they know what is good for them (cf. Katz 1982:33).

Being a *chovihano* is very dangerous work because you have to say to the sickness 'come into me', and unless the *chovihano* is very careful the spirits of sickness – which could be the spirits of cancer or other such illness – might decide to stay. A part of the *chovihano*'s training concerns learning how to cope with malign spirits to avoid unwanted ones entering his body. It is essential to have adequate spiritual protection in the form of red wool tied around the wrist, neck or any potentially vulnerable place; henna may be painted onto the skin, or kohl painted around the eyes. Any orifice has to be protected from unwanted spirit entry. The doorways and windows, as potential entry points for unwelcome spirits, are decorated with red wool; any animals or plants around are protected too. Clothing is turned inside out to confuse the bad spirits and bring *kushto bok* (good luck). Gypsies like multi-coloured clothes with 'jazzy' designs as this is thought to disorientate the spirits so that they cannot find their way into a person. Gold is thought to work against the 'evil eye' (*bengesko yak)* and is generally protective. The *chovihano*'s *ran* (wand) also has a protective function, and is used to charge and protect the people involved in the healing; salt is liberally sprinkled as an added protection.

Jasper explains that in a collective healing ritual such as this, he thinks about the sickness collecting in the centre of the room, and then travels to the sick person to collect the spirit of sickness into a ball: 'When I go into trance I get a collection of problems – a jumble in my throat, my head – and then it slowly separates and is made into people.' The main thing is to get hold of the spirit of sickness, to personalize it and send it away. Healing is 'like a good piece of drama', and the *chovihano* has to be a good actor for when he goes into trance he tries to reach out to the person's sickness. He has to put himself in the role – to be a good mimic – to get into the shoes of the sick person and the sickness, to lose his own identity completely: 'You can't be a proper *chovihano* unless you can leave yourself behind.' Emotions are freely expressed, and Jasper explains that when 'the spirit realizes that I'm not its friend there are tears and it's very emotionally charged – I appear to be having a complete nervous breakdown. By the time I get to that stage I know I'm bringing things out. I start to feel the releasing of things.'

Once the *chovihano* has tricked the spirits out of the sick person's body they are put into an object or animal such as a worm, slug, spider, or toad. The worm is placed in a pot and when the spirits of sickness are introduced into it the *chovihano* spits on it three times to seal it in before it is buried. The worm is treated with great dignity and Jasper says that when he performs healing rituals he often appoints a 'worm guardian' to look after the worm. The worm takes the spirits of sickness to grandmother Earth (*puv*) who turns them into something positive. In Romany culture the earth has special significance because it is seen as grandmother and it does not have the connection with dirtiness that it does in *gaujo* society. Gypsies do not consider soil to be unclean and they often put it into their mouths to get rid of germs; if they drop food onto the soil they would eat it, but if it fell on the floor of a wagon, or more recently a house, they would consider it polluted (*mokadi*) and it would not be consumed. Traditionally worms or slugs would be pinned on a thorn bush; a spider might have been put in a bag and worn around the neck until it died. Jasper says that he does not do that now in consideration of contemporary sensibilities concerning the treatment of animals.

We rubbed flying ointment onto any exposed skin – the face, and particularly the forehead and arms. Red wool was tied around our wrists, necks, or legs and we lay down on the floor forming a circle. Jasper spoke in a mixture of Romany and English and, beating his tamborine (*vastengri*), called on the earth (*puv*), air (*bavol*), fire (*yag*) and water (*pani*), the sun (*kam*) and moon (*shon*), the spirits of the herbs, and the ancestors (*puri foki*). He called these good spirits in (*kushti muli*), and thanked them for coming (*parraco*), by a repetitive chant '*kushti muli, kushti muli, kushti muli ... Kam ta Shon, Kam ta Shon, Kam ta Shon ... kushti Puv, kushti Bavol, kushti Yag, kushti Pani, kushti muli, parraco, parraco, kushti muli, kushti muli...*', and sent those he did not want away. This chant, and the beating of the tambourine, sent those present into a trance; we imagine the otherworld. Jasper told us that the ancestors (*puri foki*) were gathering, and that his special Ancestor was here: 'All the spirits form a spiral, they go zig-zagging up, while I step out of my self and the Ancestor takes over the proceedings. When the Ancestor is here I just clear off.' He explained afterwards that he was hovering outside, 'just where the trees are'. We are told to think about any illness we have, any healing or change that we want; we are told to focus on it, to bring it into our consciousnesses, symbolize it so that the *chovihano* can 'see' it.

The *chovihano* goes into a deeper trance; he prepares to hand the situation over to the Ancestor who hovers over us 'seeing' what has presented itself. Getting into confrontation with various spirits, one at a time, he cajoles them, laughs and colludes with them. He invites them into his body and enacts an internal battle to force them to leave; he wrestles around on the floor, shouting, screaming and sobbing. The *patrinyengri* persuades the spirits of sickness that they had better leave; they will be much happier elsewhere. Three or four such demonstrations were conducted before the *chovihano* and *patrinyengri* approach various people who, having visualized their illnesses, were sitting in a circle watching the proceedings. Hands are placed on those with physical illness. When it came to my turn, *chovihano* and *patrinyengri* sat either side of me and told me that the ancestors were there for me and wanted to speak to me. There was much emotion.

'Look into the river and see your own reflection'

On another occasion, a couple of days after the total eclipse of the sun by the moon in Totnes, when all the participants of the ritual to celebrate the sacred marriage of the ancestral spirits of the sun and the moon had departed (a ritual described in the previous chapter), I stayed behind for a healing session with Jasper and Lizzie. In the centre of the room, in their flat – one of a number created in the conversion of a brewery into domestic dwellings – a single candle flickered. The flame, when lit a little earlier, had 'bowed' with pleasure at being with us, according to Jasper. Salt used for purification and protection had been liberally sprinkled. Lizzie assisted Jasper to conduct the healing ritual to make my spirits of sickness depart. She waved a birch *ran* (wand); it was protected by red wool, and decorated with a painted green vine interspersed with gold and silver dots representing the otherworld; the small bells tied to the end tinkled to keep away evil spirits. Jasper sat opposite me gently rocking, tambourine in hand he beat a rhythm as he entered a trance state. Lizzie, eyes closed, sat to my left; she also moved to the rhythm while tuning in to what Jasper was doing. The reason for my sickness was that I was not in contact with my ancestors and so the *chovihano* made his body available to his ancestor spirit guide to speak to me – the Ancestor was going to speak through the *chovihano*. Using the rhythm of the tambourine, Jasper allowed his own everyday identity to become malleable – he described it as dough – thus providing a space in the middle for the Ancestor to come through. As already indicated, this process involved the *chovihano* stretching so that another being – in this case the Ancestor – could occupy the space in the centre, which Jasper said was 'like the hole in a Polo mint'.

Jasper rocked backwards and forwards in trance; his body became inhabited by the Ancestor; his visage and tone of voice changed, and I sensed that there was a distinct presence in the room. The Ancestor, via Jasper's body, placed his hand on my head and commanded the spirits of sickness to depart. They were told to find their own place and to leave me. All three of us rocked, deep in trance, and the air was thick with emotion. The sound of the jingling *ran* permeated the atmosphere. The Ancestor started talking about the spirits of sickness:[10]

> When they [the spirits of sickness] know that you know what they're up to (and they know that you know what they're up to at his moment in time) ... they start to become self-conscious. They know that you mean them to leave. So they start to prepare for a journey to the otherworld, where they have to go if they know what's good for them.
>
> The spirits of sickness these days are very comfortable. They know what they can do, they know what they can achieve, they know all the tricks. So it's a matter of breaking all this down and making them realize that they can't stay here because this life cannot sustain them. They will be far better off going somewhere where they can be as they want to be...

It is the modern attitude that allows the spirits of sickness to invade people; it is this attitude that sees everything as a part of a whole, whereas, by comparison, the old Romany way sees the spirits as separate and external to the self:

> The modern attitude to the spirits of sickness is not a healthy one; sounds quite funny when I say that [laughter]. You need to start to see yourself as being independent from them, so that they can realize they're not a part of you. The spirits of sickness do not realize that they're attacking you; they are such a part of you. They fit quite comfortably; this is their home.
>
> But the old way is not to see it like that. The old way is to see that you and they are very separate. Your modern way has created the condition and so they slot into this quite nicely and feel quite at home.
>
> This is not the way to do it; a change needs to be made and to see them as being very separate spirits... Start seeing them as something very separate so that you can start to gradually push them away.
>
> It doesn't happen overnight. We ancient ones know this; we know it takes time. Start externalizing these sicknesses that you have and start understanding that they do have their own beings.

The Ancestor made a distinction between the personal and the individual:

> Everything has its own being. Everything is personal but it's not individualized, it is personal. It is all of you here in this modern world that individualize, making everything a part of you. The whole world is a part of you and everything is one. This is not the way we gypsy ancestors saw it. One leads to two and three and four and five, and so on.

There is never one of anything. You have one life, one earth, one world, one house... You believe there is one life and one death. You believe there is one God, some of you. One is a trick. One is a beginning and some of you are fooled by it. It leads to many.

So there isn't just one of you there are all these spirits of sickness and all these different spirits contacting you all the time. All the spirits of the earth, spirits of water, spirits of fire, spirits of wind, rain, sky, clouds – all spirits. You're interacting with them all of the time. And of course spirits of sickness, that is perhaps the negative side. The spirits of sickness can teach you a lot if you learn.

By understanding that there are many spirits it is then possible to get wise to the spirits of sickness:

It will help if you start to see yourself as one spirit of many spirits; if you see the spirits of sickness as separate entities... Start to see these spirits as coming out of you, weaving in and out... Sometimes you don't know it and it's against your will and that's when you've got to use your senses and your wits and tell them to get lost. Tell them you're wise to them and you're not going to have them any more. They will hear you; rest assured that they'll hear you. They'll know exactly what you're talking about, and they'll say, 'no, I'm not going', and it may take a chovihano to help you to send them packing, but you can help yourself by getting wise to them...

Healing also involves the re-establishment of a spiritual community, and this is done by way of meeting with the ancestors for closer communication – the ancestors are pretty ordinary really:

[I]f we all stick together, we ancestors and you, as we used to do, we can get through, we can bring all this [the civilized way of being] to an end. We can re-unite people again, we can set people's hearts free. Make them laugh again, make them sing, and really, really laugh and sing, and get them to feel again [sigh]...

But please don't consider that I'm high and mighty, I'm pretty ordinary really [drinks whisky]. We have many jokes in the past and we ancestors like to do it this way in the Romany tradition. We like our legs pulled just as you do ... I'm not unreachable and untouchable...

[W]hat we need to do is meet in the middle. I need to come half way to you and you need to come half way to me, and we can do that quite easily if we try ... we can achieve a great deal and you can have very enriched experiences through this, and I can feel I'm helping you more.

Because sometimes I feel lonely myself, I'm wandering around and thinking I'd like it to be as it was, or as close as it can be ... I have a great desire to be closer to you as you have a great desire to be closer to me, and all ancestors. This is what's missing...

[Lizzie: 'We've grown too far apart.']

That's it [this (drink) is very good]...

The Ancestor told of the past when things were very different: there was unity, community, harmony with the earth, and spirit communication:

> What I would encourage you to do is look behind yourselves ... look behind and you see the way the earth was. You see the ancient people communicating with each other in a better way. You see unity, you see community, and you see ancestral communication – spirit communication – and everything being in harmony. You see the earth being left alone; you do not see these wicked and horrible civilized ways...
>
> If you look ahead and you see the ending of this ... present civilized way of living... Your earth deserves a future, a great future, and she deserves to come back to herself again, just as you do. You deserve to come back to yourself again. We all do. Everything does; all the spirits do.

The source of healing lies within the self: it is necessary to look to the self to find the soul within. In my case, I had rather naively asked the Ancestor what he felt about our present culture, and the New Age in particular. He was somewhat confused by the term 'New Age' and then said that I had to forget about culture and think about my soul instead. I then wanted to know how my soul related to others. I was told in no uncertain terms that I had spent too much time looking at other souls and that this was why the spirits of sickness have found their way into me:

> [I]t is down to you trusting in you, you believing in you. I think you're too concerned for others. Trust yourself more... Others will find their way... The immediate problem is that your soul needs to find its way; it needs care and attention.
>
> The way I see your soul, if you'll allow me to say this, [is that] your soul is busy looking into the river but not at its own reflection. Your soul is looking at the reflections of others and seeing their suffering... Your own reflection is crying out and is saying 'look at me, look at me'. You need to look into the river and see your own reflection... Believe and trust in yourself first and you will find that everything else will slot into place. That is the way of it. That is the way of all souls. That is not simply a Romany way, that is the way of all souls... Your soul is what you're looking for... You can see to other souls later, and because you are looking at other souls then the spirits of sickness can find their way in because you are not looking or seeing to yourself...

When the Ancestor had had his say, and had drunk his whisky, it was time for him to retreat back into the otherworld. He said his goodbyes, saying how fond he was of us all. The whole process seemed to be part of an everyday occurrence, as though an elderly and respected relative had just dropped in for a quick drink and a chat. Jasper laid down on the floor while the Ancestor was departing and after a few minutes returned to join in the ordinary conversation that was going on. There was a minimum of fuss and a notable lack of ostentatious ceremony as the candle was gently blown out amid laughing and general good humour; we continued talking into the night before going to sleep.

'Stretch out a hand ... there are other hands stretching back'

The conversation with the Ancestor seemed to break down the boundary between this world and the ancestral spirit world, and although the Ancestor was not amongst us using Jasper's body and voice, he did still seem to be there as a presence. He had said that he and all the ancestors were there supporting us in this the civilized *gaujo* world; helping us keep in touch with our souls and reminding us of our connection with the spirit world. What is important is the closeness and connection to the ancestors. Ancestors are active in everyday life; they watch over and guide their descendants, giving 'kicks up the bum' where necessary, and making sure that things are kept on track by inspiring and guiding how one should live. There are many ancestors in the otherworld: 'as you stretch out a hand to the otherworld there are always hands stretching back'; all offered experience, but some were more helpful than others. Health may be equated with following the path of the ancestors. This fundamentally restructures reality, alters perception and gives a clear moral guideline for living in harmony with the earth. The aim of my healing ritual was to put me on my true personal soul path. Here was a different vision to that provided by the *gaujo* society, whose 'civilized' ways are the source of disease. Health, according to the Ancestor, involves finding a wholeness of soul through a restoration of the 'old ways', or spiritual communication with the ancestors. The spirits of sickness cannot penetrate whole souls.

The healing ritual started with an exorcism: the spirits of sickness had to be expelled. Talking about a Sinhalese context, Bruce Kapferer points out that exorcism diagnosis can facilitate the construction of the patient's illness as a metaphor for a wider social context that links subjective experience to external events ([1983] 1991:86). The spirits of sickness may be viewed as metaphors for destruction, disorder, the 'civilized ways' of gaujo society; they represent modernity, soul-loss, a lack of contact with the ancestors, and disrespect for the earth. My soul-loss was due to my inability to see my own soul's reflection – I had to learn to trust my own experience. However, my sickness was not different in principle from the sicknesses experienced by others in the first healing ritual – we are all ill due to the way of living in 'our civilized world' – the spirits of sickness are an expression of a sick *gaujo* society. It has traditionally been the role of the shaman to put things right. The shaman is the medium who links this world and the otherworld, and the people with the ancestors; he is the link between worlds – creating the setting for the living and the dead to communicate. Through his intimate relationship with the Ancestor, the *chovihano* allows others to gain access to this wisdom and the ancestral heritage, and by so doing mediates individuals' own relationships with the ancestors. The process of healing involves him 'seeing' the spirits of sickness in a form of enhanced perceiving and knowing; he has to pull out the sickness into his own body before he can exorcise it by trickery and confrontation, and he needs all his experience of the spirit world, and the support of spirit beings, to help him in this task.

While the first part of the ritual identified the problem, the second part involved an articulation of an alternative cosmological order: the Romany way was presented as an alternative; the ancestors represented a metaphor for order, community and a spiritual health made possible through an awareness of the importance of achieving a whole soul. Learning about the ancestors concerned learning a new way of daily living – how to meet new challenges of life from the perspective of being 'soul-centred'. Being in touch with the ancestors was an experience of losing the old way of experiencing the self and finding oneself in a relationship with a group of living dead spiritual beings. These beings push a confrontation with the unknown – a transformation of consciousness. The concept of illness thus opens up a communication network between the patient and the ancestors that involves a discourse between the dead and the living. The Romany past does not refer to a specific time – knowing details about individuals and places is not considered important. The ancestors are not known individually by name or by where they lived – this information is considered to bring bad luck. The old ways emerge out of the mystery of the otherworld; they retreat back into the mists of time, and it must stay that way. To enquire too deeply into the mystery is said to bring bad luck. It is not considered advisable to look back at immediate generations either, because these beings are seen to be lost, like contemporary living humans, within civilized ways. Jasper advises looking back 1,000 or 2,000 years to those ancestors who were probably conscious of those destined to come after them, 'The earth still contains the bones of those people you came from, and we can re-establish links', he asserts.

Through the various examples used here, I have shown how magical consciousness is developed through participation; this may encompass relationships with the natural world, animals and ancestors. Using Bateson's notion of codes, it is possible to say that magic is concerned with accessing areas of the mind that 'operate' through a language of metaphor and myth. To examine magical consciousness it is necessary, therefore, to look for the pattern within the code – that is, the patterns formed through individual analogical associations. However, it also includes what Bateson has called an ecology of mind, or, in other words, a wider view of Mind that is broader and more expansive than the view that locates it solely inside the human head. In this view, Mind is shared with an inspirited nature, as argued by David Abram when he refers to a world made up of multiple intelligences (1997:9–10).

In the next chapter I continue the examination of magical consciousness through a study of a specific European mythos known as the 'Wild Hunt'; this can be seen as a 'code' or 'tradition' that shapes practitioners' world-views.

Notes

1. Anthropologist Brian Morris claims that all human cultures make some distinctions between cultural and natural phenomena; thinking requires distinctions and discrimination, but not dualism. In relation to Malawi, Morris observes that human beings and animals are not ontologically equivalent – there is no dissolution of the boundaries – but there is a dialectics: recognition of the distinctiveness of humans but also a conception that animals are kin (2000:40).
2. Tambiah has pointed out the connection between Lévy-Bruhl's emphasis on non-rational sources of behaviour and Freud's notion of the unconscious in structuring the perception of reality. However, Lévy-Bruhl's formulation of pre-logical mentality is essentially shaped by collective representations, while Freud focused on the unconscious as an attribute of individual psychology (Tambiah, 1991:93–94).
3. The two orientations to the cosmos outlined by Tambiah correspond to what Michael Harner terms 'Ordinary State of Consciousness' (OSC) – which accords with causality – and a 'Shamanic State of Consciousness' (SSC) – which corresponds with participation (see p.6).
4. Personal communication on invitation letter to a sacred trance dance.
5. This type of spirit communication can be seen among African peoples. Pointing out that a close and intimate relationship exists between animals and spiritual beings, particularly the spirits of the ancestors, Brian Morris draws on Steven Lonsdale's (1981) examples of dance rituals to show how, through the medium of the dance, masked dancers become spiritual beings in the form of animals. Morris observes that animals play an important part in the religious imagination of African peoples; an organic unity is expressed through the religious imagination. This unity with nature has, however, been severed by new religious movements influenced by the transcendental theism of Christianity and Islam (Morris, 2000:24–25).
6. Although Cybernetics, a term coined by mathematician Norbert Weiner to refer to self-regulating machinery as a system of communication, seems rather ironic as a framework for understanding living organisms of nature (Lipset, 1982: 180–181; see also Lovelock, 1995:44; and endnote 2, p.198).

7. Anthropologist Tim Ingold draws on Bateson's views of mind but makes no distinction between the organism and its environment as exclusive entities that interact. Ingold takes the whole-organism-in-its-environment as a point of departure; there is no domain of mind. He sees mind as the 'cutting edge of the life process itself' (Ingold, 2001:16–19). Thus, Ingold, by conflating organism and environment, dismantles Bateson's distinction between ideas about the world, on the one hand, and the actual physical world on the other.
8. At the University of Sussex in 2001.
9. I suggested that her experience might be viewed as being similar to the Aborigine myth of the Wauwalak Sisters that we had been studying a few weeks previously.
10. Jasper readily agreed to this session, and the eclipse ritual described in Chapter 4, being taped. I subsequently transcribed the material from the tape.

–6–

The Wild Hunt: A Mythological Language of Magic

Metamorphoses, cavalcades, ecstasies, followed by the egress of the soul in the shape of an animal – these are different paths to a single goal. Between animals and souls, animals and the dead, animals and the beyond, there exists a profound connection.

Carlo Ginzburg, *Ecstasies: Deciphering the Witches' Sabbath*

The discussion developed in this chapter will show how the mythological corpus of the 'Wild Hunt', a generic name given to numerous folk myths associated with 'soul-ravening' chases, often led by a god, goddess, or mythological figure accompanied by a cavalcade of souls of the dead, opens awareness with the cyclical process of nature through magical consciousness. The mythology of the Wild Hunt, as a language of magical consciousness, creates a framework to experience what Carlo Ginzburg, in the quote above, calls the 'profound connection' between animals, souls, the dead, and the beyond; it primarily concerns an initiation into the wild, untamed forces of nature in its dark and chthonic aspects. This mythology comprises what Ginzburg has termed a Eurasian substratum of shamanic beliefs (1992a) and forms a significant component of many contemporary practitioners' ideas about otherworldly spiritual realms. For those engaging with the Wild Hunt the aim is not only participation with animals, souls and the dead but also with the ritualized cycle of life and death. This experience runs counter to anthropologist Maurice Bloch's (1992) universalistic and dualistic assertion that there is an underlying theme to all ritual that negates biological life processes in favour of a transcendent realm of spirit.

Soul-Ravening Chases

The night flight is an ancient theme in folk beliefs and it involves an ecstatic journey made by the living into the realm of the dead. According to Carlo Ginzburg, in Europe from the eleventh century onwards apparitions of furious armies were frequently referred to in references in Latin literary texts. A 'throng of the dead' consisting of anyone from soldiers killed in battle to unbaptized children were led by various mythological characters on a journey to the beyond (1992a:136). One such leader is Gwyn ap Nudd, who in Celtic folklore is a wild huntsman who rides a demon horse and hunts in waste places at night with a pack of white-bodied and red-eared 'dogs of hell'. Cheering on his hellhounds in a fearful chase, he hunts souls. A British god of battle, the otherworld and the dead, Gwyn ap Nudd is a psychopomp who conducts the slain into Hades and then rules over them. 'He knows when and where all the great warriors fell, for he gathered their souls upon the field of battle, and now rules over them in Hades, or upon some 'misty mountain-top" (Squire, 1912:255). Later semi-Christianized stories place Gwyn ap Nudd over a brood of devils in the Celtic otherworld of Annwyn, lest they should destroy the present race. In Arthurian romances he was king of the Underworld and had a duty to control imprisoned devils and prevent them from destroying humans (Briggs, 1976:212–213).

There are many leaders of the Wild Hunt in folklore.[1] In Teutonic mythology it is Woden (Odin or Wotan) who leads the hunt, accompanied by fearsome ghostly dogs:[2]

> Mortals can hear the hunt thundering across the sky, and dogs will often begin to howl at the noise of the ghost hounds, but to see the procession is to invite death or disaster, perhaps even to be caught up with it and swept away (Jones, 1996:455).

In some accounts Woden is accompanied by beautiful spirit maidens called Valkyries or Waekyrges who, mounted on white steeds, took heroes slain on the battlefield to Valhalla, the battlefield reserved for the worthiest. The Valkyries are portrayed as ravens or wolves in some accounts (Jones, 1996:444; Farrar and Farrar, 1991:145). Herne the hunter,[3] a descendant of Woden,[4] is also said to lead a faery pack across the hills of Britain (Matthews, 1993:47) and is identified with Hermes (Graves, [1961] 1981:151). The leader of this ghastly rout was sometimes female; in northern Germany she was the wife of Wotan, sometimes it was Holda, Holle, or Holt, 'the friendly one', goddess of marriage and fecundity; in the south she was called Perchta, Berhta, or Berta, 'the bright one'. During the Middle Ages there were female ecstatic cults of night-flying goddesses, whose followers believed they were riding out with Diana, Herodias, or Holda, accompanied by a train of souls of the dead. Hekate, or Hecate, a goddess originally worshipped in Asia Minor and later in ancient Greece (Ronan, 1992:5), was a leader of the 'famous witch ride' of the Middle Ages (Smith, 1992:61). Hekate, an Underworld goddess originally associated with crossroads, 'flies about by night on the wind' accompanied by a 'host of Hekate', the restless souls of the dead (Rohde, 1992:67–69). These beliefs about night-flying goddesses were distorted and re-elaborated by the Inquisition to create the stereotype of the diabolical witches' sabbath (Ginzburg, 1992a; Greenwood 2001).

Many modern witches have incorporated this folklore into their present-day rites. According to Doreen Valiente, a well-known witch and one-time high priestess to Gerald Gardner, the founder of modern witchcraft, Herne, the leader of the Hunt (also known as the Horned God, the Oak King, and the Greenwood Lord), carries off the souls of the dead into the Underworld and leads the hounds out on the chase at Candlemas. Gwyn ap Nudd and the Wild Hunt are also called upon to prowl beyond the witchcraft circle as a 'protective element keeping all that has no right to enter the circle away' (Valiente and Jones, 1990:59, 154). Valiente, who lived in Sussex, England, notes how on Ditchling Beacon, the highest point on the Sussex Downs and an ancient earthwork, is haunted by a 'phantom hunt, known locally as the Witch Hounds'. She says that 'listeners hear the cry of hounds, the hoofbeats of galloping horses, and the call of the hunting horn, but nothing is seen' (1962:55).

I now turn to see how a group of contemporary Pagans in Norfolk used the Wild Hunt mythology as a means of confronting the dark of nature as a process of initiation.

A Wild Hunt Challenge in Norfolk

East Anglia has a reputation among some for being a strange and magical place. The magical realms of eastern England are said to be the land of handywomen, horse-whisperers, wizards and witches, cunning men and wise women (Pennick, 1995). The Essex witch trials have been well documented by Alan Macfarlane (1970), and the infamous self-styled 'witch-hunter general', Matthew Hopkins, hailed from and worked in this area too (Deacon, 1976). In the King's Lynn Tuesday Market a diamond-shaped brick keystone above a first-floor window allegedly marks the spot where, in 1590, the heart of Margaret Read, the last witch burnt in Norfolk, exploded. Another story, current to the beginning of the previous century, claimed that it rolled down a lake leading from the market place and plunged into a river (Porter, 1974:137–138). According to folklorist Jennifer Westwood, there is a well-recorded history of magical activities of witches and their familiars, but less on the cunning folk – the wise men and women who practised 'un-spelling' or 'un-bewitching'. However, some cunning folk, such as Cunning Murrill who apparently dressed up for the part wearing 'terrifying goggles', attained some notoriety. Westwood notes that it was a common belief in Norfolk that the toad and all creeping things were in the service of evil. In 1879, Eckling Green was fined a shilling for assaulting a woman who had charmed him by using a toad, and in East Dereham, as recently as after the Second World War, a man was brought to court for assaulting a woman whom he had accused of being a witch.[5] East Anglia today is said to have become a particular target for devil worship, with its many abandoned churches regularly being found daubed with pentagrams and other magical symbols.[6] For such a dispersed and largely rural area of the country, Norfolk also has quite a number of practitioners of contemporary Paganism, and I met a number of them at a pub moot (the meeting was advertised in the Pagan magazine Pagan Dawn) organized by one couple.

Richard and Louise, who are both in their early forties, run a small post office called Wizard's End in a small Norfolk village. Wizard's End is like any other post office apart from the fact that it has a large wizard painted on the outside wall,[7] and that it sells magical paraphernalia – such as incense, essential oils, candles, wands, wizard figurines and Pagan journals – alongside stamps, postal orders and regular national newspapers. Richard also makes special Wizard's End skin cream from a blend of essential oils and herbs in a natural base using 'age-old knowledge'. Louise casts horoscopes.

At the moot in the back room of the pub Richard told about how he had been struck by lightning. He had walked outside the post office whilst looking up at a storm and a lightning bolt had struck him. At this point in the conversation Richard pointed to the top of his head and showed us a small round bald patch, the place where the bolt had hit him. Thinking that he had died and gone on to the next world, he tried to phone some of his friends to check whether he could communicate with the living; they were all out, and he said he did not know whether he was alive or dead. This had awakened his interest in religion and magic, and both he and Louise had attended a Pagan Federation course on witchcraft in a nearby village. However, they felt that the person running the course did not know anything and was 'on the lookout to initiate young women'. Then Louise had a communication from a hereditary witch in the north of England via citizen band radio, and subsequently Richard and Louise took up a training offer given by these hereditary witches, who had passed on their tradition fearing that it was dying out through lack of family interest. Communicating with the witches by taped recordings, the first time they met their trainers was at their joint initiation. Richard said how they had been worried about meeting the witches but had nevertheless undergone an initiation; this had included being tied up naked while a sword was pointed at them as they were introduced to the circle watchtowers.

After the death of one of their initiators and unresolved differences with the other, Richard and Louise decided to go their own way. They explained that hereditary witchcraft originated with the Iron Age tribes, of which the Iceni was the most local one in Norfolk, and that they had their own ways of doing things. They followed the Celtic 'Herne Path', which was apparently similar to the Romany way of life, but also different. They described it as an eclectic path that incorporated many ideas and practices of different times. Richard said that it involved a cosmic fight between good and evil – Herne, the force of good, seeks out and battles with the forces of darkness (which inhabit vulnerable bodies or those close to death). They follow a Wiccan ritual pattern but are also involved with nature, and they spoke about getting to know trees and trying to understand the energies of woods, etc. They frequently compared themselves to another group of Norfolk Pagans who allegedly always conducted their rituals indoors. According to Richard, they were so scared that something powerful might arrive that they conducted their rituals in a church hall 'just in case'. Richard added that 'they [the other Pagan group] go out and hug trees, we go out and the trees hug us – we know what the outside is'.

Richard and Louise invited those interested to an open event that involved getting to know the spirits of a wood near Norwich through a Wild Hunt Challenge; it was to be held on the 31 October at Samhain (Halloween), when it is said that the veil between this world and the otherworld is thin. They spoke about previous experiences with the spirits of another wood near Norwich in which they had conducted similar challenges in previous years. The aim of the Challenge was to gain mastery over an area of Gwyn ap Nudd's hunting ground. The plan was to walk the wood route during daylight to learn the way, and then repeat it at night in a timed challenge. If completed successfully, the challenged person earned the right of the cooperation of the spirit beings of the area, and to cut a staff from the wood.

Richard, who said that he had been researching the folklore of the Wild Hunt on the Internet, explained to me that the challenge was a 'guided mediation' where the challenger tried to interact with the elementals of the wood to open up other ways of being and to learn how to use the senses:

> We are used by Herne and the Hunt to find things on this plane. It's like a territorial army exercise – learning to use them, to work with them, and them learning to trust us. It's a challenge.
>
> Normal people don't go into the wood at night. You take on the ambience of the wood and learn. You come back charged. You survived! You learn. You hear different things, your senses go on overdrive and your ears are the size of elephants' ears. Last time I heard fairy bells. I strained to hear them and then I saw other people straining to hear... It was a lovely sound. Then there were fire flies...

Richard informed me that the challenge was by invitation only and that people had to do it for the right reasons. In a previous year, one group had participated for excitement rather than spiritual intent, and when Richard had refused to let them join in the following year they had gone around Norwich dressed up as vampires instead. Richard said that he and Louise had cycled around the route in the wood and that the wood had a positive energy. He did not know how long it would take to walk at night. On previous challenges he used to time the pace by how long it took their old lurcher dog to walk, but she had died. They were going to walk it the following night with a group of people. Then they were going to walk it for two more nights before the big challenge at Samhain.

At the next Pagan moot the conversation was mainly focused on a discussion of the Wild Hunt. Five people had walked the course the previous afternoon. It was agreed that the wood was friendly and wanted to communicate with us. Richard and Louise spoke about issuing the challenge to the wood. We decided to walk the route in the dark on Friday, Samhain eve. People recounted what had happened in previous years in a different wood, but nearly all of the conversation was on the forthcoming challenge as people aired their fears and their fantasies about what might happen. This was part of a process of building up the tension and excitement. There was an air of anticipation, of shared purpose, spiritual quest, an expedition into the unknown. When we ventured into the wood what would we find? What would find us? Would we come back? Richard and Louise handed out the following challenge information:

The Wild Hunt

Samhain 1998

This is a competition betwixt the shaman, and the elements of the Fairy Folk who hunt with Gwyn Ab Nudd [*sic*].

This is called the Ultimate Sport of the Magician or Sorceress (all sons of Herne and Maids of Moira were thus qualified).

The Magician wishes to gain mastery over an area of Gwyn Ab Nudd's sporting and hunting grounds, if ... the shaman is triumphant, the Elemental Kings must yield mastery of the territory to the Magician for his lifetime.

If ... the land succeeds in preventing the magician/sorceress from finishing, and the said applicant survives the chase, then he should repay the land according to the terms set out before the challenge begins.

The area has been carefully chosen and an offering will be laid out before the hunting date, bread, fruit etc. The terms of the challenge will be issued aloud i.e. boundaries, time, forfeit or prize.

Dark clothing is to be worn in salutation to the time of the season. Kindle a fire at the starting point, dedicate it to Gwyn Ab Nudd thus:-

Place the posy into the flames and as it burns this releases the dark spirit of the Hunt in its smoke. Be off and hasten about your business, from here on you are alone, use your wits.

Turning around or looking over your shoulder will be viewed as surrender! The Challenge is betwixt you and the Hunt, both you and they will know if you succeed!

Should you win, you may expect full co-operation of non-physical being within that area for your lifetime.

Losing is evident if the circuit is not completed in the specified time, or any other surrender, a precious offering is given to appease the triumphant Hunt, such as honeycomb, wine, etc.

Some have lost their lives or have actually joined the Wild Hunt instead of being chased by it, but, please think of this as a great honour.

On the reverse side was a map of the route sitting between these words:

Failure exists only when
Success is measured by
The words of a Non-God!

But remember this, you are only following in the footprints where we your Elders have trodden before.

The emphasis was on competition, sport and mastery – a contest between the Magician/shaman and the land with its Elemental Kings or nature spirits. This was a challenge shaped by the mythology and folklore associated with Gwyn ap Nudd, and it also showed the influence of computer language: 'Be off and hasten about your business, from here on you are alone, use your wits'. The reference to the ancestors 'following in the footprints' of the Elders stressed the continuity between the land, past generations and the present. The implicit danger in this quest – the possibility of joining the Wild Hunt and not returning – added to the *frisson*, the excitement of an initiation encounter.

Walking the Wood

Three of us who were considering undertaking the challenge – Mary (a shamanic practitioner, artist and musician), Sophie (a hereditary witch and an artist), and me – decided to walk the wood route in the daylight to see what it was like. We called in to Wizard's End *en route* to see Richard and Louise. Richard had announced that he had had two messages: one was from ordinary reality, and the other from the otherworld. The first was that Andy had checked with the warden from the wood that permission had been given for us to be there. The other message was from the otherworld: Gwyn ap Nudd had communicated, via the ouija board, saying that we would each be met with challenges according to our ability.

Driving to the wood, the clouds gathered over the wide Norfolk horizon, momentarily dispersing the sunshine. There appeared to be an ominous dark cloud over the wood as we approached and a flock of rooks flew overhead. However, on arrival at the car park the clouds disappeared and the atmosphere appeared to become more benign. We walked leisurely around the wood and, as instructed by Richard and Louise, I gathered material to put in a magical bag or 'posy'. I collected oak leaves, mushrooms, holly leaves, soil from a molehill, acorns, silver birch bark, and twigs. Mary had already collected hers on the first walk, and Sophie had decided that she did not need to do the challenge (as she claimed to be a hereditary witch). We followed the special challenge map that Richard and Louise had given us; it showed a route on which significant places had been marked. It started at 'Wild Hunt car park' and went in a straight direction along the perimeter of the wood before a left hand turn to 'Thor's Furnace' (a charcoal-burning oven). The path from Thor's Furnace led between piles of felled pines into the dark interior of the wood. To the right was a 'Circle of Power', a small circle of tree stumps, and a bit further on was the 'Magical Tree'. This silver birch had had honeysuckle growing around its trunk in its formative growing years, leaving it with an unusual twisted shape. After the Magical Tree, the path led towards the right and came eventually to a 'Log Seat' to one side of a low-hanging branch. From here on the route in the wood was difficult to follow – there was no clear path and many twists and turns which were cut through scrub and woodland which looked the same (this was to prove to be a real test in navigational skills). It came as a great relief eventually to find 'Woden's Standing Stone' (a tall narrow slate sculpture which appeared to be invisible if approached from the wrong angle). Another area of criss-crossing paths eventually led out onto a wider track – with muddy swampy areas – which eventually completed the circuit leading back to Wild Hunt car park.

On the Friday Mary and I drove to Wizard's End and Richard and Louise took us to the wood in their car. Richard wore a red jester's hat with many bells. On this occasion the mood was light-hearted although not much was said, and it was in stark contrast to the serious event that loomed the following night. When we arrived at the wood the others were waiting in two cars in the car park. Mike, in his early twenties, was unemployed but interviewed people who had had UFO sightings for the Norfolk UFO Society. Colin was about the same age as Mike but was very quiet and not very talkative. Janet and Malcolm were in their mid-fifties. Janet said that she and Malcolm had known Richard and Louise for about six years and that Janet looked after the cards in the post office shop at Wizard's End. They had initially got to know Richard and Louise because they had asked them for help with difficult neighbours who were interfering in their life. Richard and Louise had done a spell to try and get them to move. The spell had not worked in the sense that the neighbours had moved, but they were much quieter afterwards.

We walked around the circuit in the wood in the moonlight together. Some people collected things for their posies. When we reached the Magical Tree everyone stopped to admire it. I decided to walk ahead to see if I could find my way by myself. Janet and Malcolm followed some distance behind. There were three difficult turns – right after the low branch and left at the first fork and right at the second. When I was sure that I knew where I was going, I slowed down and waited for Janet and Malcolm to catch up, and we started talking. They said that they had been in the wood since 3.30 p.m. and had done a practice run in the light and were now doing it in the dark. They had tried the previous Sunday with their grandchildren but had gone in completely the wrong direction. As we walked we chatted about the route and how we would remember where to go the following night. When we arrived back in the car park we had to wait for the others to arrive. When everyone had come back we agreed to meet at 8.30 the next evening.

Richard and Louise gave myself and Mary a lift back to Wizard's End. After showing us their rescued tawny owls (Odin, Phantom and Min), which were kept in an aviary in the back garden, they invited us in for tea in the back part of the post office. The sitting room was finished in pine and had a Scandinavian feel to it. The large fireplace was decorated with pistols, a mace and an enormous sword. There were Egyptian pictures on another wall, pictures of owls and lots of wizard figurines (like the ones for sale in the post office shop). On one windowsill overlooking the garden was a model of Wizard's End post office. In one corner of the room was an enormous globe. An open-plan pine staircase led upstairs. Louise showed us a copy of the women's magazine *Chat*, drawing our attention to a Halloween special on spells for curing cellulite, how to get pregnant, how to deal with a hostile mother-in-law, etc. We laughed at the way the article had been written, and the contrast between this popular interpretation of magic that drew on rather superficial stereotypes of witchcraft, and our forthcoming challenge – which seemed like a confrontation between life and death – seemed stark. Richard played some music by The Enid, a New Age Pagan band.

Confrontation with the Wild Hunt

On Samhain morning Mary and I made our posies. We bound the leaves, bark and fungi, etc. into newspaper and then wrapped it up in hessian, stitching it with turquoise thread into a parcel. As the day drew on and darkness descended our anticipation and anxiety about the forthcoming challenge increased. We spoke about 'the wild' and what it meant to us. Mary saw the wild as neutral. She said that when it sees destruction – ecological or whatever – the Wild Hunt comes in and sweeps it all clean. It is earth energy – tornadoes, flood and earthquakes. It is a wild energy – of rain and storm. The wild comes in as an uncontainable force. I said that I saw the wild as all that was repressed by society; it was the potentiality of humanness; it was like walking off the path into the wood, where the path represents the social and the wood the unrepressed part of the self. Mary said that she had experienced elementals in the wood. She picked up one of her many drums and tried to channel the elemental by drumming:

> The first thing is that it wants reassurance that I'm not taking the piss. It wants me to ask questions.
> What is it and where does it come from?
> It won't answer.

It's not communicable that way. It's an energy that moves around in woods. It was in holly, but not a holly thing. It moves around. It is the eyes of the wood checking us out to see who we were.

It wants a honey sandwich [laughter]. I'm going to take a selection of sandwiches with me!

It's not the wind blowing through the holly. I did some gazing at it – it's a presence – I saw it but not as I see you. It's like a sense of being slightly sparkly inside the bush and when I see something like that I get shivers up and down my spine. It didn't feel bad or good – neutral – and it feels as though it's sussing us out – the eyes of the wood, but won't say more than that. It wasn't very convinced that we were taking it seriously.

I don't see fairies – I get the feeling first then change in shape or lights etc. It was definitely in the bush. It wasn't hiding but drawing attention to itself. I've sent a power animal round the wood and she says it's ok.

I said that I was not worried so much by what was in the wood, but in confronting my imagination about what might be lurking – my own fear of being in the wood. I was allowing myself to opt out of the challenge until the last moment to see how I felt about walking in the wood alone at night. I knew that my active imagination would see rapists and other monsters at the slightest noise from the undergrowth; supposing I met some one on the path? Mary said that what starts off as a psychological battle could shift a person into another place where a different type of communication was possible. She said that that had been her experience of a shamanic 'sitting out' vision quest where she had faced her biggest fear and had managed to walk through it to see 'images of beauty'.

As darkness fell it started raining lightly, no moon was visible. How would we see in the wood? Fears about being lost in the wood were voiced by both of us; we decided to go and buy a torch each 'just in case'. We arrived at the wood at 8.15 after a drive in near silence as a light drizzle played on the car windscreen. Andy was standing outside Colin's car; Mike, Colin and his girlfriend had taken the opportunity to practise the route. We chatted as we waited for everyone to arrive and Andy told me that he'd been involved in all sorts of magical practices from Druidry to Gardnerian Wicca. He was now more concerned with 'putting theory into practice' and was studying an environment management course. The course was small compared to other courses at the college, and he thought that this might be because many people were not interested in the environment. He said that he thought that Pagans were not very interested in acting on their ideas about nature.

As we were talking, Richard and Louise arrived with their barbeque that they set up in the car park. They proceeded to light a fire so that the posies could be burnt to release our spiritual connections to the wood. In the meantime the others came back. Everyone was very talkative and quite animated. Richard said that he would go first and then it had to be female, male, female, etc. (reflecting the Wiccan notion of sexual polarity). Mary said that she wanted to go after me because I'd go quickly (because of my fear); so I said I'd go after Richard. The others decided the 'running order' between themselves. Richard read out the dedication to Gwyn ap Nudd and placed his posy in the fire to burn, thus releasing his spirit connection to the wood, and he took off. Some time later it was my turn, and after placing my posy in the flames I walked down the first track, rather relieved that at last it was happening. As I was walking away from the others I felt resolute that I was going to do the challenge, quietly determined to face my own fears about walking in the wood at night. I tried to blank my mind to my fears – was that shadow someone or something sitting down watching me, or was it a local axe man? I visualized myself strong and with a blue light protecting me. This feeling of strength and determination became stronger as I entered the deeper, darker part of the wood; there was no turning back. There was very little light, but it was possible to make out the path and the shapes and outlines of the trees. The rain was falling softly and there was a wet, misty feel to the woods – dark but gently inviting. The ground was very wet underfoot and boggy in places. I found my way easily, and between the Log Seat and Woden's Standing Stone I imagined I saw a shadowy figure. I had a moment of panic – was I going to let my biggest fear overtake me? Was I going to panic? I decided to carry on and resolved that I was going to enjoy the experience. I felt relatively confident of the route and thought I would just enjoy the darkness and the wood and let myself be aware of the energies and sounds. I felt the wood and its energies through a misty, glistening darkness – it was a wonderful experience.

When I eventually arrived back in the car park some people were still in the process of setting off on their challenge. As I walked into the circle around the fire faces looked expectantly for my report on my experiences. As more came back so the discussion and comparison of experiences grew. Richard said he felt a dark presence following him, which he thought was a large black dog. Darren, a friend of Colin and Mike, who had arrived late and was wearing a black army-style balaclava, saw a medieval knight sitting on a horse behind him to his right. He spoke to Richard about it afterwards and offered to take Richard back to the spot where he had seen it. Richard said that this was no good, as it had been Darren's experience, and that the knight would have vanished. Richard advised Darren to look at the armour in a history book to find out what the knight was. Richard spoke of the last challenge and how, in a different wood, he had seen some Vikings. He had reached out to touch them but they had backed off, making his hand and arm glow golden.

In the meantime, Mike had got lost and found himself in brambles, but had eventually found the 'Wild Hunt car park'. He talked to me about his pet subject of UFOs and seemed quite disappointed that he had not seen one on this occasion. He spoke about how he went out UFO hunting in the night with a group of friends.

They had gone to a local beach and meditated on calling down UFOs. A large cube had materialized with four bright lights and a cigar-shape in the middle. This had convinced his friend who had been sceptical. Mary came back saying that she had been fine until the last section when she had heard a dog barking and also she thought that she might have been followed. Richard said that the previous year the Wild Hunt had left a dog with a challenger to look after for a year as a learning experience. Mary said that she had been overtaken by a figure and she was not sure who or what it was (it later transpired to be Mike who had got lost). Janet and Malcolm were quiet about their experiences, but spoke about hearing noises and seeing lights. In the meantime Andy had got thoroughly lost. There was a discussion about whether he had been taken by the Wild Hunt. Richard was just on the point of going to look for him when Andy stumbled through the undergrowth. He had not encountered horses or dogs, but had gone in totally the wrong direction and seen a badger's set and a deer instead. When everyone got back we made our way up to the Circle of Power close to Thor's Furnace. Mary drummed and sang while everyone sat on tree stumps. We walked to the Magical Tree and then all present agreed that the energy in the wood had changed – it was no longer welcoming, it was time to go.

Initiation into the Process of Nature

Maurice Bloch, in a study of the Merina of Madagascar (1986) (which he later developed into a universalistic theory of ritual (1992)), maintains that transcendent spirit must conquer nature as biological life processes. According to Bloch, Merina circumcision ritual demonstrates that blessing is the true transcendental source of eternal life through descent and this is established by the denial of nature as represented by women, fertility and sexuality. However, this is only suitable for the ancestors not the living. Nature, as the biological facts of life, cannot be expelled but it has to be controlled, and this is done by a violent reassertion of ancestral spirits. This assures obedience to the past, the dead and senior generations; it makes certain that the ancestors are not forgotten and that their authority is established via a complicated symbolism that tries to overcome that which cannot ultimately be conquered. Bloch sees the ritual as an attempt to establish a source of fertility 'free from nature, women and biology and based entirely on descent blessing and authority'; however, this cannot be done because of the inevitable reliance, in this world at least, of the living on natural fertility. As a result the symbolism 'seems to be forever chasing it own tail, recovering what it has thrown out and celebrating what it has denigrated' (1986:103). Bloch's assertions have been challenged as ahistorical and dualistic (Morris 1999:158–162), and it seems to me that they demonstrate not so much an indigenous understanding but rather a specific neoplatonist interpretation of ritual.

In the case of practitioners of nature spiritualities, the aim is to re-establish a contact with the process of nature. There are neoplatonic aspects within the broad category of nature religion, as discussed in Chapter 8, but they tend to focus around anthropocentric and monotheistic tendencies within a wider and more holistic world-view. The majority of practitioners of nature religion see the world in holistic terms where everything is interconnected, but people living in modern Western societies are separated from the natural world and are no longer directly dependent upon it for day-to-day survival, therefore a relationship with nature has to be created. The Wild Hunt challenge was an initiative aimed at creating such relationship by opening up a different sort of understanding with nature – it was an initiation into the process of life and death. Entry into the wood was a type of initiation into magical consciousness through the mythology of the Wild Hunt: to be hunted, to be taken by the hunt, is to face the dark chthonic realms of the otherworld. It is difficult for this to happen within the confines of a witchcraft ritual circle marked out inside someone's living room with all the furniture pushed out of the way. It has to happen out 'in nature'. The wild wood is the ideal place – it is dark, the realm of elemental spirits, a space apart, and, according to Richard, 'normal people don't go into the wood at night'. One has to turn from the everyday world – 'the normal' – to put oneself into a position to 'be taken' by the train of the ghostly dead. In a manner of speaking, it was an exposure – not only to 'see' in a different way by an opening of the senses but also to be taken up by a state of awareness shaped by the rhythm of moving from one state to another; that is, from light to dark and also from life to death. The wood represented a different world, a single ontological domain of otherness but cross-cut by different perceptions and experience. A relationship with the spirits contained in the wood had to be achieved through a mythology; it could not happen automatically (cf. Humphrey and Onon, 1996:113). The mythology provided the context and the language for the experience.

Richard had said, via his spirit communication, that we would all be tested according to our ability. Several people reported experiences of hearing noises associated with the Hunt – references to black dogs, barking, dark presences. The 'sightings' of a medieval knight could be explained in terms of an Arthurian romantic and heroic overlay on an original mythical nucleus theme of a journey into the realm of the dead (Ginzburg, 1992a:107–108). The challenge combined heroic quest with a spirit of openness. The wood, as the antithesis of society and the social order, is a liminal space where anything can happen, and the initiate is told that she or he may not come back – to see the Wild Hunt is said to invite death or disaster, or to be caught up with it and swept away. As we were warned in the challenge handout, 'Some have lost their lives or have actually joined the Wild Hunt instead of being chased by it, but, please think of this as a great honour.' This had echoes of brave Viking warrior heroes who, escorted by Valkyries, were taken to Valhalla, the favourite home of the Norse god Odin, where they could battle without injury, feast, drink, and spend their evenings hearing songs of great battles while being waited on by the Valkyries (Jones, 1996:444). The heroic element can be likened to an ascetic preparation for mastery of the spirits of the wood. As the historian Richard Kieckhefer has observed, with reference to Odin who hangs on a tree, fasts and is exposed to the elements, a magical force is seen to issue from one who has performed heroic disciplines, mastered their body and strengthened their soul. With intense effort of will access to otherwise hidden energies is gained (1993:53).

In a way, we all saw what we were prepared to see. Andy, the environmentalist was ambivalent about the challenge, got lost but saw a badger's set and a deer instead. Mike got lost too in his search for UFOs. Despite a more frivolous component of the acting out of computer Dungeons and Dragons type game-playing, the wood was a place of real disorientation where unconscious and conscious fears could be aired – and might be overcome. The challenge raised psychological issues – in the words of psychotherapy it brought the contents of the unconscious to consciousness – and combined them with magical techniques for naming and symbolizing the unnameable in a manner common to shamanic healing rituals conducted in non-Western areas of the world (Vitebsky, 1993; 1995:98–103). In my case, I had to overcome my social conditioning that woods are indeed dangerous places to be in at night. They are full of the fearful creatures that lurk in the dark recesses of the subconscious. Only when I had decided that I was not going to allow myself to be frightened by my imagination did I relax and enjoy the elemental feel of the woods. The image of the soft greys and shadow, the damp smell of vegetation, the fine misty rain, and the shapes and sounds of the trees and the rustling undergrowth is an enduring memory; it is one that gave me a very different understanding of nature and of my place within it – it was a wonderful experience.

Ideologically nature religion embraces life and death; there is no transcend-ence, neither is there a radical separation between the living and the dead – the dead are the essence of life and are a part of the living everyday world. They come alive through the mythology of the Wild Hunt as it sweeps through the darkness gathering those who would open themselves up into the ghostly train. This encounter with the dark and with death is a form of initiation into magical consciousness; this is another way of knowing, one that is all encompassing and immanent, rather than transcendent as Bloch would have it.

A search for nature often stems from a feeling of disconnection. It originates in the eighteenth-century Romanticism movement's protest against the Enlightenment ideal of disengaged reason. Here the meaning of natural phenomena is not defined by nature itself, or the ideas which they embody, but is given signification by the effect of the phenomena on humans and the reactions they awaken: 'attunement with nature consists of being able to release the echo within' (Taylor, 1989:299). However, as the example of the Wild Hunt has shown, there is more to nature than releasing echoes within – there is the issue of participation and magical consciousness. In addition, Bloch's assertion that the essential core of ritual is a violent transcendent conquering of nature as natural processes of growth, reproduction, ageing and death does not account for why the Norfolk Pagans entered into the spirit of the Wild Hunt challenge. Their aim was to open the senses and to expand consciousness to other realities and living beings. The world of the wood represented 'nature', wildness and another way of knowing and feeling that is cyclical rather than linear, and holistic rather than dualistic – to link into the spirits of nature through the mythology of the Wild Hunt.

The domain of nature was also to be controlled through a discourse of mastery and power, but it is also a moral area and one demanding respect as laid out in the terms of the challenge. Initiation has to be worked at through conquest and encounter, but also through an intentional opening to evocation. As Richard said: 'You hear different things, your senses go on overdrive'; it is an experience that is hard won (cf. Humphrey and Onon, 1996:113). As the hunted we were also to become hunters as part of the act of transformation. We would gain a relationship with the spirits and, as Richard said, would be used by them paradoxically in a dualistic cosmic battle between good and evil.

The theme of hunting is important and one to which I will return. Firstly, I look at how the mythology of the Wild Hunt has influenced two shamanic practitioners working in environmental education and healing.

Creating Connection

Midwinter is the 'hunting time', and from Samhain onwards the Wild Hunt forms a cycle of meditation says shaman Gordon MacLellan, who has been initiated by the Wild Hunt. Gordon told me that he had seen skull-headed people waiting in a rank, smelly and crowded cave. He had seen flashes of eyes and bits of limbs but did not know who was there. It was the Wild Hunt. He was accepted into their midst and he saw them ride. He told me that he had been hunted and had experienced shamanic dismemberment, 'The first dismemberment is shocking and it must be to drive you out of your shape. You have to rebuild your body after dismemberment; it is a teaching about embodiment – a disconnection to commitments to shape (see previous chapter especially pp.95–96, 105). It is different to processes such as illness or death which are awakenings to a wider world'. He could feel the Hunt coming; he could feel a tremble in his bones, like a horror film. When in a supermarket he might feel them, but he has the right to stall them and set a time for the encounter in the immediate future so that they do not get him in front of a class that he is teaching.[8] The purpose of the Wild Hunt is like a spiritual or magical tornado – anyone could be taken up on a hunting night, either hunting with or before it as entertainment. It was not a 'nice experience' but a 'part of things as is'. He explained that part of being a shaman was to be available to the spirits, and if they needed a victim he was available. If he was asked he could not refuse – the oaths he had taken made it inconceivable for him to refuse. Gordon is here referring to the deeper, darker aspects of the Hunt, a world apart from a superficial New Age workshop culture that does not engage with the dark in its frightening aspects.[9] Gordon said that the Hunt was something that happened to a person. It was a process that he would not seek to wake or facilitate in others, and definitely not with children. The Wild Hunt is not a subject for the workshops that are so popular with practitioners of nature spiritualities because it involves dissolution of the self and an associated confrontation with fear, although he commented, cynically:

> it may only be a matter of time before someone tries to reinvent them [the processes associated with the Wild Hunt] as a safe personal discovery process and dismemberment becomes a cheerful form of self-examination. O, wait for that howling on the edge of the senses that says the Hounds are running and then you remember that They are real. Trouble is, so many people never stop long enough to listen, let alone actually *hear*.[10]

Jo Crow, who is a shaman and who works individually and with Gordon in environmental education, told me how she first encountered the Horned God, who 'felt like the Holly King, the Oak King and the Green Man', in a women's Dianic witchcraft coven (this was rather ironic and she felt that her coven sisters would not have been best pleased as they did not work with male deities). The Horned God said to her, 'I am the Hunter and you are the Hunted; you are the Hunter, and I am the Hunted'. Jo said that some of the ways that she had encountered the gods were as Herne, Cernunnos, and the Horned One. For her they came as the spirit of the land, the greenwood, and the Hunt, amongst many other things. She said that she had only 'touched the tip of the iceberg of possibilities'. The gods could be the connection with the otherworld, and the process of being in process:

> The Hunt comes after you, hunts you. You run with it, run from it. There is a feeling of everything that you pass gets caught up in a whirlwind; you are a part of it. It feels like nothing is left untouched by the Hunt. For me, the Wild Hunt is the pulse that runs through life. The Wild Hunt is frenzy in the pack, the frenzy of the prey. It is an exhilaration that can carry anything in it. At any time the hunter can become the prey and the prey can become the hunter. The spirit of the hunt is in every aspect of life – the hunter and the hunted, that is life.

Jo told me that when she was visiting another witchcraft coven as a guest, they called the Wild Hunt to hunt those who in ordinary reality were hunting and leaving deer injured. She said it was a terrifying and exhilarating night:

> Wolf came inside me. It was terrifying. He was right in my face, standing on his hind legs staring at me face to face … I smelt his breath; his fangs were dripping. He was going to devour me. He said, 'You have to let me in. You let me in once before'. On another occasion, in a dream I had mated with wolf on a village green. It was an ecstatic and wonderful experience. He showed me this dream and, although I was quivering with terror, I allowed him in. He came behind me and went into me at the base of my neck. I became filled with wolf and went on the Hunt. I ran with the Wild Hunt and I went on the rampage. I was taken by the Hunt.

It took her some time to return to everyday reality:

> When I came off the downs, one guy could see that I was not out of wolf and tried to bring me back. He joined his forehead to mine to try to call me back but wolf came out of me and almost bit his head off. Eventually I went to bed and I still had wolf in me and every time I looked in a mirror I saw wolf. I still had wolf inside me and came back down later. Sometimes he comes as a companion but does not sit inside me. Wolf helps me to walk in two worlds.

Wolf, for Jo, is a presence who comes to her at times and helps keep her connection with another reality; such an experience may bring insight. Jo said that when she works in environmental education she takes groups of people and sends them out hunting to discover their connection with nature 'through their psyches' to bring out their connections with the wood. Jo says it involves two dimensions: the physical collecting of material and the imaginative opening of the senses; she asks people to interpret what they have experienced into something three dimensional: 'This acts as a connection between the worlds.' Making a fetish of gathered leaves, twigs or any other material may represent the experience; the aim is to make a connection with nature that people will remember.

Jo works on what she calls 'inner landscape', and this often involves the Wild Hunt: 'The Hunt is an opening up time – an exposure to spirits.' Jo said that sometimes she would take a client's hand and take a look at the Hunt. It was a process of 'getting them to hunt for themselves, a quest'. She said that when she works with someone it involves going inside to learn about strong physical feelings and emotions. When a person is comfortable with these she asks them to go out in nature to find a place of connection. The inner landscape has to connect with outer; the outer resonates with the inner and this leads to empowerment:

I encourage them to go out into nature once they're open. We are not separate, we are all on the web and impressions will come. There are lots of ways of connecting. It just involves a change in consciousness, a connection with a shamanic world-view – to deepen and open. If we really know we are connected and not separate from everything, how can we purposely do harm? It's about rebuilding connections, making bridges, or maintaining a knitting pattern so that the flow can come through – removing obstructions, or knots in a string.

This hunt is conducted within to find a self lost in restricting social roles and expectations. It represents a process of self-examination as confrontation with the wild inside, and a connection with a wider web of connections.

Hunting and Rites of Regeneration

The Wild Hunt mythos encourages a different way of knowing and an insight into an alternative way of being in the world, one that appears to be unfamiliar to Westerners but familiar to hunting and gathering cultures. In Malawi, according to Brian Morris, the hunt is a rite of transformation conducted within a pantheistic world-view that expresses life as an ongoing process that includes the living and the dead. Hunting is highly ritualized and is an activity that links individual, social group (including ancestors) and the natural world (cf. Turner, [1967] 1972[11]). The village must be peaceful with no illicit sexual activity taking place, the hunter must go about the hunt with no anger in his heart, and offerings must be made to the spirits of the ancestors for their help in the hunt (Morris, 1996:28–31). The spirits of the ancestors are associated with the woodland and with animals. Death is not seen as the antithesis of life but is viewed as a part of this world and necessary for humans to be mortal. The spirits of the dead ancestors are 'dead' but have life – they are reborn as living human beings; they are an aspect of life that includes humans and spirits. There are different modes of being between the dead and the living but there is not a radical dualism between a static transcendental order and the ordinary world, as claimed by Bloch; rather, they are seen as two aspects of a cyclical process – the spirits of the dead are a part of this process and reflect life's essence (Morris, 1999:160).

Aiming to create a non-detached anthropological account of hunting, anthropologist Tim Ingold draws on the lifeworlds of the Cree people of north-east Canada – who say that an animal offers itself up intentionally in a spirit of goodwill, or even love, to the hunter – to illustrate the differences between embedded lifeworlds in the environment and dominant dualistic scientific perceptions which find the Cree view – that an animal should voluntarily offer itself to be killed – incomprehensible. Pointing out that the entire world for the Cree, not just the human world, is 'saturated with powers of agency and intentionality', Ingold calls hunting a 'rite of regeneration' (Ingold, 2000:14, 67). The Cree hunter is perceptually skilled and detects clues in the environment that reveal the movements and presence of animals. The hunter also narrates stories of hunting journeys and encounters with animals – often in a performance which aims to give form to human feelings about caribou as living sentient beings. When it comes to the point of eye-to-eye contact with the animal at the point of killing, the hunter feels the animal presence; there is an intermingling of being with the animal tantamount to love, and also sexual intercourse in the human domain. In telling of the hunt that feeling is expressed (ibid.:24–25). The hunter consumes the meat but the soul of the animal is released to be re-clothed in flesh. Animals will not return to hunters who have treated them badly: if proper respectful procedures in the process of butchering, consumption and disposal of the bones are not followed, or if undue pain and suffering is caused in the act of killing. Animals are offended if there is unnecessary killing, and if the meat is not properly shared. Hunting aids regeneration – consumption follows killing as birth follows intercourse, both are seen to be integral to reproductive cycles of animals and of humans (ibid.:67). Human beings and animals are enmeshed in relationships of reciprocity:

> The animals in the environment of the hunter do not simply go their own way, but are supposed to act with the hunter in mind. They are not just 'there' for the hunter to find and take as he will: rather they *present themselves* to him. The encounter, then, is a moment in the unfolding of a continuing – even lifelong – relationship between the hunter and the animal kind (of which every particular individual encountered is a specific instance) (Ingold, 2000:71).

People and animals are enmeshed in highly particularistic and intimate ties with both human and non-human others; the hunter does not transform the world, or dominate it – rather, the world opens up to him through knowledge (ibid.:72).

Referring to the Rock Cree of northern Manitoba, studied by Robert Brightman (1993), Ingold calls hunting an 'epitome of progeneration':

> In the unfolding of the relation between hunters and prey both humans and animals undergo a kind of perpetual rebirth, each enfolding into its inner constitution the principle of its relationship to the other. Actual events of birth and death, therefore, are merely moments in the progenerative process, points of transition in the circulation of life (Ingold, 2000:143).

Human beings and animals are linked in the same process of birth, death, and rebirth. Life is a matter of 'coming and going' rather than starting and finishing (Deleuze and Guattari, 1988:25). All of existence is suspended in this process: 'animals come when, following the successful hunt, they enter the human community, they go again with the eventual disposal of the remains'; the animal does not cease to be, it still exists, but in another form, and, 'for this reason, there is always the possibility of its return' (Ingold, 2000:143). Death does not mean the replacing of one generation by another, as in Western genealogy, but is rather an affirmation of the continuity of the progenerative process. The life of every being, as it unfolds, contributes to the progeneration of the future as well as to the regeneration of the past (ibid.). All humans, animals, plants, and other persons,[12] leave trails of intersecting pathways that resemble a rhizome (Deleuze and Guattari, 1988; Samuel, 1990:2). Persons pass along lines of movement and meet with other persons who may further their growth and development by experience or by contributing substance by being killed and eaten. Knowledge is generated in the process:

> Knowledge, from a relational point of view, is not merely applied but generated in the course of lived experience, through a series of encounters in which the contribution of other persons is to orient one's attention – whether by means of revelation, demonstration or ostention – along the same lines as their own, so that one can begin to apprehend the world for oneself in the ways, and from the positions, that they do. In every such encounter, each party enters into the experience of the other and makes that experience his or her own as well. One shares in the process of knowing, rather than taking on board a pre-established body of knowledge (Ingold 2000:145–146).

Ingold's example of the Cree relations with non-human persons of the environment demonstrates both the nature of this reciprocal cyclic relationship, with its emphasis on participation and sharing in the process of knowledge, and the difference between a detached and dualistic Western point of view.

Hunting in this sense has not always been understood by Western scientific thinking. A stereotype of indigenous peoples being primitive and barbaric in their hunting practices has had devastating effects on indigenous aboriginal peoples. Ilarion (Larry) Merculieff, an Aleut, one of three distinct aboriginal races in Alaska, who was born and raised on the Pribilof Islands in the Bering Sea, argues that there is a breakdown of communication between what he calls the ingrained linear structures of Western scientific thinking – with its specialization and refinement of scientific methodology divorced from a direct involvement with nature – and the cyclical understandings of native peoples, who he points out, live by the seasons and respond to their immediate environment. There is a symbiotic and functional relationship between humans and animals that involves the hunting of animals, and among the Aleut this includes seals. This form of hunting has been the target of Western animal rights campaigners (Merculieff, 1996:406–413), many of whom are Pagan.

Western scientific attitudes to nature stem from being physically cut off from living on the land. A degree of variance of perception between Western and non-Western cultures appears that yawns like a vast chasm of cultural difference, reflecting a Western alienation from nature – an absence of knowing about nature as the natural world. Due to the influence of industrialization, and its cultural reaction in the shape of Romanticism, nature in Western cultures is other to industrial urban life; it is not lived in and confronted on a day-to-day subsistence basis, as among rural Malawians or the Cree, for example. Westerners tend to either control and dominate the natural world on the one hand, or romanticize it on the other. For a long time Western cultures have been divorced from a complex interconnection with nature as process, and any form of relationship is sometimes hard to achieve. The mythology of the Wild Hunt goes some way in working towards this. As far as practitioners of nature spiritualities are concerned, the Wild Hunt offers an initiation into the wild and an opening up of the senses; a sense of dissolution of self in confrontation with fear and death, an exposure to a 'whirlwind pulse that runs through life'. In short, engagement with the Hunt is a bid to restore a reciprocity and harmony between humans and nature. To be hunted and to be a hunter involves a metamorphosis – a shift from one to the other, as explained by Jo Crow through her encounter with the Horned God and the movement from being hunted to finding herself a hunter. Paradoxically, one becomes the other in a process of coming to know the rhythm of nature – of the movement from life to death. A confrontation with the Hunt may confer certain powers as the result of a relationship with spirits, and, perhaps more importantly, an understanding of the fluidity of the processes of life. A successful completion of the Wild Hunt challenge earned the right of the cooperation from the spirits of the wood; and for Jo the metamorphosis into wolf enabled her to hunt those who had been leaving deer injured in ordinary reality.

The Hunt has an aim of restoring reciprocity between humans and nature through the cyclical process of relationship between the living and the dead – the hunter becomes hunted and vice versa. This is fluid and ever changing, not a static dualism between a transcendent and a material world, as outlined by Bloch, but rather represents a different form of knowledge and relationship with nature enabled by magical consciousness. This is an ecological model for Western cultures that have historically lost their participation with nature; they have to reconnect in whatever ways are available.

Inevitably, practices and mythologies are mixed and contradictory reflecting a deep historical past antipathetic to or romantically attached to nature. As I have indicated, some Pagans condemn hunting; they may be opposed to any taking of animal life. Interpretations of the Wild Hunt vary too; they may be dualistic, as in Louise and Richard's hereditary witchcraft tradition. In the latter, Herne was associated with the forces of good, and Richard, who identified with Herne, spoke about engaging in a cosmic confrontation with the forces of darkness. Richard clearly also wanting to engage with the process of nature. This would appear to demonstrate a Christianized overlay on the original shamanic theme outlined by

Ginzburg. According to Ronald Hutton, a dualistic interpretation can be traced to Alex Sanders, the founder of Alexandrian witchcraft, and his view of a universe divided into warring good and evil forces (1999:335). (The neoplatonic influences on nature religion will be discussed in Chapter 8.) Despite these later overlays, the mythology of the Wild Hunt provides the framework and language for a 'profound connection' between animals, souls, the dead and the beyond – a language of magical consciousness.

In the following chapter I investigate three different ways in which practitioners of nature spiritualities use stories to relate to the environment in the process of learning to become indigenous.

Notes

1. Le Grand Veneur hunted with dogs in the forests of Fontainebleau in France; Hackelberg sold himself to the Devil for permission to hunt until doomsday in Germany; and in Britain King Arthur served as goblin huntsman. The same mythology is said to prevail among all Aryan peoples, with little difference in detail. The souls of the dying, according to Wirt Sikes, were carried away by the howling winds or the dogs of Hermes. Hermes conducted the souls of the dead to the world below and was, at times, interchangeable with his dog. This relates to the early Aryan conception of seeing the wind as a howling dog or wolf which speeds over the housetops causing the inmates to tremble with fear lest their souls should follow them ([1880] 1973:144).

2. The spirit of this folklore has been captured recently by the poet Martin Newell in a poem about 'Black Shuck', a ghostly black hound of Odin. The story of Black Shuck apparently originates with the Vikings who brought the tale with them when they invaded East Anglia – as they 'sprang from their long ships and stormed ashore in the mist, they brought with them the legend of their ghostly dog'. Black Shuk has remained part and parcel of the local folklore of the region. 'Padding the quiet roads at night', he is described as having a shaggy black coat and eyes as big as saucers that glow like red-hot coals. He must be treated with respect because a sighting of him is thought to mean that you, or somebody who you know, will shortly die. You might meet Black Shuck at a crossroads, on a bridge, ford, or in a lonely country lane. He is said to haunt the boundary lines of ancient parishes, and is often encountered on marshlands, fens and misty low-lying coastal ground. A verse from Newall's poem captures Black Shuk's association with death:

> Then Shuck will run behind me
> And I may not look back
> But press on into darkness as I must
> As others have before me
> And others yet to come
> Who flower once, before they turn to dust
>
> (Newell, 1999:8)

3. The first reference to Herne comes from Shakespeare in *The Merry Wives of Windsor* Act IV, scene 4:

> There is an old tale goes, that Herne the hunter,
> Sometime a keeper here in Windsor forest,
> Doth all the winter-time, at still midnight,
> Walk round about an oak, with great ragg'd horns –
> And there he blasts the tree, and takes the cattle,
> And makes the milch-kine yield blood, and shakes a chain
> In a most hideous and dreadful manner...
> You have heard of such a spirit, and well you know
> The superstitious idle-headed eld
> Received, and did deliver to our age,
> This tale of Herne the hunter for a truth.
>
> (Quoted in Matthews, 1993:47)

Matthews indicates that Shakespeare drew upon an older story associated with an oak tree in Windsor Great Park, called 'Herne's Oak', which was supposed to 'commemorate regular sightings of a mysterious and terrifying huntsman and his ghostly hounds' (1993:48).

4. Odin was gradually replaced by the Devil and in time later local and national heroes supplanted the Devil. In many places a ghostly coach and four superseded the huntsman's pack. Francis Drake was seated in a black coach and lashing a team of headless horses into a wild gallop, accompanied by hideous howls of Yeth Hounds or Wish Hounds which scream on the wind and hunt down the souls of unbaptized babies across Dartmoor (*Reader's Digest*, 1973).

5. At a Norwich day seminar 'Ritual Protection of House, Farm and Church from the Sixteenth to the Nineteenth Century', Wensum Lodge, 17 October 1998.

6. *The Guardian*, 24 November 1998.

7. For a time, in the autumn of 1998, it was also distinctive for its blue post box that was located in the wall beside the wizard painting. The Post Office authorities objected and painted the box red. According to Richard, it was originally so badly painted that he had to repaint it and the only colour he had was blue! An official from the Post Office was sent to warn Richard and Louise that they were contravening regulations. When Richard told the official that

there was no mention of colour in the regulations, the official allegedly got extremely annoyed and threatened to prosecute. The post box has now been carefully painted by the Post Office in its original red colour.

8. This important point demonstrates the difference between a shaman and someone who has no control over the situation and is 'possessed' by spirits. A shaman is a person who is in control of when she or he communicates with the spiritual realm.

9. By comparison, the solitary witch Ann Moura, author of three volumes on 'green witchcraft', gives a meditation that takes the reader into a safe 'shadow side' of witchcraft. Using language that gives agency to a male hunter and sees death symbolized jointly as Crone and earth, Moura's meditation gently introduces the reader to the Wild Hunt and takes them to an unthreatening dark entrance. Through this experience, a person should come to understand that death is a necessary part of life (Moura, 1999a:31–32).

10. Gordon MacLellan, personal communication.

11. Victor Turner's work on the Ndembu of Zambia – who practise subsistence cultivation growing cassava as well as hunting – shows how hunting is a highly ritualized activity that links hunter, the shades of the dead, and society with esoteric knowledge. Turner has noted how hunting cults have developed that involve propitiatory rites to a specific hunter ancestor and involve grades of initiation into esoteric knowledge. Hunting rites are a high-status and usually masculine activity in a society dominated by matrilineal descent, and an adept, perhaps accompanied by an apprentice, is assisted by guardian shades of a deceased hunter kinsman and by magical charms to seek out animals to hunt. He performs rites to propitiate the shades of hunter-dead before venturing into the wild bush, which is believed to harbour witches, sorcerers, ghosts, werelions and persecuting ancestors ([1967] 1972:281–284).

12. Personhood, for the Cree, is not confined to humans but is open to animal and non-animal kinds (Tanner, 1979:137–138, cited in Ingold, 2000:49).

−7−

Learning to be Indigenous

The Pagan 'renaissance' of the last two centuries has been manifested in creative literature, especially Gerald Gardner's *High Magick's Aid* (1949), Dion Fortune's *The Sea Priestess* (1959), and Tolkien's *The Lord of the Rings* (1954–5), according to religious studies scholar Graham Harvey who asserts that these authors provided 'metaphorical binoculars through which the realm of Faerie became visible again'. Such writing, he claims, is not mere escapism but might be a 'mechanism for exploring possibilities and potentials: as a form of ritual or prelude to a transformative rite of passage', or a 'catalyst for change' (2000:3–4). Harvey says that 'fantasy' literature is 'perhaps the nearest contemporary literary form of story-telling' and that Terry Pratchett's Discworld series in particular 'enables a more participatory, perhaps transformative, knowledge and experience' (ibid.:2; see also Bates, 2002). Gregory Bateson defined a story as a 'little knot or complex of that species of connectedness which we call *relevance*' (Bateson, 1988:13); in other words, stories make sense to us. But can stories teach people to find relevance in nature? Do stories help people to feel indigenous in the sense of seeing themselves as part of nature? And, perhaps more importantly, is it possible to engage fully with a surrounding ecology from within a literate culture?

In literate cultures, fairy stories may hold a key to relating to the land through experience. Fairy tales come from a literate tradition but they are based on folk beliefs about fairies derived from oral traditions. Usually written by a single identifiable author, fairy tales adapt oral stories and apply the standards of literacy. Between the years 1450 and 1700 the standardization of language and the invention of the printing press helped fairy tales to become a popular genre among the elite; the fairy tale is therefore a relatively modern genre (Zipes, 2000: xx). Fairy stories have a potential to offer a new dimension to experience; this is what led Freudian psychoanalyst Bruno Bettelheim to argue that they speak to the unconscious through the imagination, giving inner psychological phenomena a body in symbolic form ([1976] 1991:36, 71). Nevertheless, the fairy tale speaks not only to the individual, it has wider implications for how people relate to the wider world too. However, something may have been lost in the process of translation from oral story to literary fairy tale; the message of communication has become enshrined in the printed word. This has implications for how we relate with nature, and the root of the problem lies in language. Philosopher David Abram argues that language in literate cultures is visualized as a static structure; by contrast, the language of oral culture is not objectified as a separate entity by those that speak it, nor is it seen to be exclusive to human beings (1997:139, 154).

In this chapter I explore three examples of how fairy tales and stories are used by practitioners of nature religion. Doreen Valiente, a witch and prominent Pagan writer, has observed that the 'fairy creed' is a composite of several factors: the actual spirits of nature; souls of the pagan dead; the folk-memories of aboriginal races; and an apparently world-wide belief in a hidden underworld within the earth. The different strands become intertwined until 'they are like the twisting magical knots upon some old Celtic or Saxon carving, with strange faces and forms peeping out between' ([1973] 1986:123). And so it is that the different strands are intertwined in practice. The first account of such intertwining shows how Jasper, the Romany shaman, gets participants in his workshops to journey using the fairy tale of Sleeping Beauty as a metaphor for reawakening the earth; the second intertwining concerns how Reclaiming, a centre for feminist spirituality in San Francisco, uses fairy story narrative in exploratory journeys of empowerment in Avalon, 'the gateway to the Otherworld' (Ivakhiv, 2001:105); while the third examines how shaman Gordon MacLellan seeks to encourage a celebration of nature in children through stories and encounters with nature spirits. The question of whether stories create a sense of being indigenous, when being indigenous means knowing the land through participation, will be discussed.

Thinking with Nature

Joe Sheridan argues that learning to be indigenous means knowing the land by its stories; knowledge is vested in landscape.[1] Stories involve understanding the narrative within nature; they blur the lines between humans and non-human nature, giving primacy to an experiential relationship with nature. Stories unify perception and experience, and link with an ancestral past. By discussing certain nature writers, he shows how it is possible to learn how to find the spiritual within the material world, and how to overcome the views of modernity which are devoid of mythic meaning. Tellers of Native American stories Raven Mackinaw, Grey Owl, Ernest Thompson Seton, and Gary Paul Nabham have 'thought with landscape and mammals'. Sheridan talks about the importance of learning an experiential nature-based vocabulary and a system of representation that requires a deep familiarity with the landscape. This functions as a precursor to revealing that language's many levels of meaning; it is necessary to learn a grammar consistent with an ecological relationship with the rest of nature (Sheridan, 1998:306). Drawing on a conversation with Cree elder Raven Mackinaw, who said that if environmental education wanted to 'get it right' it needed to understand that wilderness was the same as storytelling, learning to be indigenous meant knowing the land by divining the stories that live 'in' and 'as' the land. Identity and knowledge are vested in landscape, and specific stories have a phenomenological presence in certain places.

These stories are not fiction, but are spiritually resonant entities, 'perhaps better understood as intelligences, composed "of", "within" and "by" ecosystems. In other words, stories are the spiritual and cognitive dimension of natural systems in which humans are ecological members.' Thus ecologies communicate – but not to the 'narrowed sensual perception of the literate modern' who has 'elevated what the eye can see to the level of near absolute truth and sole arbiter of the "real"'. By contrast, oral culture has a listening and holistically sensual relationship that stays true to the integrity of both the perceptual ecology of the senses and the communicative ethic of the land. This type of language unifies perceptions and experiences; it harmonizes and transcribes nature's phenomenological reality and creates an ontological structure; place is a central theme in Native American concepts of cultural development and continuity with an ancestral past. 'Developing landscape so biodiversity is eviscerated makes a ghost of ecological intelligence and the communicative ethic once composed by that place' (Sheridan, 1998:303).

Ernest Thompson Seton, who had extensive knowledge of ecosystems, was a writer of animal stories and he used this knowledge to tell anthropomorphic tales about animals. Influenced by James Fenimore Cooper, a writer of novels about noble Native American indigenousness, and Charles Eastman, a Dakota or Sioux Indian, Thompson Seton was also a charismatic naturalist, artist, conservationist, public speaker and first chief scout of the Boy Scouts. One of his major goals was to instil manhood in boys through woodcraft and outdoor life inspired by Indians (Krech, 1999:19). Concerned by anxieties created by late nineteenth-century urban industrial capitalism and the alienating effects of technology, Seton created the 'Woodcraft Indians' in 1881.[2] This youth development movement started from his attempts to tame a group of local vandals whom he had invited to camp on his land. Organizing them into a make-believe tribe, he told them tales about Indians; they made costumes and played nature study games. The emphasis was on the natural world and a sense of freedom (Deloria, 1998:96–98, 102). Seton attached great importance to play-acting and costume; however, he used the Indians not a role models but as 'points of entry into a magically transfiguring mimetic play for children' (ibid.:98). He sought an authentic social identity that had meaning in the face of the displacement of modernity (ibid.:101). Seton's ecological world-view considered that 'we and the beasts are kin'. He saw animals as having complex and intricate forms of communication, aesthetic sense, social systems, learned as well as instinctual behaviour, emotions, a moral sense, subjectivity, and unique personalities; and they often formed close relationships with humans (Morris, 2000:38).

Grey Owl, who was British rather than Ojibwa, was accused of faking his real identity – of 'playing Indian' – but, as Sheridan has pointed out, he revealed the 'Indianness' in every white reader by reversing the superiority of colonialism and showing how it was possible to learn to be Ojibwa, 'Thinking *with* the beaver was a step towards understanding creation and thereby comprehending the narrative within nature' (1998:310). Both Grey Owl and Ernest Thompson Seton were influenced by Ojibwa, Iroquoian, and Saulteux language; they learnt how to hunt and trap, and composed stories from the land working with animal intelligences. They 'thought with wildlife' (ibid.:305; see Morris, 2000:36–40; see also Chapter 9). These languages have adjectives that describe the dynamics of ecosystems and have an experiential nature-based vocabulary that requires a deep familiarity with landscape to reveal many levels of meaning (Sheridan, 1998:306). For Grey Owl 'the experience of modernity was devoid of mythic meaning. His encounter with the First Peoples of Canada was grounds for a conversion where he re-gained a grand narrative his own culture had lost from its ancestral past' (ibid.:313). Sheridan concludes that to literate, settler culture 'the absence of deep ancestral time/presence in a place tends to make for cynicism with regards to the authenticity of the experiential link between culture and landscape' (ibid.:12).

Sheridan does not discuss the political dimension of regaining an ancestral past. However, it is an important issue, as raised in my initial correspondence with Jasper, the Romany gypsy, in Chapter 4. Aboriginal peoples have suffered racism, loss of land, way of life and genocide at the hands of white settlers and colonialists (Vizenor, 1995:2–8; Churchill, 2003). It is my view that white Westerners must learn from this shameful history and not repeat it through spiritual appropriation too. However, despite his European ancestry – his non-Native Americanness – there is much of value in Grey Owl's message of thinking with nature for white Westerners. Like Seton, he provided a way for Westerners to think in different ways about nature. Both used play-acting to create a point of entry into another world-view, one that is more in tune with the land and its animals.

A central issue for literate cultures is the distinction made between scientific and spiritual understandings of the land and how this affects language, as Wendell Berry, a writer on ecological issues whose motivation stems from 'a desire to make myself responsibly at home in this world' (Trimble 1988:225) demonstrates when he sets the language of religion against the language of an empirical science. Berry calls for a community-based ecology with a language to speak of the particularities of place. Science, he claims, with its language of abstraction, does not deal with the preciousness of individual lives and places. By contrast the language of religion – with its delights in individuality and the variety of creatures – sees creation as holy. He calls for a 'whole, vital, particularizing language'. The world's multitude of places and creatures need to be known not just conceptually but imaginatively too; they must be pictured in the mind and in memory and they must be known 'by heart', so that 'in seeing or remembering them the heart may be said to "sing", to make a music peculiar to its recognition of each particular place or creature that it knows well' (Berry, 2000:39).[3] This is different to the language of objectification and abstraction.

While noting that the simplification of differences is dangerous, anthropologist Veronica Strang, who has studied white settler and Aboriginal relationships to the land in Australia, claims that it is possible to outline certain themes that aid the process of abstraction. The first is fragmentation and discontinuity, a greater need for individuation, boundaries, explicit language, less collectivity and uses of metaphor; the second concerns a larger scale which demands more specialization and quantative evaluation, as well as intellectual distance and objectivity; the third highlights a lack of continuity and the discontinuity of a fast-changing society that gives few opportunities to build up long-term qualitiative environmental interactions (1997:285–287). Strang comes to the conclusion that affective values are complex but they are concerned with qualitative issues: the land is used in economic and physical terms as well as providing emotional and intellectual sustenance – it is the 'medium for every cultural form, the common ground for all discourse' (ibid.:286).

Strang has observed that the white Australian settlers and the Aboriginal people inhabit the same geographical space but have two different 'landscapes' of knowledge. Pointing out that language makes explicit human values and relationships with the material and imaginative world, she shows how Aboriginal classification systems group together trees, shrubs, insects and crustaceans that have tree-like qualities. This classification system is created by relating seasons of the year to natural events marking an interrelationship between people and the environment. Aboriginal country is defined by its story places, its mythological associations and by groups of people; it uses metaphor, analogue and implicit language – it is specific and speaks for the particular. There is a lack of quantative words – there is one, two, and three but after that 'a big mob of things' (ibid.:178–182). Readings of the land tend to flow from one aspect to the next and concern information on society, spiritual, historic and economic meanings. The country is described in terms of lines, ridges, waterways and storylines which connect one place to the next; each place is a 'repository' of information which Strang observes is rarely commented upon elsewhere or in the abstract but is 'released or stimulated by the place itself' (ibid.:200–201).

It is hard not to invoke dualisms between Western and non-Western views of language; and also between science and religion, as Wendell Berry seems to do when he stereotypes religion – which comes over as Christianity – and science. Indeed, when Berry writes that the mystery of the unitary truth in God leads to the glorification of the multiplicity of his works (2000:33) he echoes the seventeenth-century Protestant reformers who saw God manifest by his work: 'The deep rooted religious interests of the day demanded in their forceful implications the systematic, rational, and empirical study of Nature for the glorification of God in His works and the control of the corrupt world' (Merton, 1949:329, quoted in Tambiah, 1991:12). In Berry's case the rational and empirical study of nature is replaced by affection of the heart. This conflict model ignores both the history of the development of science and the richness and complexity of the relationships between them, as well as the animistic world-views of oral cultures. In the seventeenth century natural philosophy integrated science and religion to explore questions about the attributes of God and his relation to the physical world (Brooke, 1991:7). Also during the seventeenth century there developed what Antoine Faivre terms a *physica sacra*, which he says might be considered to be the chronological link between the cosmological views of the Renaissance and German *naturphilosophie*, a philosophy of nature that takes an intuitive but rigorous approach to understanding nature (Faivre, 1989c:24). Contemporary science must expand its classification systems and not just rely on abstraction; according to Murray Bookchin it must take an ecological approach (Bookchin, 1997:71).

David Abram, taking a phenomenological approach, argues that literate cultures with formal writing systems objectify the field of discursive meanings: 'In the absence of any written analogue to speech, the sensible, natural environment remains the primary visual counterpart of the spoken utterance, the visible accompaniment of all spoken meaning. The land, in other words, is the sensible site or matrix wherein meaning occurs and proliferates' (1997:153). By contrast, an oral culture might interpret the environment as an animate terrain that not only speaks but listens too. Language, in oral cultures, is experienced as a property of the sensuous lifeworld not just that of human beings (ibid.:153–154). Linguistic patterns of oral culture are more responsive and responsible to the bioregion: 'Stories hold, in their narrative layers, the sedimented knowledge accumulated by our progenitors' (ibid.:178, 181) – and these are not always exclusively human.

Thus the language of literate cultures is, as Grey Owl noted, often devoid of mythic meaning. Many practitioners of nature spiritualities try to reconnect with folk memories, but it is sometimes difficult to relate emotionally to the land; they may have to 'bracket' certain approaches and understandings, or perhaps allow themselves to return to a sense of child-like wonder at nature, perhaps through the world of faery, as suggested by Graham Harvey. However, stories about fairies as the spirits of nature are not culturally embedded in the land, or in Western psyches, so how do practitioners of nature religion come to feel the land? Is it possible through creative writing?

The Creative Imagination

Historian Simon Schama starts his book *Landscape and Memory* with the observation that it was only when he got to secondary school that he realized that he was not supposed to like Rudyard Kipling. This came as a blow. He did not mind leaving Kim and Mowgli behind, but *Puck of Pook's Hill* was different; he had been given the book for his eighth birthday: 'For a small boy with his head in the past, Kipling's fantasy was potent magic.' He recounts how, 'Apparently, there were some places in England where, if you were a child (in this case Dan or Una), people who had stood on the same spot centuries before would suddenly and inexplicably materialize. With Puck's help you could time-travel by standing still. On Pook's Hill, lucky Dan and Una got to chat with Viking warriors, Roman centurions, Norman knights, and then went home for tea' (1996:3). Such is the power of the literary imagination that links place and fantasy in a small boy's mind. In Western cultures the imagination is created and shaped through myths and fairytales as well as creative writing for children. Does such an engagement with the imagination lead to escapism – a withdrawal from everyday life – or could it change people's perception of the world in which they live?

In her study of occultists, the anthropologist Tanya Luhrmann notes that most modern magicians read certain novels avidly and that in many cases their enthusiasm led them into magical practice. She claims that magicians often seem to be 'people self-sufficient within a withdrawn, subjective fantasy world who are conflicted about their own desire to have impact within the larger social world' (1989:87). Luhrmann observes that magical books encourage an embracing, dream-like absorption, a disassociated day-dream, and that magical practice attempts to elicit an uncritical imaginative absorption in ritual which suspends 'judgmental reality-testing criticism' (ibid.). This may indeed be true, but it is only one of a number of possible options and outcomes from such reading and does not account for the work of many Pagans in environmental education or in protest against environmental destruction. Gordon MacLellan's environmental work is not about withdrawal from the larger social world or an absorption in ritual, but rather a commitment to helping people rediscover a child-like sense of wonder at nature.

Gordon and Jo Crow both told me that they had been influenced by magical fiction. In Gordon's case this was primarily through Alan Garner's *The Moon of Gomrath*, a magical adventure story about the Wild Hunt (see Chapter 6) that he had read as an eight-year-old 'from cover to cover without stopping'. This had had a profound effect on him. In this story Colin and Susan are two children who get caught up with the Brollachan – a universal power of darkness. Eventually, after a battle between good and evil, the Wild Hunt, led by an antlered Herne the Hunter, wins out:

Colin heard another sound, so beautiful that he never found rest again; the sound of a horn, like the moon on snow, and another answered it from the limits of the sky; and through the Brollachan ran silver lightnings, and he heard hoofs, and voices calling, 'we ride! We ride!' and the whole cloud was silver, so that he could not look.

The hoof-beats drew near, and the earth throbbed. Colin opened his eyes. Now the cloud raced over the ground, breaking into separate glories that whispered and sharpened to skeins of starlight, and were horsemen, and at their head was majesty, crowned with antlers, like the sun. (Garner, 1963:152–153)

Such stories open up an imaginative world of moral forces of unseen powers and battles between dark and light. The work of the psychoanalyst Bruno Bettelheim ([1976] 1991) emphasizes the need for such fiction for healthy child development in the answering of existential questions about the self. Myths, like fairy tales, he suggests, may express an inner conflict in symbolic form and offer options on how it may be solved; they may create steps in development 'toward a higher humanity' (Bettelheim, [1976] 1991:26). Magical fiction, myths and fairy tales can also free an individual from restraining social conditioning.

Jo Crow told me that she had been deeply influenced by the magical novels of Diana Paxson (see pp.48–49), but also by the psychologist Clarissa Pinkola Estés's best-selling book *Women Who Run With the Wolves*. Pinkola Estés claims that fairy tales, myths and stories provide understanding which leads into deep self-knowing – that of the wild and 'innate instinctual Self'. For women this is especially important, because women have been 'forced into unnatural rhythms to please others'. Pinkola Estés likens healthy women and healthy wolves, and claims that they share certain characteristics: they are relational and intuitive by nature, and both have been 'hounded'. She claims that the instruction found in story is reassuring because it leads women deeply into their own knowing: 'the tracks we are all following are those of the wild and innate instinctive Self' (Pinkola Estés, 1995:1–4). Thus novels may engage and expand the magical imagination into an exploration of deeper parts of the self (see Harvey, 2000:4–5).

A major influence on many practitioners of nature religion has been Brian Bates's *The Way of Wyrd*, a novel written to introduce the reader to an Anglo-Saxon animistic world through the imagination. *The Way of Wyrd* chronicles the apprenticeship of Wat Brand, a Christian scribe attached to a monastery mission, to an Anglo-Saxon sorcerer in the late 600s. Wat Brand is initially marked out and acknowledged by the spirits of death in the form of Woden and the Wild Hunt, who are 'custodians of knowledge' and who must be experienced ([1983] 1996:59):

The moon had slunk behind clouds, pitching the forest into darkness. From a distance wolf howls split the night air and echoed mournfully through the tree-tops. I lay still as a grave-stone while the forest fell eerily, ominously silent. Then, almost imperceptibly at first, the whole forest began to tremble. I lifted my head and stared blindly into the surrounding blackness, beyond the fading embers of the fire. I could see nothing. A rumbling noise grew rapidly louder and louder, like thunder, until the forest shadows rocked and swayed and I thought the trees would come crashing to the ground. I lurched to my feet and my crucifix slipped from my chest; frantically I scrabbled in the leaf litter until I found it and then slumped against the tree trunk, my shouted prayers snatched away by the uproar. Giant black clouds still blotted out the moon and in the darkness the air around me seemed crowded with spectres, invisible tormenters hissing from tree to tree, shrieking in front and then behind me so that I did not know in which direction to turn. Then, crashing into the clearing came a pack of monstrous black dogs, pounding past me with a horrible, rasping howl, and on their heels thundered a herd of enormous horses, black as night, with the same hideous, staring eyes as the horse-head of my nightmare. Astride the leading horse rode a shadowy figure, cape flooding out behind him like the wings of a demon, bearing straight down on me. At the last moment the horse veered to my left and charged past, followed by twenty or more horses and riders, kicking up the embers of my fire into the black night air (Bates, [1983] 1996:42–43).

The reader, who is encouraged to identify with Wat Brand, is led through the imagination into a story of spiritual transformation by the use of the folk myth of the 'soul ravening' chase of the Wild Hunt. A different view of the world is revealed, one that is based on participation with the interconnecting patterns of 'wyrd' (see Chapter 8).

This alternative world is peopled with other-than-human folk such as elves, dwarves, and fairies. Andy Letcher, the well-know Druidic bard introduced in Chapter 3, who has spent a winter in a bender[4] up a tree in a Newbury Bypass protest camp,[5] points to the importance of fairies in the creation of alternative mythologies. He says that protesters used folk mythology about fairies to explain their experience of the land. Letcher explains that for Pagan protesters the land is often seen as an enchanted place; many report sightings, 'fungally assisted or otherwise', of 'other-than-human folk, mythological beasts and fairies'. He points out that many protesters take their inspiration from fairy mythology; this is reflected in the use of words like 'pixiemagick' or 'pixieing', phrases used to describe the nocturnal activities of eco-saboteurs, and, 'If the pixies of folk tale turn the milk sour, or tie an unsuspecting person's shoelaces together, then the modern day pixies let down the tyres of bulldozers or snatch a helmet from a security guard's head (a reminder that fairies are not necessarily "nice people")' (Letcher, 2000:3). The language of another reality sometimes finds expression in Robin Hood myths and the outlaws of the forest – living in the trees and opposing the Under-Sheriff of Berkshire. However, new myths are creating a 'geography of enchantment' for the present rather than some imagined past:

It is tempting to see protesters as an expression of the Robin Hood myth, but they do not simply reinvent the old; they help to establish the new. Our relationship to place takes on new meaning when, for example, we know that this is the hill where Arthur's Camelot was alleged to have been. A tree becomes more than a tree when we know that the magna carta was signed beneath its branches. Similarly as one travels the route of the Newbury bypass one crosses the sites of the protest camps, with all the stories that they created. Gotan, the Pixie Village, Skyward, Kennet, Rickety Bridge each have their own stories, their own mythology. Each have contributed to a 'geography of enchantment' that comes from the now, not from an imagined past. (Letcher, 2000:3).

In terms of Pagan protest, fairies and the land of faery mark the connecting point between the protesters and the land they are protecting; the language of fairies represents another mode of reality, an alternative one to mainstream culture with its road-building and development schemes. Folklore and mythologies are used to create and talk about a different way of experiencing the world as a language of the otherworld, a language of participation.

I now turn to examine three approaches to story-telling. The first concerns the fairy tale of Sleeping Beauty.

Romany Gypsy 'Old Animistic Ways'

Long ago, Sleeping Beauty, a spirit recognizable to all of us who have European roots, came under the spell of a wickedly clever fairy, whose spirit worked through many gullible sorcerers. These sorcerers threatened to kill the beautiful princess – or to take the beauty of the imagination away.

Patrick 'Jasper' Lee, *We Borrow the Earth*

Learning to be indigenous involves learning stories about the land to structure otherworldly experience. In the case of the gypsies, Jasper says that fairy tales are the common medium. A particular favourite is *Sleeping Beauty*.[6] Jasper has reinterpreted this as the Great Forest Mother, a friendly spirit and the energy in Western Europe, who is also within us. Jasper explained to me how he thought that a spell, cast by self-centred sorcerers, had been put on Western Europe; he thought that it catches everything in a vicious whirlwind and is responsible for individuals and nature being enchanted by illusion and consequently suffering soul loss. It is a hard spell to break – but all spells can be broken, and Jasper is constantly working at weakening it to let the more natural energy surface. Jasper and Lizzie hold workshops where people can learn to rescue Sleeping Beauty, the natural energy of the land, through shamanic journeying. According to Jasper, Sleeping Beauty had a spell put on her when people started living in the civilized world but when a handsome prince kisses her she will wake up, and so a new beginning will occur, both within the person journeying and with the Spirit of the Forest.

Six people lay on the green Persian rug around a flickering candle in the living room at Jasper and Lizzie's new home in Sussex, England and journeyed to rescue Sleeping Beauty from her castle. Afterwards, in gypsy fashion, so we were told, we recounted what had happened.[7] The following is the account of Annie, a Pagan trained in the feminist witchcraft tradition of Reclaiming (see pp.157–158):

As usual I got into my little boat,[8] which carried me across the river, down stream, to the other bank. I got out, tied up, and walked thro' the wood to my bender. 'Faery Fox' was inside waiting for me, and we sat together waiting for Jack to arrive. We all set off at a fast pace thro' the wood and came out at the foot of a hill. At the top was a strangely ornate castle, like a fantasy drawing. Up the hillside, it was surrounded by an ancient gnarled thicket of thorn bushes, wild rose and brambles. We crouched low and followed 'Fox' thro' hoop and loops of lower branches, where we were joined by lots of small animals. When we reached the base of the castle, the rats living inside showed us the way in, thro' the tunnels of a drainage system. We all steadily climbed up stairs and corridors, avoiding holes and broken floors, broken and crumbling in the dark. There were lots of little creatures with us by now. Up a winding staircase to a tower top. In the dark, I could see a large four-poster bed covered in dead climbing plants and thick cobwebs. I gingerly broke my way through. There was a shrouded figure in the bed, wrapped around like a mummy, but it felt warm and supple.

I had a problem in moving it. Jack and I heaved it over his shoulder. The rats guided us all down thro' the castle to a small door at the base. I heaved it open, and it fell off its hinges. We were facing east, and the sun was just starting to rise from below the horizon. The ancient bushes were beginning to crumble, as we pushed thro' them down to a small grassy knoll or mound with a raised stone bench on top. The sun was rising and the sky was full of dawn colours. Small flying creatures, birds, butterflies, flies and little transparent flying beings with hands but an indistinct body outline, flew around us all. Jack and I laid the shrouded figure on the stone slab, and the little beings started to pull at the wrappings. We all helped, and clouds of dust blew around us. The small animals took the wrappings away as we opened them up and revealed a pale female form. The animals sat on her to warm her, and wings fanned her head.

Jack and I decided to look for water, so 'Fox' led us downhill and we found a small river. Jack filled his water bottle, and we came back and wet her lips and sprinkled her face. Her colour was returning, pale skin, pink cheeks, red lips and dark hair. Jack kissed her, and I stroked her hair. She opened very blue eyes, and everything danced around her in a whirl of energy. I stepped back and away to watch. I decided that she was all right by now, so Jack, 'Fox' and I went off for a walk, down to the river, to follow it to see where it went. The sun was up and felt warm, with the scent of flowers and grass in the air. I saw my wood in the distance, the river flowed into it. I heard the signal to 'return', so we all ran back to my bender. I said goodbye to Jack and 'Faery Fox', and ran to get into my boat to return.

Annie said that she has a group of spirit animals that she meets and they develop in ways appropriate to each world; she described 'Faery Fox' as 'like a cartoon fox who lived in a bender when I wasn't there'.

My own journey reflected some of the gypsy wiles or techniques of survival in a *gaujo* world – such as mesmerizing, originally used to capture rabbits but also effective in getting one's way in the human world – that Jasper had been teaching us about:

> I walked along the path and met up with Robin Hood,[9] who took me to the forest to meet his band of merry men. We realized that we couldn't rescue Sleeping Beauty without a plan, so we had to work out a strategy. The problem was to overcome a large black monster that was sprouting many heads; it was like an octopus and black tar, both at the same time, and it was guarding the golden castle where the Sleeping Beauty was imprisoned. We had to trick the monster by using different strategies: by mirrors to reflect it back to itself, so it could only see itself; and by mesmerizing it by asserting our will; and by walking around it and pretending we weren't interested in it [these were techniques that we had learnt during the workshop]. These strategies were better than direct fighting and confrontation.
>
> Everybody was using different techniques for distracting the monster, dancing, and singing. The monster was confused and a pathway appeared, like a black sea opening up to allow a path through into the castle. Robin Hood rushed through. He raced up the stairs, around and around the garret staircase, until he came to the highest room in the castle where Sleeping Beauty was lying. Robin kissed Sleeping Beauty and she turned into a beautiful green tree, and the castle turned into a forest. All the merry men started dancing and everyone celebrated.

Jasper and Lizzie frequently ask participants in their courses to rescue Sleeping Beauty; the more that she is rescued the more that the old animistic ways of being will be rescued. The process works within the individual as well as for the greater whole – we are both the tree and the forest. 'It can't be done too many times', says Jasper. The aim of the journey is transformation of consciousness by the development of the imagination and a rekindling of the old animistic ways. This process is said to involve the affirmation of all bodily senses and goes beyond mere fantasy. Otherworldly reality, Jasper claims, goes beyond being fantasy when the experiences that it engenders take on whole body intensity: 'There is an honesty involved which comes from giving of yourself – of having the courage to lay yourself on the line.' He says that when he sees this in someone's journey he knows that 'something is happening'. Jasper said that in the past gypsies would originally have journeyed in a group – each person would bring back their own story and then share and relive it with the community.

Stories are also used within the Reclaiming feminist witchcraft workshops in ways that are designed to reshape experience and provide a theme of continuity.

Reclaiming Tradition

> Once upon a time, there was an island, a misty, secluded spot only half in this world, where priestesses, heroes, heras, and mages would go to be trained in magic. Called Avalon, Mona, the Isle of Women, its hidden groves would shelter the wise as they learned the language of birds and the speech of nature, the arts of sensing and shaping unseen energies, of moving at will through the spectrum of consciousness, of bending reality and shifting fate.
>
> Starhawk and Hilary Valentine, *The Twelve Wild Swans*

Reclaiming is a centre for feminist spirituality in San Francisco and offers a framework for a radical paganism, hence Jani Farrell-Roberts's invitation to Starhawk to visit the Lyminge protest camp (as described in Chapter 3). Reclaiming is a loose community of like-minded people who share the common goal of uniting spirituality with politics. There are feminist Pagans, direct-action Pagans, performing arts Pagans and anarchist Pagans who share a joint cultural identity as a Witch and/or Pagan working towards uniting politics and spirituality (Salomonsen, 1996:115; 2002). As a community of women and men working to unify spirit and politics in a vision of the Goddess as immanent life force, Reclaiming seeks to work for a new culture to overcome oppressive social structures of domination and control by using magic, which is defined as 'the art of changing consciousness at will. The collective works with political action based on the understanding that the earth is alive and all of life is sacred and interconnected. The Goddess is seen to be immanent in the earth's cycles of birth, growth, death, decay and regeneration, and magical practice 'arises from a deep, spiritual commitment to the earth, to healing and to the linking of magic with political action' (*Reclaiming Quarterly*, Winter 1997–98 p.20). This type of radical activist witchcraft is very different from the type of British witchcraft from which it is derived. Witchcraft, as developed by Gerald Gardner, was a countercultural religion based on a reworking of Hermetic high magic, but it was very much a product of its time and did not question conventional political understandings of gender, sexuality or relationships with nature.[10]

A founder member and formative influence on Reclaiming is Starhawk. Her books – *The Spiral Dance* (first published in 1979 and republished in 1989), *Dreaming the Dark* (1982), and *Truth or Dare* (1990) – offer a different approach to more conventional witchcraft by putting more emphasis on using magical techniques for social change. Starhawk's work, like that of the social ecologist Murray Bookchin, combines a social ecology that draws on Marxism and anarchist traditions to synthesize a political philosophy. Like Bookchin, she sees imbalance in the natural world as caused by imbalance in the social world, but whereas Bookchin is against what he views as mystical romantic nature worship Starhawk uses magic – as a means of actively changing consciousness – to create a way of empowering the individual to resist and ultimately transform the oppressive patriarchal social structure. Her work is Goddess-centred and incorporates ecofeminism, giving positive value to the connection of women and nature: the male domination of women and the domination of nature are interconnected, and this is part of a general oppression of human communities and the environment. Thus for Starhawk witchcraft is a 'psychology of liberation', a healing from social alienation and fragmentation. The path home is associated with the natural, the original, and a 'return' to beliefs already held, perhaps unconsciously, by the inner Self (Salomonsen, 1996:109).

In a trance journey recording tape made in 1991 called 'The Way to the Well', Starhawk creates an inner landscape where alternative images produced by the imagination may be formed to change consciousness. This story focuses on three wells: the wells of 'power over', 'power within', and 'power with'. These wells map the inner landscape and open the senses to smell, feelings, visions, etc. The symbol of the well represents the different forms of power: power within is the empowered self, power over represents the exploitative social relations of patriarchy and capitalism, while power with expresses working with community from a position of power within and mutual respect, decisions being reached by consensus. The aim of working with power within and power with is to transform the structures of power over – the social institutions of patriarchy with its wars and aggression. Power within is when you are who you really are; it comes through a sense of embodiment inside the self – the inner landscape opens up and the deep part of the self connects to that beyond the self. Looking in this well reflects the true empowered self. This inner sense of being is symbolized as the Goddess.

Feminist witchcraft's mythical origins lie within a golden matrifocal age when women and nature were revered, before urban cultures of conquest, with their patriarchal religions, divided spirit from matter, shattering the former symbiotic wholeness with their emphasis on a divine force outside the world. Judaeo-Christian traditions were seen to have deepened the split, finally establishing the duality between spirit and matter. Women became identified with matter, nature, the body, sexuality, evil and the Devil, and had to be controlled, while the male God was uncontaminated by birth, menstruation and decay and was removed to the transcendent realm of the spirit. Feminist witchcraft, in common with Wicca, has a holistic philosophy: the symbol of the Goddess unites all; seeing deity as female is a political statement as well as a spiritual reality (see Greenwood 2000).

Part of the process of changing consciousness from patriarchal thought forms involves the use of fairy and folk tales. Starhawk and Hilary Valentine, authors of *The Twelve Wild Swans: a journey to the realm of magic, healing and action,* say that what remains of the stories our ancestors told are passed down in such stories. Working with fairy tales is a process of 'uncovery': 'It's as if we're trying to sail an old, old ship so encrusted with barnacles and seaweed that the true shape of the keel can only barely be discerned' (2000:xxi). The scraping-away process does not mean removing the uncomfortable elements as power is seen to arise from the aspects that induce uneasiness. The Reclaiming method does not take the characters of goddesses and gods, or Jungian analysis, or use morality plays; rather it looks for the 'true form' of the ship through an encounter with aspects of the story using ritual, reflection and meditation. The aim of the process is to explore issues and challenge stereotypes, turning pain and rage into growth and empowerment. Encoded in the fairy story of *The Twelve Wild Swans* is a set of instructions for becoming 'a healer, a shaman, an artist, a Witch: one who can walk between the words and retrieve lost souls, one who can restore balance and justice to a world made ill' (ibid.:xxii). These stories form the structure for Reclaiming Witch Camps.[11]

Witch Camp in England is held in Somerset, close to the site thought by many practitioners to be the 'sacred Isle of Avalon', the 'Isle of Apples', the gateway to the otherworld and south of Glastonbury Tor. The Tor is a place connected to Celtic mythology and particularly the fairy Gwyn ap Nudd, one of the huntsmen associated with the Wild Hunt discussed in Chapter 6. A guardian of the Gates of Annwyn, Gwyn ap Nudd is associated with 'fairy hills' in Wales and other places; he lives in a glass castle in the otherworld (Ivakhiv, 2001:105). Some Reclaiming witches gain inspiration from Marion Zimmer Bradley's novel *The Mists of Avalon* (1984) in which she portrays Avalon as an island where women were trained as priestesses in magic.

Annie, who has been a participant in Reclaiming Witch Camps at 'Avalon' and in the US, and has also been involved in organizing the camps for others, told me of her experiences of fairy stories at camp. She said that a fairy story would be taken as a continuing thread to focus the camp and hold everything together. Stories such as *The Twelve Wild Swans*, or those found within the *Mabinogion*, would be treated as an imaginative theme structuring the work of the camp. The camps are usually, but not always, organized along the lines of three paths or tracks: the first is an 'elements path' that teaches the basic magical skills and tools necessary to work magic and create ritual; the second is the 'inner path' concerned with personal healing, inner vision, and teaching the self-knowledge necessary for change; the third is the 'outer path', which involves service to community, ritual skills, and confronting the larger structures of domination. Annie explained how the theme would be worked into each of these paths if possible, as well as in mumming plays and skits: 'Each track goes off to be trained in magical skills, such as sensing energy, and trance work', and parts of the story are used in a particular track: 'For example, in voice work, you might go into trance to find out what song a bird of Rhiannon might sing, this might involve turning into a bird to find your inner voice. You might also have homework from the path work – you might have to go off and observe something – such as a plant – or you might have to think about something'. The themes are used as teaching material and might teach, for example, that there are many ways of obtaining something. Annie gives the example of the *Mabinogion* story of Pwyll and Rhiannon in which Pwyll learns that after trying to chase Rhiannon on his horse and failing, if he goes and sits on a certain mound – and this is interpreted as a fairy mound – she will come to him and take him to the Underworld.

Annie says that Witch Camps create communal magical space; they are a week of heavy-duty visionary experiences. Reclaiming organizes the structure of the camp but does not take a specific line: people are encouraged to have their own vision using the theme of the stories. Some of the stories might be highly political; others might be ecological. Ritual is another opportunity to engage with the story. The evening ritual, Annie says, is planned by the Reclaiming teachers to develop a particular dimension of the tale. Everyone is in a light trance; the events of the day have put people in the right frame of mind for what is to come. This is helped by the fact that participants have time to spend in that 'liminal' space – they have not had to worry about shopping or cooking, for example. Everyone gathers around a fire at twilight, and the night becomes dark. The teachers will have spent some time planning what is going to happen and will either tell the story, enact a part of the story, or ask the participants to act it out. Then the beat of the drum changes and someone will tell a bit more about the story until a cone of power is raised whereby the energy reaches its peak. Gradually, people will be brought back, and safely grounded. The teachers take on different roles to make sure that people are fully out of trance, and later there is grounding with 'treats' of bagels or flapjack or suchlike, when people can share their experiences together. There is a sense of completion of one part of the story before starting on the next. Feedback meetings and after-lunch discussions are held the following day where participants can talk about their experiences – of what worked and what did not – so that the teachers can adapt rituals for the next night. Annie comments that 'there is a sense that everyone is weaving the story together'.

Increasingly, Reclaiming is becoming more involved in what it terms 'magical activism'. Starhawk, who is 'first among equals' as a Reclaiming teacher, is charismatic. She is said to be a quiet person, almost shy, but she has a gift for communication. At her talk at St James's Church, Piccadilly, London, in 1996 she was wearing a greyish-yellow-brown muted patterned dress fastened up the front with ornate metal buttons, and a long blue cotton sweatshirt. Over the top she wore a long sage green robe, knotted at the corners. On her feet were long brown socks and flat suede shoes. Around her neck she wore various necklaces – one was a goddess figurine pendant, another was made from what looked like pieces of white coral. Her manner of speaking was quiet, with a soft American accent; she appeared to be inspirational to her audience. This inspirational quality was evident even in dreadful conditions in jail. Arrested for her part in the anti-World Trade Organization (WTO) demonstrations in Washington in 1999, she wrote an open letter to the Pagan community whilst she was in jail. In it she manages to find ways to teach about overcoming adversity:

> In one of our rituals, my friend Willow had invoked the Green Man and reminded us that oxygen is his breath and he is everywhere. When I lay in my airless, torturously overheated cell at night, coughing and feverish and struggling to breathe, I could call upon him through such air as there was and visualize the cool, moist scent of the redwoods by my home. I'd close my eyes and see the ancestors marching with us in great rivers, turning the tide.[12]

The Reclaiming journal, *Reclaiming Quarterly*, regularly runs information on environmental and spiritual protest. One such protest was inspired by the situation of the U'Wa of Columbia, which has been resisting oil drilling on their lands by a petroleum company. An 'Invitation to Spell' was sent out at the Winter Solstice on the Reclaiming International Discussion List, and all Pagans were asked to join in both political and spiritual support for all indigenous people trying to protect their land and struggling against displacement. The spell circulated was formulated by Yarrow:

> Let there be a rebirth of the land's wisdom. Let the land's wisdom stay with those who live it. Let the land's wisdom return to those who remember it, or whose grandmothers remember it. Let the land's wisdom come to those who seek it. Let all who would live wisely on their land be free to do so, free as of right.[13]

Finally, I turn to the environmental work of shaman Gordon MacLellan.

Creeping Toad Environmental Education

> Aim: to use traditional stories of the shaping of landscapes and the nature of things to work on a 'local folklore' of 'why' and 'how' stories.
> ... Stories touch people on quite a separate level from the organisation and precise knowledge that a scientific approach calls for and to neglect either in favour of the other deprives people of whole realms of experience.
>
> Gordon MacLellan, *Talking To the Earth*

Gordon MacLellan is a dancer and storyteller as well as a well-known shaman; he trained as a zoologist and as a teacher and now runs Creeping Toad environmental education. He sees the role of the shaman in modern Britain as one of communicator and 'patterner' with nature. Seeing himself as working on the relationships between people and the world around them, his aim is to help people find a relationship with nature and to understand and appreciate a connection. By using investigation, awareness, discovery and personal creativity, he encourages people to learn to enjoy the natural world (1996:143). For Gordon, being a shaman is a practical job of mediating between the human world and the world of spirits, and he says that a modern shaman has to find new ways of engaging humans with the living world. In his introductory guide to shamanism (1999) he points out that this can be very difficult in a non-shamanic society where there is little physical support. Everyday concepts and people's behaviour can block the process of communication between the everyday world and the spiritual otherworld. In the West there is no shamanic tradition. Nearly two thousand years of Christianity have effectively changed people's relation to the earth and nature, and so 'traditions' have to be invented and new situations are created to re-establish a connection with the land.

The work of Creeping Toad environmental education develops children's imaginations and the art of creative play; it uses fairy tales, myths and those 'other-than-human beings' to bring the natural world alive in a child's imagination by building on their animistic thinking,[14] and actively encouraging them to interact with the natural world. Creeping Toad workshops give children an opportunity to expand their imaginations in ways that lead to a growing environmental awareness. Gordon emphasizes the need to help people step out of a world-view that encourages separation from the world and re-experience a childlike sense of wonder at nature. In his workbook for environmental educators, *Talking to the Earth* (n.d.a), activities are suggested which are concerned with 'making and doing, jumping up and down and singing songs with colour and shape' as ways of 'talking to the earth: giving shape to feelings about ourselves and this planet home' (ibid.:5).

Gordon explains that boggarts are people from the world of faerie – 'that strange, wild, reckless place that lies behind the enchantment of lonely moors and silent woodlands and speaks in the wind that rustles the leaves of autumn'. Gordon notes that stories about fairies are a wonderful way of drawing people into the magic of their own places. Looking at the world from the perspective of a boggart is a 'good way of breaking conventional imagery and approaching the familiar with an inspired imagination' (ibid.:65–66). He describes a one-day workshop, 'The Midwinter Boggarts', as a means of taking the idea that the boggarts, as spirits of nature, are busy during the spring and summer but sleep in autumn and winter. However, this year they are disturbed and wake from their usual slumber in December amid the glamour and excitement of the midwinter season. The boggarts set out to explore the celebration by having their own party. Gordon describes a workshop on this theme:

> The workshop stayed very carefully within frivolous and seasonal limits – we were exploring the nature of the midwinter season and something of what humans get up

to. We avoided unleashing boggart perceptions upon the religious background to Christmas. An underlying desire for celebration at this darkest time of the year and the need to watch out for the sun during these longest of nights, arose out of the children's own reflections on the season, letting them shape their own interpretations of the turning wheel of the seasons and lending another layer of awareness to the final performances.

Format:

story: a good boggart tale of silliness and folly to get us all going, introduce the idea of what boggarts are, where you might find them, and what would they think of a modern December?

    invent-a-boggart: body sculpture in groups to shape a boggart out of your imagination – show the place where the boggart lives and the boggart within it. This produced under-the-bridge boggarts, cake tin boggarts (who always eat the last piece), hay field boggarts, muddy puddle boggarts and more...

    winter: small group brainstorms – impressions of the season

    the boggart dance: a created parade with lots of stamping and arm-waving and sudden wary stillness...

    walk: a walk into winter using environmental awareness activities to explore the changing seasons, thought of weather, impressions and the like

    life in winter? different groups now look at ponds, grass, hedgerows and stones in more depth – each group also works a poem of their place

    shaping winter: those groups now become the boggarts of the various habitats and work together to make boggart decoration inspired by those habitats, use their poem to create a performance piece with body sculpture and words, and throw in anything else that reflects their boggart perceptions of their homes at this time of year.

    Finale: the boggarts gather for the boggart dance, parade their gifts..., present their own interpretations of winter with words and movements and end with a quiet story of stillness and a final dance. (MacLellan, (n.d.a):71–72)

By contrast to both Jasper and Reclaiming, Gordon is not primarily interested in tradition. Gordon takes an eclectic and practical approach to his shamanic practice and argues that shamans working in Western societies where there are no clear surviving traditions must find new ways of building bridges to the spirit world.

Boggarts in a Kent Wood   Gordon had been employed by Paddock Wood Town Council to work with some children at a local school on a project at Foal Hurst wood. Foal Hurst is a small wood of 30 acres in Kent that once formed part of an impenetrable forest covering the Weald; it was purchased by Paddock Wood Town Council in 1997 as a 'place for people and wildlife',[15] and it boasts a number of wildlife attractions, among them the rare dormouse, tawny owls, spotted flycatchers, speckled wood butterflies and fly agaric mushrooms. The wood was officially opened at a May fair, which included Saxon village artisans, tablet weaving and bone and antler carving. There were also such crafts as hedge-laying and longbow-making being demonstrated. According to the programme, the event aimed at blending a 'spirit of youth and heart of oak' in 'this area of old England in the Weald of Kent' that 'will link our history with our future, and environmental issues'.[16] Gordon, Jo Crow, and another environmental arts worker, Sue, had been working with sixty children (thirty ten-year-olds and thirty eight-year-olds) the previous week, making masks and woodland creatures in preparation for the fair.

On the morning of the fair in Kent Gordon, Jo and Sue met the children by the main arena (in which Morris dancers were giving a demonstration by a maypole) and formed a carnival procession, accompanied by a woodland musician and her dancing bear, around the stalls and into the wood. Here they took up positions hidden in the undergrowth, behind trees, and amongst the profusion of bluebells. Some time later, as the mayor, council officials, visitors and other interested parties walked into the woods, they encountered the children who had been mysteriously transformed into snakes, birds, frogs, dragons and other creatures. There were boggarts (spirits of nature from the world of Faerie) in the form of rod puppets which, animated by the children, engaged in an enchanted playland world. There were toadstools with friendly faces, blue and green fish, large butterflies with translucent and brightly coloured wings, and giant bluebells which swung gracefully in the breeze. The children were clearly enjoying the whole process. They took every opportunity to respond to visitors' reactions (such as feigned or real shock at the surprise encounter with a boggart peering around a tree), either as play, if the visitor interacted with their character, or by answering questions about how they made the model etc. When all the visitors – some 200 people – had gathered around a small clearing Gordon and the children enacted a collectively produced drama which, drawing on local history, told a tale about important lessons to be learnt from the wood and its nature spirits. The children had made up the story themselves. Gordon, Jo and Sue had helped them bring their story to life, finally dancing it in front of the visitors. Gordon explained that the children had decided that the wood wanted to be respected: 'A collective story emerged about an offensive little girl named Natalya who went riding through the wood crushing bluebells. At the end the other creatures followed her and swallowed her up' (MacLellan, 2001:255).

English Nature Bronze Age Project   I visited Gordon and Jo at an event organized by English Nature on Thursley Common national nature reserve. The English Nature Sussex and Surrey teams had combined to work on a Bronze Age project funded by a millennium grant. The aim of the event was to explore Thursley Common from the perspective of the Bronze Age, and to use inspiration from older times to look at a familiar landscape in a new way; to encourage people to experience the richness and variety of the habitat, and explore ideas about sustainability and the use of resources.[17] By getting the children to appreciate their local environment – both 3,000 years ago and at the present – the plan was to enable them to communicate this to the visitors that were going to arrive the following day as part of an open day with attractions such as the appearance of celebrity naturalist David Bellamy, and making traditional and ancient crafts (along with not-so-Bronze-Age tractor rides).

I arrived at Thursley Common in the morning and met an English Nature warden who was directing children and parents to the camp, which was about half a mile into the heath. Giving me a lift to the site in his four-wheel drive vehicle, he explained to me that he and fellow teams of wardens had been working on the Bronze Age thatched roundhouse 12 hours a day for the last two months. They had constructed the roundhouse in authentic detail under the advice of archaeologists with the aim of using it for education about the past. However, someone had complained that they did not have planning permission to build on the heath, and the warden told me that they were in the middle of fighting to make sure that it stayed up.

When we arrived at the roundhouse groups of children and parents were arriving and in the process of registering and getting changed into their Bronze Age clothes (the interpretation of Bronze Age clothing was quite liberal, and some looked more medieval). Gordon gave me a white shift to wear over a green skirt before going off to check children into the event. Jo was drumming at the entrance of the roundhouse. After some time had elapsed, everyone was asked to gather around an oak tree to one side of the roundhouse and by the side of a brushwood pen enclosing some Manx sheep. A cuckoo was calling as the light gently filtered through the leaves of the oak tree onto the assembled group below. Gordon introduced himself, Jo and some of the wardens who were helping for the day. He explained that we were going to be a Bronze Age tribe for a day and that we would be divided up into four clans. There were about sixty children present from two local schools and their teachers, and there were also quite a few English Nature workers, and one environment studies student who was on her second year placement.[18] The children were told that they would be able to try a number of activities such as exploring the heathland, tracking animals and making plaster cast footprints; they could also help to put the finishing touches on the roundhouse: wattle and daub, hurdles for walls, doors or gates, putting more heather on the roof; working on a communal standard and magical defence posts to ward off ill-luck and enemies from the homestead, and making baskets, pots, rushlights, flint-knapping, rushlight dipping, fire-making, and decorating clay panels for a communal 'altar' were other activities that they could try their hand at.

Gordon asked the children what sort of animals they would expect to find in the woods and on the heath, and they responded by making lots of suggestions – from deer and foxes to eagles. He also asked the children to think about a name that they might want to call themselves that would associate them with a particular animal. One girl called out 'I'm Jessica, and I'm an eagle' – she became known as Jessica Eagle. The children were asked to think about clan names for their groups – such as the 'damp feet' clan (this was a suggestion offered by Gordon).

Telling a story is the ideal way of setting the imaginary scene, and Gordon told one about an orphan boy who was an outcast in his tribe, nobody looked after or cared for him. His uncle, the leader of the tribe, was a hunter whose 'arrows never missed' and what he hunted he always killed. One day the uncle took the boy hunting as his 'dog'. The boy was delighted at the unexpected attention from his uncle, but also a little worried because they were going to hunt in the north, a place that had a bad reputation. The uncle sent the boy down a hole, and when he was out of view, rolled a stone over the entrance. The boy, unsure at first about what to do, started singing, as his mother had taught him before she died. As he sang louder, the stone rolled away from the entrance but there was no sign of his uncle. The boy was helped by an assortment of animals – mole, eagle, wolf and a bear. Each asked him to come and live with them. Eventually he chose to be a 'bear person' and went to live with mother bear and her cubs. In time he grew hairy and was as a bear, and he was happy. Mother bear told her children about hunters and how to recognize them by the sounds they made in the wood – all that is except one who 'made no sound and always hit what he aimed at, and what he aimed at he always killed'.

One day, mother bear sensed that the hunter had come. She told her children to run and they ran and ran, and eventually hid in a hollow tree. The hunter followed them and lit a fire at the bottom of the tree to smoke them out. The boy realized what was happening and climbed out of the top of the tree and confronted the hunter who was his uncle. His bear hair fell off and he shouted at his uncle to leave the bears alone. The uncle could not believe his eyes and was pleased and delighted to see the boy because he regretted his actions. He said he had been back to the hole and seen the stone removed but thought the boy had died. He asked the boy to forgive him and to return to the clan. The boy asked the bears what to do. Mother bear told him to go, but to never forget that he had been a bear. This story had the effect of gently dislocating the children from the human world and encouraging them to enter into the lives of animals – to make friends with the animals, imagining what it would be like to become a bear and to live with them before returning to human society.

The next activity organized by Gordon and Jo further reinforced this by asking the children to work together by creating animals from their own bodies. Jo or Gordon shouted out 'rabbit, four people' and four children had to work together to form a rabbit, and so when Gordon or Jo called 'bear, seven people', and 'eagle, three people' the children formed the appropriate animals. There was much laughing and cavorting as the children struggled to manoeuvre into animals. Then the children broke up into their clan groups, Gordon took a clan of ten children on an exploration of their environment, while Jo took another clan to make clan totems, other groups went on walks through the heath with the wardens. Gordon asked his group to form twos and threes, to link up and walk along with their eyes closed until he shouted for them to open their eyes and to focus on the first thing they saw. He then got them to point at what they saw with their feet, knees and elbows, etc. Sitting the clan down under a tree, the children made up stories and poems about what they had seen. Taking themselves off into the wood, some sat amongst the branches of fallen trees, others climbed like monkeys along the horizontal trunks, while others huddled amongst the bracken exchanging ideas and reading out what they had written with their peers. After their endeavours had been shared with the group, they made drawings on long strips of paper looking at cave paintings for inspiration.

After a 'Bronze Age' lunch of vegetable soup and gorse tea, both prepared on an open fire, the tribe reassembled back at the meeting point under the oak tree to the beat of Jo's drum. Gordon gathered together a different clan of children and took them into another part of the wood, where he sent the children off to practise becoming invisible. One boy huddled against a tree trunk, cap over his head, and looked indistinguishable from the tree; others found it more difficult to merge with the surroundings. When they had all gathered together again amongst a group of young trees Gordon encouraged them to make their own stories about Thursley Heath, its people and wildlife. He gave them a story framework and asked them to think about where they were going to place their story, the hero or heroine, a problem that had to be solved, an attempt at resolving it, another attempt, and finally, what happened.

When they had written their stories down and were discussing them, I went back to the encampment and helped Jo with explaining how to make dreamcatchers – Native American-inspired twig and thread weavings that were thought to catch dreams. One girl asked me what the time was, and I replied that I did not know what she was talking about. Exasperated, she exclaimed: 'Oh, I couldn't have lived in the Bronze Age without knowing what the time was!' A very interesting discussion developed between the girl, the other children, Jo and I, and we said that there was time and time, and that in the Bronze Age we would probably have measured time by the sun, the moon, and the seasons, and that they had a different conception of how the world was. It was at moments like these that the realities of what life would have been like in the past really sank in; it was through the practical engagement in everyday activities that a deeper understanding appeared to be achieved.

The following day was the public event, and the tribe was engaged in talking to the visitors and introducing them to the camp and the heathland. David Bellamy, whose time had been bought through a charity auction by an English Nature worker, looked around the site and listened to what people had to say. He later incorporated this into his talk about the heathland. Some time later, I asked Gordon whether he ever worked with the children again after an intensive weekend such as this. He replied that he did not on an organized basis – he moves from place to place, and from school to school – but he said that sometimes a child would come up to him and say: 'I know you, you're Gordon (or you're the Toad) do you remember me?' To which he replies: 'Yes, I remember you, but remind me of your name...'

Being Indigenous?

Drawing on Mervyn Meggitt's (1962) work on the Walbiri Aborigines of central Australia, anthropologist Tim Ingold notes how every locality has its own story created through the earth-shaping activities of the ancestors as they roamed the land during the Dreaming. Observing the waterhole while the story of its formation is told or enacted, the novice, as part of his initiation preparation, 'witnesses the ancestor coming out of the ground' and, 'casting his eyes over the distinctive outline of a hill or rocky outcrop, he recognises in it the congealed form of the ancestor as it lies down to rest' (Ingold, 2000:21). The task for the novice is, according to Ingold, not one of decoding but of discovery and revelation – to find out the meaning behind superficial appearances. Clues are keys that unlock perception: 'A clue, in short, is a landmark that condenses otherwise disparate strands of experience into a unifying orientation which, in turn, opens up the world to perception of greater depth and clarity' (ibid.:22). Truths are immanent in the landscape and are gradually revealed; every place has its own stories.

Practitioners of nature religion do not have this culture – in general stories are not located within the landscape. Given this, can practitioners of nature religion ever learn to be indigenous? Being indigenous means knowing the land through participation; stories unify perception and can give a perspective from inspirited nature. In Western cultures the language of science and the language of religion are prevalent – but not a language of 'listening' to the land, of participating with the land, of knowing the particularities of place. As Veronica Strang points out, language makes explicit human values and relationships, and Western cultures have lost the rich description that aids this process in relation to the environment. Perhaps this is due, in part, to the fact that fairy stories, although originating in orally based folk tales, have become part of a literary genre, one that is a stage removed from direct experiences of the land. While offering potent sources of inspiration for the creative imagination and ways for self-empowerment through psycho-spiritual healing, ultimately they have lost a capacity that they may once have had to help people gain experience of the land. Doreen Valiente is surely right when she says that there are several factors associated with fairies, including beliefs in nature spirits and the folk memories of aboriginal races ([1973] 1986:123). It is these more animistic elements that are more ecologically and environmentally resonant, and it is these aspects that have perhaps been diminished or overlaid in the development of the fairy tale as a literary genre. Referring to the translation of tribal stories from the memories of oral culture, Gerald Vizenor comments that 'the eternal sorrow of loss haunts the scriptural translation'. How, for example, could a word heard or a scene imagined in an oral story or performance have the same meaning in a written language? The original communal context cannot be translated, metaphors in oral stories are multiplex – they may be mundane, abstruse, mysterious and unnameable – but few translations reveal the rich context, they speak the language of domination instead (Vizenor, 1995:6–7).

If learning to be indigenous means knowing the land by its stories and having an experiential relationship with nature, then neither Jasper's nor Reclaiming's use of fairy tales would appear to aid such a process. Both are too anthropocentric. Jasper's model is of a passive and female earth 'Sleeping Beauty' who has to wait for heroic rescue to be awakened. Reclaiming, with its universalistic central notion of the Goddess as immanent life force, puts emphasis on individual therapeutic experience combined with political action, despite rhetoric that Avalon is a place where the 'language of birds and the speech of nature' is taught (Starhawk and Valentine, 2000:xv). There seems to be little space for reflection on a wider non-human inspirited world. Neither can be said to offer a truly relational or ecological world-view.

The Reclaiming community is recreating an alternative conceptual and experiential framework to that of the dominant mainstream culture. It also claims to be drawing on tradition, but this time a suppressed tradition; one that is seen to have been politically denied and silenced. The theme is of an 'uncovery' of a past golden age of the Goddess, a time in the distant past when things were different and women and men related harmoniously with nature (see Chapter 8). Interpretations of prehistoric data are overburdened by the desires and assumptions stemming from the attempt to redefine female aspects of deity that have been deliberately repressed by patriarchal monotheistic institutional religions. In seeking to uncover the roots of the male domination of women in the overthrow of matriarchy, feminist witches found answers to why and how the gender hierarchy had developed (Eller, 2000b:182). As Cynthia Eller points out, the problem is that origin stories reduce historically specific facts to timeless archetypes not tailored to specific cultural environments but to a totalizing image of 'patriarchy'. Eller argues that ancient matriarchies should be viewed as a myth which stems from a nostalgia for a lost past: 'Feminist matriarchalists, like other myth-makers, begin with a vision of the world as they would like it to be, project it into the past, and then find a way (narratively speaking) to make present conditions emerge from ideal ones' (ibid.:185). The matriarchy myth serves to reintroduce biological determinism (ibid.:183–184) (that women are innately more pacifistic) and gender stereotypes (women are more nurturing while men are more aggressive), thus emphasizing differences between women and men. The myth rests on the notion of 'the natural' as a way of being in harmony with a nature uncontaminated by alienating patriarchal culture. The language of the Goddess does not sit easily with the more ecological and shamanic Faery aspects of feminist witchcraft.

In contrast to Jasper and Reclaiming, Gordon's work encourages a direct relationship with the natural world through identification with the other than human world: by 'becoming' animals by getting together with other children, by listening to a story of a boy being adopted by bears, and through creating stories about the land, as well as in many other ways such as drawing, painting and performance.

In the next chapter I continue the discussion of ecological issues through an examination of some of the historical ideas underlying the complexities and paradoxes within nature religion.

Notes

1. Thanks to Geoffrey Samuel for sending me this article.
2. After being serialized in the *Ladies Home Journal* during 1902, Seton's Indian programme spread. According to Deloria, it was later transformed into an autobiographical novel, *Two Little Savages: being the adventure of two boys who lived as Indians and what they learned* (1903) (Deloria, 1998:96–97).
3. I am grateful to Gordon MacLellan for directing my attention to this article.
4. A bender is a portable dwelling, usually made from pliable tree branches and covered with waterproof material.
5. The Newbury bypass consists of a nine-mile stretch of road that passes through North Wessex Downs, an area of outstanding natural beauty, and covers three sites of Special Scientific Interest, a Stone Age settlement, eleven other archaeological sites, and two Civil War battlefields. It also destroyed the habitats of kingfishers, nightjars, hobbies, bats and dormice, and one of the last remaining colonies of the Desmoulin Whorl snail (Evans, 1998:103).
6. This is a tale that first appears in the fourteenth century. 'Briar Rose' features in the Catalan *Frayre de joy e Sor de placer*; she is also 'La Belle au bois dormant' in *Histoires ou contes du temps passé,* written by Charles Perrault in 1697 (Goldberg, 2000, in Zipes, 2000:467).
7. As is usual in such sessions, time is allowed for people to make notes on their journeys for future reference. This usually happens before group discussions.

8. Jasper taught us to start our journeys by imagining that we were in a boat sailing down a river. At some point we would get out of the boat and find our bender, a special place from which to venture forth and to return to.

9. It is common for heroic characters from different stories to be freely interchanged. I could have used Jack, from the fairy story of Jack and the Beanstalk, or the Prince from Sleeping Beauty. I chose Robin Hood, with his association with woods and his outlaw status, because I did not feel comfortable identifying with either Jack or a prince.

10. The historian Ronald Hutton writes that the political views held by Gardner, and the magicians from whom he had drawn many of his ideas, were right-wing and conservative. Hutton notes that Samuel MacGregor Mathers, a founder of the nineteenth-century Hermetic Order of the Golden Dawn, was fascinated with militarism and aristocracy, and that other members of the Golden Dawn had similar politics: William Butler Yeats had right-wing tendencies and flirted with fascism, Aleister Crowley was a lifelong high Tory, Dion Fortune had similar attitudes, and Alex Sanders expressed admiration for monarchy and hierarchy. For most people, the interest in Paganism and magic was part of a wider rejection of modernity, and their spiritual interests 'marched closely' with three aspects of right-wing ideology – namely, 'nostalgia for a better past, elitism and suspicion of the masses, and a desire for a free market, in magic and sex as in economics'. Hutton observes that Pagan witchcraft travelled from Britain to the United States as a branch of radical conservatism, and returned as a branch of radical socialism (Hutton, 1999:360–361).

11. Witch Camps originally started as classes in the US; this led to the formation of covens. People who could not make all the classes were invited to 'intensives' (long weekends instead of the classes). This led to week-long camps held in the wilderness, in the middle of nowhere (for example in the Californian redwood forest).

12. http://www.reclaiming.org/starhawk/update.html

13. This spell was reproduced in the British Reclaiming Newsletter, Beltane 2001.

14. Piaget claimed that a child's thinking remained animistic until puberty (Bettelheim, [1976] 1991:46).

15. Foal Hurst Wood information leaflet produced by Paddock Wood Town Council.

16. Foal Hurst Wood May Fair Event Programme, Monday, 3 May 1999.

17. From notes for group leaders, prepared by Gordon.

18. She explained to me that she had been given Thursley Heath to work with for a dissertation, and that she had been delighted to find out that she would be working with English Nature on such an exciting and unexpected project.

–8–

A Tangled Web: Paradoxical Elements

Does nature religion affirm the sacred nature of the earth as is claimed by many Pagans? When the earth is seen as sacred does an ecological attitude follow as a matter of course? Is nature religion ecological? If nature religion is based on views of the world as animate, inspirited and seen as comprising an ecosystem then it would be possible to assert that it is *ipso facto* an eco-religion. However, the basic ideas and principles of both Paganism and the New Age derive from the esoteric-ism of the Western Hermetic tradition which, having neoplatonic monotheistic influences,[1] shifts the emphasis from relationship *between* phenomena of the natural world to one directed *to* God – or increasingly, *the* Goddess, even as She is manifested in things, or found within. This is non-ecological. Indeed, the social theorist and political philosopher Murray Bookchin has levelled scathing attacks on what he calls pantheistic and animistic cults (as well as Deep Ecology) when he argues that these ideologies 'subtly enchant' the naïve with supernaturalism.[2] For Bookchin, neo-pagan belief systems provide a surrogate 'reality' whereby the rational is replaced by the intuitive (cf.Ernest Gellner's indictment of psycho-analysis ([1985] (1996)). While Bookchin's extreme naturalistic rationalism is evident – he sees a 'preening emphasis on the subjective' as 'clothed in the mystical vapors and inchoate vagaries of fevered imaginations, any recognition of reality is dissolved by beliefs in the mythic' (1997:66) – he does make important points in relation to ecological systems, and these must be addressed if nature religion is to be considered ecological. Asking questions such as these opens up a whole 'can of worms': to question the ecological credentials of nature religion strikes right into the heart of many practitioners' identities and deeply held attitudes; it also raises issues concerning magical consciousness and what constitutes knowledge.

In this chapter I shall compare the discourse of esotericism, as already discussed in Chapter 2 and as found in the mystery religion tradition (those whose secret initiatory rites sought to bring participants into direct union with an ultimate being), with an organismic discourse. The term 'organismic' comes from the Greek *organikos*, referring to 'organic' as constitutional, inherent, structural, organized and systematic, and includes notions of an organic unit or whole and 'organism' as an organized body with connected interdependent parts sharing a common life. The early Greeks had an organismic conception of the cosmos as a coherent whole; it was 'a form of thought before matter and spirit had been distinguished' (Morris, 1994b:23). Environmental historian and philosopher Carolyn Merchant points out that organic thought, referring to bodily organs, structures and the organization of living beings ([1980] 1990:xxiv), had its roots in Greek concepts of the cosmos as an intelligent organism. This view was revived, modified and assimilated into Renaissance thought of the fifteenth and sixteenth centuries. According to Merchant, three root traditions of Platonism, Aristotelianism, and Stoicism became the basis of later syncretic forms of organicism. When synthesized with Hermeticism, gnosticism, neoplatonism, and Christianity the root traditions produced a 'spectrum of Renaissance organismic philosophies' based on the premise that all parts of the cosmos were connected and interrelated in a living unity (ibid.:103).

As already noted in Chapter 1, nature has had many different meanings, and Merchant notes that in ancient and early modern times it referred, amongst other things, to a vital power in persons, animals and things, as well as the dynamic creative and regulatory principle in the material world. A distinction was commonly made between *natura naturans* (nature creating) and *natura naturata* (natural creation) (ibid.:xxiii). Biologist Rupert Sheldrake points out that the scientific revolution of the seventeenth century denied nature animation; matter became inanimate and passive, acted upon by external forces in accord with the mathematical laws of motion. By contrast, in the Middle Ages souls had played the role of *natura naturans*, organizing the development and behaviour of organisms. According to Aristotle, souls were not outside nature, they were physical and a part of nature. Sheldrake says that 'when the founders of mechanistic science expelled souls from nature, leaving only passive matter in motion, they placed all active powers in God'; nature was thus only *natura naturata*. The invisible productive power of *natura naturans* was divine rather than physical (1990:61–62). Many non-Western small-scale societies share an approach to the world that does not separate spirit from matter. Nature spiritualities draw their inspiration from these, as well as what is known of those of the early Greeks, the Celts and the Anglo-Saxons. Today, organismic discourses are often referred to as 'holistic', a term that refers to a tendency in nature to form wholes that are more than the sum of their parts

In contrast to esotericism, which has a sustained history (albeit one that is underground or countercultural), Western organismic world-views are inevitably fragmented and fractured due to countervailing religious and scientific approaches. They are more generally understood through oral storytelling and mythology, and so when it comes to relating to nature in accord with these cosmologies practitioners have to re-imagine or invent traditions. Inevitably, there are problems in reconstructing a holistic organismic world-view, an issue highlighted in Chapter 5, and this raises issues of academic versus practitioner understandings of the past.

I shall use the example of the Anglo-Saxon world-view of wyrd as understood by psychologist Brian Bates to argue that an understanding of magical consciousness enables a different insight into this material, one that overcomes the rationalistic tendency in the social sciences and offers an insight into the ecological potential of nature religion. The comparison made here between esotericism and organicism highlights many contradictory and internal inconsistencies that may throw doubt on the validity of the claim made by many practitioners that nature spiritualities are somehow inherently ecological.

Practitioners' Attitudes to Nature

How do practitioners view nature? Nature religion has developed and expanded in the late twentieth and early twenty-first centuries and environmentalism and ecological issues are now high on the agenda, as many Pagan political activists against road-building and the destruction of countryside have shown. At an anti-war against Iraq demonstration in London in 2003 several groups of Pagans formed part of the protest, along with left-wing socialist groups, Palestine liberation movements, the Campaign for Nuclear Disarmament (CND), and a Stop the War coalition, among others. A leaflet about Paganism was handed out to interested bystanders explaining Paganism as 'an ecological religion that affirms the sacred nature of the Earth'.[3] The fate of the planet depends upon a spirituality that is rooted in a love of nature and a love of the land, so says an information leaflet published by the Order of Bards, Ovates and Druids (OBOD). Druidry, it claims, is based upon a love of the natural world, and offers a 'powerful way of working with, and understanding the Self and Nature – speaking to that level of our soul and of our being which is in tune with the elements and the stars, the sun and the stones'. Through working as a Druid it is possible to 'unite our natural, earthly selves with our spiritual selves while working, in however small a way, for the safeguarding of our planet'. This echoes a claim made in a beginner's guide to druidry by Cairistiona (Christine) Worthington, a modron[4] of OBOD, that 'when we come to know the earth as sacred then conservation and ecology, sound management of the earth's resources follow as a matter of course' (1999:48).

This view, like so many others held by practitioners, holds that nature religion is naturally an ecological religion – when we come to know the earth is sacred then conservation and ecology follow as a matter of course. These views are at odds with those of Murray Bookchin who claims that such cults are based on mysticism and supernaturalism (Bookchin, 1997:66). Bookchin distinguishes ecology from environmentalism. The former 'deals with the dynamic balance of nature, with the interdependence of living and nonliving things', while the latter is reformist and deals with the serviceability of the human habitat. According to Bookchin, ecology 'opens to a wide purview the vast disequilibrium that has emerged from humanity's split with the natural world'. The split has led to the necessity to speak of 'social ecology', a discipline that employs a 'dialectical naturalism'; this is a way of knowledge that sees nature as a process in which all life forms participate in their own evolution as active agents. There is no opposition between nature and human society, culture or consciousness: all are products of natural evolution working towards self-reflexivity (ibid.:32).

Is a spiritual approach to nature compatible with an ecological view such as that expressed by Bookchin? In many ways Bookchin expresses a more radical political interpretation of the position taken by feminist witch Starhawk (1982) who refers to the shift from seeing the world as a dead machine to experiencing it as a living organism. This involves a corresponding political change in consciousness from one of patriarchal domination, which she terms 'estrangement', to one of 'immanence', as 'the awareness of the world and everything in it as alive, dynamic, interdependent, interacting, and infused with moving energies: a living being, a weaving dance' (1982:5, 7–9). However, there are non-ecological tendencies in this view – as there are non-ecological tendencies within other 'tenets' of nature religion that must be addressed in the process of determining whether nature religion is ecological.

According to anthropologist Roy Rappaport, humans see nature 'through a screen of beliefs, knowledge, and purposes'; and it is in terms of images of nature, rather than of the actual structure of nature, that humans act, and 'Disparities between images of nature and the actual structure of ecosystems are inevitable' (1979:97). This 'screen of beliefs' shapes the process of participation; there is a rich array of ontologies revealing many different approaches to nature held by practitioners of nature religion. The sociologist of religion Michael York, while claiming that both Paganism and New Age are 'religions of ecology' (1995:109), highlights important differences. These are concerned with locus of deity, tradition, attitudes to this world and the otherworld, and issues concerning light and dark. York observes that New Age pursues a transcendent metaphysical reality within a new distinct religion that inclines towards a hierarchical understanding and adopts a more passive approach through meditation, for example. It also emphasizes the spiritual and white light. By contrast, Paganism (he calls it 'Neo-paganism') sees deity as immanent, stresses tradition and links to the past, is relatively more democratic and emphasizes light and dark (ibid.:148–172). The strongest areas of overlap between Paganism and New Age lie in what York terms the Earth Religions: Native American Spirituality and Shamanism (ibid.:164). York points to José Argüelles, as a leading shaper of New Age thought, who combines psychic phenomena, UFOs, psychedelic drugs, interspecies communication and the ecology movement: 'our life will merge the shaman's environmental resilience with the pageantry of medieval court life ... a kingdom in liege to the Sun, and the entire Earth its single realm, (Argüeles, 1987:192, quoted in York, 1995:85). Given such a diversity of positions and views, how is it possible to examine whether nature religion is ecological, as is so frequently claimed by practitioners as well as by practitioner academics such as Michael York (see also Dennis Carpenter (1996:65) for example)?

Margot Adler, in *Drawing Down the Moon*, a study of Paganism in America, which was first published in 1979 and then updated in 1986, explained that she came into Paganism (she calls it 'Neo-Paganism') from a search for a 'celebratory, ecological nature religion that would appease my hunger for the beauty of ancient myths and visions'. Adler believed that Paganism could heal the breach between the spiritual and the material worlds and would 'celebrate those interrelationships that would heal into synthesis all oppositions: primitive and civilized, science and magic, male and female, spirit and matter'. She saw in Paganism a philosophy that would join ancient and modern values in a religious way of life that allowed a regaining of kinship with nature ([1979] 1986:374–375). Adler had what she calls a 'strong bias' towards viewing the Craft as an 'ecological religion' and assumed that 'The worshipper in a religion that venerated nature would surely consider the protection of the earth a religious duty', and that both ecology and Paganism sought restoration of the balance of nature. However, from her research she found that there was a split between Pagans 'committed to ecological principles' and those whose 'commitment was limited to a religious vision'. The former 'often felt that the latter were not living up to their commitments', while the latter 'generally felt that no extreme measures were needed'. The real difference was political, between those who believed in a complete change in lifestyle and those who felt that change was unnecessary, or would evolve by itself given time (ibid.:399–400). Adler concluded: 'Clearly, a position that assumed the necessity of political and economic and religious transformation was not typical of the Pagans I had encountered' (ibid.:403).

My own assumptions were similar to Adler's when I first got involved in Paganism in the mid-1980s, and I found from my later research among London Pagans in the early to middle 1990s that there was more emphasis on ritual and psycho-spiritual 'internal' nature as personal experience rather than a connection, or interest even, in the environment. When writing up my findings I observed that contemporary witchcraft practices were a continuation of the eighteenth-century Romantic movement, to which the philosophy of Nature as source was essential. Romanticism affirms the individual's feelings and imagination against the emphasis on rationality. The human being is a part of a larger natural order, which is inherently harmonious. 'God, then, is to be interpreted in terms of what we see striving in nature and finding voice within ourselves' (Taylor, 1989:371; see Greenwood, 2000:111–113). It was these initial observations that led me to conduct further research on nature religion to assess the impact of environmentalism and increasing ecological awareness.

Andy Letcher, the Druidic bard and environmental protester mentioned in Chapters 3 and 7, points out that although the narrative of the sanctity of nature is central to Paganism, he has found that radical Pagans – those involved in direct action – are a minority. Letcher suggests: 'If Paganism as a movement is not at the vanguard of environmentalism then surely it can be labelled as a "virtual religion", a faith without substance or credentials.' He adds that Pagan perspectives of the land and relationships with it are often naïve and derived from novels, films and television rather than from direct experience. The prevailing attitude towards the land is an urban one, and there is consequently a disassociation from what is venerated. Pagan practice, for Letcher, must be derived from real experience of the land for it to be non-virtual. Deciding to live in a protest camp is an introduction to 'real' Paganism (1999:1–3).

Aware of the issues surrounding a focus on masculine heroic direct action,[5] and pointing to the precedent set by the women at the Greenham Common anti-nuclear protest, Letcher says that 'real Paganism' does not necessarily mean taking to the trees – it is possible to be a real Pagan without engaging in such direct confrontation. However, he is clearly against too much focus on 'inner work' as a possible ally of consumerism and an enemy of sustainable ecological living. In a conversation discussing these issues, Andy told me that the high ideals of environmental awareness are not always worked out in practice:

> Obviously there has to be a space for inner work and healing – I know from experience that there are profound moments to be found on the inside – but my concern is that one generates a self-obsessed culture, sitting on its arse navel inspecting while the world falls apart. Take for example the OBOD [Order of Bards, Ovates and Druids] course. It repeatedly states that by following the teachings and ancient wisdoms (*sic!*) of Druidry we can learn a more harmonious way of living with the earth. In fact (I have only experienced the Bardic grade) the course offers no pointers at all on living ecologically. Sustainability is never mentioned, nor are ways to reduce consumption. Consumerism is so insidious that it takes a bold step to detach oneself from it, however slightly. The course is all about 'inner' work and I am just not convinced that inner work will save the day.[6]

Letcher's comments seem to contradict those of Cairistiona Worthington (see p.173) when she suggests that coming to know the earth as sacred automatically leads to an ecological perspective.

In other areas of Paganism too there may be more emphasis put on individual development than ecological action. Jani Farell-Roberts, the Pagan protester at Lyminge, when comparing her camp with the one that Starhawk held at Glastonbury to which she and two other protesters had been invited, said that Starhawk's camp was primarily addressed at self-development through ritual and discussion. Although they worked with plants found locally, Jani said that

Starhawk did not utilize the wild wood, despite having a 'wonderfully magical ancient forest' close by; neither did they link so much with the spirits of place as those protesters at the Lyminge Camp (1997:15). Starhawk's approach in Witch Camps was more psychotherapy based; as discussed in Chapter 7 the focus was more on 'inner nature' and healing the self from the ills of patriarchal society, although there are indications that this is changing.

More recently, there appears to be a sea change in some practices of nature religion in general – at least in ideology if not in practice – towards a more practical relationship with nature. From a cursory glance at recent Pagan magazines there seems to be more engagement with 'outer nature' – as well as 'Earth Healing' days, which the Pagan Federation have been running for a number of years, there were plantings of new oak groves[7] for the year 2000 organized by the Order of Bards, Ovates and Druids – and also more political activism to stop the destruction of woodland for road development, as well as anti-capitalism and anti-WTO (World Trade Organization) demonstrations. This is in line with Adler's findings in the US. She notes a change in Paganism since 1979 and the first publication of *Drawing Down the Moon*; by 1985 she observes there was more political activity and also more concern with environmental issues.

Notwithstanding, it appears that a focus on nature as the environment is a relatively recent concern. In the New Age there is more emphasis on individual healing and 'the light', as demonstrated by the healing work of Julia in Chapter 3. When I asked Julia whether God was in nature she replied in the affirmative, but she also said that God was a higher spirit being and that we evolved upwards as we became more spiritual. Western Shamanism, on the other hand, tends to concentrate more on soul retrieval and journeying for self-development, and merges with aspects of New Age thought – for example in the work of Leslie Kenton, a Core Shamanism teacher. Kenton talks about shamanism as a technology for bringing a person closer to their soul through an expansion of consciousness into 'quantum realms'. Quantum consciousness is the transcendent, mystical non-ordinary reality that gives access to spiritual experiences unmediated by restricting world-views. Making contact with nature, for Leslie Kenton, is part of a shaman's technology for accessing this type of consciousness (see Chapter 3). If we turn to look at historical aspects of the Western cultural tradition we will see how these ideas have come about.

A Discourse of Esotericism

Esotericism, in particular, is central to the debate on whether nature religion is ecological; it is intimately associated with mysticism and a religious attitude. William James noted early in the twentieth century that nature seems to have the peculiar power of awakening mystical moods, and that religious experience has its roots in mystical states of consciousness ([1902] 1977:379).[8] The word 'mystic' has its origins in the Greek mysteries[9] and referred to a person who had gained an esoteric knowledge of divine things acquired through an initiation ceremony (Happold, 1979:18). There are many different forms of mysticism, but some forms take a non-ecological approach in their focus on deity rather than the natural world, such as in some interpretations of modern witchcraft, a contemporary version of the mysteries whereby entry into the various degrees is frequently effected by initiation (see Greenwood, 2000:28). A focus on inner nature and on the ritual invocation of anthropomorphic deities appears to direct attention away from seeing nature as including other sentient beings. Nature can thus become an abstract force consisting of impersonal energies, not as other human persons and beings within a particular relationship of contiguity *within* the natural world. Likewise, New Age scientific theories explain the interconnections between all beings within a network symbolized as the goddess Gaia, the spiritual aspect of which is expressed through a neoplatonic and panenthiestic[10] harmony and light. While it would not be accurate to say that the New Age in general was against the natural world, it does place an emphasis on a mystical oneness with angels or devas as nature's representatives and spiritual evolution, rather than *natura naturans* – nature as nature in itself as already discussed. This view is non-ecological in terms of its tendency to separate spirit from the natural world.

I now turn to issues of 'one unity' and 'spiritual evolution', as two key elements of the Western mystery tradition, to illustrate how they mitigate an ecological approach. The former, manifesting through the influence of neoplatonism, is evident in certain ideologies within nature religion, while what has been termed an 'optimistic gnosticism' characterizes the occultism derived from the Renaissance; this has shaped much New Age and Pagan thinking. Nature is, in essence, a part of divinity, and this philosophical ontology is akin to panentheism, the view that all things are in God, and that nature is an emanation of divinity, usually interpreted as a Goddess.

One Unity: Neoplatonism and Gnosticism

The neoplatonic conception was that the whole of creation – the earth, the heavens, and all of nature – represented a macrocosm whose unity was reflected in a variety of possible microcosms of which man was the most perfect. A collection of many religious beliefs, myths, rites, cults of Greek and oriental polytheism, alchemy, and magical correspondences between the planets, etc., neoplatonism offers a coherent image of the universe and the human place within it, and a method for achieving salvation by a restoration to an original divine condition. Plotinus

(CE 204–270), the founder of neoplatonism, allegedly turned aside from the spectacle of ruin and misery of the disastrous period of Roman history in which he lived to contemplate an eternal world of goodness and beauty. Following Plato, but concentrating on religious aspects, the eternal world of ideas became the real world.

The metaphysics of Plotinus begins with 'the One', the supreme principle, that passes into multiplicity and becomes the Intellect (*nous*) from which it passes into further differentiation as soul (*psyche*), and then into the universe of nature (*physis*). This theory of emanations concerns the movement of manifestation from the One as a timeless flow; it is not an intentional creative act, nor is it solely transcendent – it is immanent too. The One is inaccessible to rational thought, and is only accessible by rapt contemplation or absorption into unity (Merlan, 1991). The visible world may be a beautiful living thing – the abode of blessed spirits coloured and breathing with living harmony (Russell, 1946:308–315; Smart, 2000:137) – but it is constrained by its material nature. Plotinus did not denigrate the material world like Plato; he saw it as spiritual – the thought processes of a spiritual mind. The human soul has an archetype on a higher level, and spiritual discipline enables the harmonious merger of mind with higher levels of being. The ultimate aim of the soul is the mystical union with the One, who becomes fully present to the human soul (Solomon and Higgins, 1996:121–122).

Theologian Gordon Leff points out that by the second half of the thirteenth century the influence of neoplatonism was seen in the widespread diffusion of some of its leading concepts – from the Aristotelianism of Albert the Great to Thomas Aquinas. It also directly inspired a mystical outlook among the Rhineland Dominicans culminating in the speculative mysticism of Eckhart (Leff, [1967] 1999:310). Neoplatonism was influential during the Renaissance, especially in the work of the magus Marsilio Ficino who drew on a Christian interpretation of neoplatonism.

An influence during this period was the *Corpus Hermeticum,* a work of central importance to Renaissance magicians. It was probably Greek rather than Egyptian, as was commonly thought in the Renaissance, and was written in the second to third centuries CE. A composite of individual treatises offering no coherent system of thought,[11] it did, however, contain two distinct lines of thinking which A.-J. Festugière, in *La Révélation d' Hermés Trismégiste* (1950–1954), has termed pessimistic and optimistic gnosticism (Yates, [1964] 1991:22). This distinction portrays a fundamental tension between world-rejecting and world-affirming religious outlooks. The former is dualist and sees the material world as evil; it must be escaped from by an ascetic way of life which avoids all contact with matter until the 'lightened soul rises up through the spheres of the planets, casting off their evil influences as it ascends, to its true home in the immaterial divine world' (ibid.). By contrast, for the optimist gnostic matter is impregnated with the divine and 'the earth lives, moves, with a divine life, the stars are living divine animals, the sun burns with a divine power, there is no part of Nature which is not good for all are parts of God' (ibid.).

The *Corpus Hermeticum* was translated by Marsilio Ficino (1433–1499) in 1460, and the resulting work was called *The Pimander*. However, historian Frances Yates suggests that it was the *Picatrix*, a comprehensive treatise on sympathetic and astral magic written in Arabic probably in the twelfth century, which postulated that primal truth was to be found in One Unity, which inspired Ficino's approach to 'natural magic' – a neoplatonic philosophy concerned with drawing down the natural powers of the cosmos. For Ficino, all derived from One Unity, and truth and divinity were received in the 'perpetual movement of generation and corruption' within a hierarchy in which 'lower things are raised to higher things; and higher things descend to lower things'. The magician was concerned with gnosis – an insight into the nature of this Unity (ibid.:51). Ficino reconciled neoplatonism with Christianity by placing the ascent towards God within a mystical cosmic vision.

Ficino had a hierarchical vision of the cosmos, and in *Platonic Theology on the Immortality of Souls* (1482) he saw the human soul standing in the centre of the universe between God and the angels on a higher level, and beneath minerals and qualityless matter (Smart, 2000:215). The Christian mystic Pico Della Mirandola (1463–1494), who was Ficino's student, turned to the Kabbalah as a means of calling upon the higher powers of angels to aid the magical process. Essentially a 'sacred map' or a geography for conceptualizing both the human body and the cosmos, a study of Kabbalah facilitates the union of the two by providing a framework for linking the external cosmos with the internal, subjective feelings of the individual. It consists of ten spheres (sephiroth) and twenty-two interconnecting pathways that become the focus of specific meditational practice. Originally a Jewish system for contacting God, the Kabbalah has been adapted by Christians and Pagans, as well as practitioners of nature religion who frequently combine it with ritual workings.[12]

Spiritual Evolution

Another major influence in the history of nature religion is the notion of spiritual evolution found in Theosophy.[13] Blending neoplatonic spiritual evolutionism, science, and Eastern religious philosophy, Theosophists worked on the basic premise of occultism that all is interconnected and aimed to reconcile Eastern with Western religious traditions.[14] Founded by Helena Petrovna Blavatsky (1831–1891) and Henry Steel Olcott (1832–1907) in 1875, the Theosophical Society played a major part in disseminating esoteric doctrines at the turn of the nineteenth century, summarizing spiritual and religious ideas (Noll, 1996:67). At its inception its objectives were the following: to form a Universal Brotherhood of Humanity without distinction of race, creed, sex, caste or colour; to encourage the study of comparative religion, philosophy and science; and to investigate unexplained laws of Nature and the powers latent in Man (Ransom, 1938). These last two objectives were later developed by HPB, as she was popularly known, in *Isis Unveiled*, subtitled *A Master-Key to the Mysteries of Ancient and Modern Science and Theology* ([1877] 1988), in which she attempted to integrate science and religion.

The essence of Blavatsky's theosophy was that 'Man must know himself'. The religion of the day was 'dogma' with no scientific foundation. Science, too, was unsatisfactory because it ignored the unseen, being based on an observation of just the material world. For Blavatsky, the whole was constituted of the visible and the invisible, the facts of nature being grasped from within the human body as well as without. Believing in spiritual evolution of the psyche rather than physical evolution of primates, she was adamantly anti-Darwinian (Washington, 1993:46). Blavatsky claimed that her cosmology was based on her contact with a Brotherhood of Himalayan Masters,[15] which she called the 'Great White Brotherhood'. The Masters formed a 'cosmic radio' to link humans and the chiefs of the divine hierarchy that rules the cosmos (ibid.). Blavatsky published *The Secret Doctrine* in 1888 and sought to explain universal creation as a scheme by which 'the primal unity of an unmanifest divine being differentiates itself into a multiformity of consciously evolving beings that gradually fill the universe' (Goodrick-Clarke, 1992:19; cf. Dion Fortune's *The Cosmic Doctrine*). In this view, human history is but one phase in the spirit's attempt to rise up again through a vast series of rebirths moving through the cosmos from planet to planet (Washington, 1993:92) to recover from the fall from divine grace.[16]

The Theosophical Society promulgated the neoplatonic idea that within an Absolute there were innumerable universes, and within each universe countless solar systems. Each solar system was the expression of a being called the Logos, the Word of God, or the Solar Deity, who permeated, existed above and outside it. Below this Solar Deity there were said to be seven ministers, called planetary spirits, 'whose relation to him is like that of the nerve centres to the brain, so that all his voluntary acts come through him to them'. Under them were vast hosts or orders of spiritual beings called devas and angels. For Theosophists, devas represent a lower order of angels who are responsible for handling the realm of elemental nature spirits, as already discussed in relation to Findhorn in Chapter 5. According to the leading theosophist Charles Leadbeater, devas are a mighty kingdom of spirits in different degrees of evolution (1987:331). They may take the form of fruit, vegetables, flowers, mountains, trees, or valleys; some are concerned with landscape, while others are found beneath the ground. They are seen to express the will of the creator, and they channel manifested Nature. 'The plan is then disseminated by a kind of mental osmosis to all the ranks below them, each lower group having its leader, responsible to the group above. The more evolved devas are said to become guardians of special groups of humans, or even of nations, working on evolution and acting as messengers carrying out the will of higher angelic beings, (Tompkins, 1997:123–125).

Rudolf Steiner (1861–1925), a theosophist who was influenced by Goethe, and who formed a splinter group of the Theosophical Society called Anthroposophy, was particularly interested in nature spirits. Unlike some theosophists he was concerned with this world and the spiritualization of the earth. He attempted to explain the important role of nature spirits in human and planetary life by claiming that without these 'workaholic' elementals the planet would be bare and sterile (Tompkins, 1997:112). In *From the Akashic Record* Steiner claimed that there exists an earth memory, written in an earth aura, that is accessible to a trained clairvoyant, and that could provide a new scientific perspective for the study of human beings (Annett, 1976:114). Tompkins points out that Steiner's aim was to 'show how the threshold from the physical to the supersensible can be crossed in order to communicate first with the elemental beings and then with the hierarchies in their ascending ranks and functions throughout the cosmos' (Tompkins, 1997:132). The idea of devas and nature spirits has been taken up by the New Age, and the varying approaches to nature – both internal human nature and the natural world – are complex.

The Theosophical Society has played a formative part in the development of esotericism, particularly through the Hermetic Order of the Golden Dawn. This magical order was founded in London in 1888 by three members of the Societas Rosicruciana in Anglia, a Masonic–Rosicrucian body formed by Robert Wentworth Little in 1865 and based on the legend of Christian Rosycross. They were William Wynn Westcott (1848–1915), a doctor, coroner, mason and member of the Theosophical Society; William Robert Woodman (1828–1891), a doctor, a mason, Kabbalah enthusiast and Supreme Magus of the *Societas Rosicruciana*; and S.L Macgregor Mathers (1854–1918), a mason who 'spent almost half a lifetime in the British Museum and the Arsenal library in Paris, delving into magical and alchemical texts'. Mathers was responsible for constructing a coherent magical system from the various elements of Rosicrucianism, Masonic symbolism, Kabbalah, Tarot, astrology, numerology and ritual magic. A fourth founder member, a country vicar who died soon after the establishment of the Order (King, [1970] 1990:47), was the Revd A.F.A. Woodford.

Mathers and Westcott were both friends of Madame Blavatsky, and while she lived there was a friendly alliance between the Eastern section of the Theosophical Society and the Golden Dawn (Cavendish, 1990:143; King, [1970] 1990:48). The roots of the Golden Dawn and the Theosophical Society are deeply intertwined, and the two organizations saw themselves as an elite secretly working towards humanity's spiritual evolution. However, there were tensions between Eastern and Western attitudes, and magician Francis King comments that 'those who had been attracted by the spiritual and intellectual content of Blavatsky's Theosophy but repelled by its oriental form began to find their way into the Golden Dawn ([1970] 1990:43).

The Legacy of Esotericism

The idea of one unity and spiritual evolution was to reach its fullest development in the work of the highly influential magician Dion Fortune. Forming a Christian Mystic Lodge of the Theosophical Society in 1923 'to interpret Christianity in terms of Theosophy and vice versa', she eventually rejected the Theosophical Society's 'Himalayan Masters' because they were 'alien' and 'hostile' to her 'race'[17] (Richardson, 1987) and joined the Golden Dawn. In 1927 Fortune left that organization to found the Fraternity of the Inner Light, which is still in existence today (as the Society of the Inner Light). Fortune wrote her own interpretation of spiritual evolution in *The Cosmic Doctrine* ([1927] 1976) from teachings allegedly received from the Inner Planes by one of the 'Greater Masters'. According to Fortune, the Western system is more simplified, while retaining the principles of the Eastern. Essentially, it concerns the 'double evolution' of the divine power of God descending to matter on the one part, and the development of human consciousness rising to unity with God on the other (Fortune, 1987:159).

Dion Fortune opened a hostel and pilgrimage centre and espoused a vision of Avalon (Glastonbury) as a centre for the reconciliation of Christianity and what she saw as native paganism (Ivakhiv, 2001:81–82). Sacred places – such as Avalon, and also Christian churches which were built on pagan sacred sites – were seen by Fortune as harbouring a secret energy which lay deep within the earth, and which was known about by ancient peoples such as the Druids. For Fortune, the ancient Druids had methods for contacting 'the great subconscious of the world, where the Past, Present, and Future lies ready to be unfolded' (ibid.:113–114). She wrote that each human being had a particular rate of vibrations and that each person could tune in to the vibrations that interpenetrated the world. Each place was inhabited by the vibrations of beings 'like, and yet unlike, ourselves, invisible and unknown', and that whenever a place has had prayers and concentrated desires directed towards it, it forms an 'electrical vortex that gathers to itself a force, and it is for a time a coherent body that can be felt and used by man. It is round these bodies of force that shrines, temples, and in later days churches are built; they are the Cups that receive the Cosmic down-pouring focused on each particular place' (ibid.:115).

In essence, Fortune's view of magic is concerned with psychic integration with one unity, a larger spiritual and cosmic being: the 'Cosmic down-pouring' of electrical vortex is a form of neoplatonic esoteric Christianity rather than a localized ecological perspective, but it is, nevertheless, influential in nature religion (Crowley, 1998:170). It marks the distinctions between an animistic and inspirited world and a monotheistic notion of a universal divine force. Dion Fortune's influential work has fostered an esoteric reconciliation between Christianity and Paganism, helping revive a certain mystical earth-centredness in the writings of John and Caitlin Matthews, Gareth Knight, and R.J.Stewart, among others (Ivakhiv, 2001:108).

Thus the cultural context in which nature religion has developed is largely formed through the Western Hermetic esoteric tradition rather than in any indigenous native practices as claimed by some practitioners (see Greenwood, 2000:111–112). Esotericism – the idea that there is an arcane realm of knowledge or mystery emanating from a higher (or deeper) level – is manifested in two attitudes found among many practitioners of nature religion today: the first is a certain monotheistic attitude demonstrated in an emphasis on the Goddess; the second, which is related to the first, is an anthropocentric view that fosters and prioritizes introspection. In the section that follows, I outline some of the issues that must be addressed if nature religion is to be considered ecological.

Monotheism: The Goddess

Dennis Carpenter, in a discussion of monotheism and emergent nature spirituality, points out that there is considerable variation regarding the extent to which Pagans might be considered monotheistic or polytheistic. The Goddess may be worshipped as the One, allegedly a celebration of diversity in unity (Carpenter, 1996:56), but while '[s]ome Pagans direct their worship toward a single aspect of deity; many focus their worship upon a Goddess–God pair; and others direct their worship to an entire pantheon' (ibid.:57). There are two main points that support the monotheistic single aspect of deity approach as dominant, rather than the polarity and polytheistic versions. The first is that, as I have shown in the preceding section, the Western esoteric tradition has a history of monotheistic and neoplatonic – mostly Christian – approaches to deity. During the Renaissance Marsilio Ficino and Pico Della Mirandola used magic as a means to contact God in a higher spiritual realm; while Theosophists attempted to reconcile Christianity with Eastern religious traditions, it was in neoplatonic terms of a spiritual evolution of the psyche towards enlightenment. In addition, the Hermetic Order of the Golden Dawn, a potent influence on modern magical practice, was shaped by Rosicrucianism, an esoteric Christian tradition also based on inner mystery as a way of returning to an original state of paradise before 'the fall'.

The second point in support of the view of inherent monotheism in nature religion is the political implications that have occurred as a consequence of a patriarchal interpretation of God.[18] Practitioners of nature religion frequently place a great deal of emphasis on the Goddess; this is a reaction to what is seen as a denial of the female attributes of deity. Jungian psychology, of which Dion Fortune was a foremost proponent, has been extremely influential in promulgating the 'return of feminine', in the shape of the Goddess, as a source of psycho-spiritual power for both women and men, as well as a particular brand of esoteric Christianity (see Greenwood,2000: Chapter 6). Caitlin Matthews, a Pagan and writer on the Western Mystery tradition, says that the Goddess is venerated under a multiplicity of different aspects – she is one and many – but modern Goddess consciousness in the West 'understands that the Divine Feminine principles stems from a central source' (1997:40), thus diversity is celebrated through unity. Historian Ronald Hutton locates the origins of the veneration of the Goddess within the eighteenth-century Romanticism movement as a reaction to early modern scientific rationalism. Exalting the natural and the irrational, a mystical love of the natural world was symbolized by the Goddess. This was interpreted in both conservative – women were a reactionary force in the world – and radical feminist discourse (1998:96–99).

Feminist witchcraft is perhaps the most developed practice of Goddess religion in this latter respect; it seeks to resolve all dualities and to re-unite spirit with matter through the Goddess. The Goddess is an image of female power – not the 'power over' of patriarchy but of a 'power within' – based on the assumption, frequently drawing on the work of archaeologist Marija Gimbutas, that in ancient civilizations where goddesses were worshipped women were empowered, and that feminine power is inherently harmonious and peaceful (Wood, 1996:9). Feminist witchcraft brings together two discourses: feminism – a political ideology and practice concerned with issues of power and advocating social justice – and witchcraft – a spirituality which views nature, women, and 'the feminine' (as intuition and emotion etc.) as sacred. This new form of witchcraft was created in the late 1970s and integrates politics with spirituality: for feminist witches, seeing deity as female is a political statement as well as a spiritual reality. The Goddess is seen to reflect women's experience and female aspects of divinity denied or repressed in patriarchal religions; she is personal and political. The Goddess does not rule the world like the patriarchal God; she *is* the world in all its manifestations (Starhawk, [1979] 1989:9, 11) and the affirmation of the unity of being underlying the multiplicity of life (Christ, 1997:112). The Goddess is a 'doorway out of patriarchal culture' (Starhawk, 1982:74).

Goddess worship is the product of radical feminism's criticism of patriarchal theology: as the monotheistic concentration and centralization of cosmic power in one personal, law-giving will, characterized as male (Raphael, 1999:59), and outlined in Mary Daly's influential book *Beyond God the Father* ([1973] 1986). Theologian Melissa Raphael notes that thealogy derives from women's experiences and reflection on the 'femaleness of the divine and the divinity of femaleness'. Not founded on the authority of a sacred text but rather on the direct experience of the Goddess in themselves, as well as in the natural environment, some 'experience nature (her)self as a comprehensive thealogical text – [t]hey find and know – or better – *inhabit* the Goddess in the wild, untamed landscape' (ibid.:10–11). Feminist thealogians such as Asphodel Long see ancient matriarchies as models of peace and harmony with nature. Nature was female, the giver and sustainer of life as well as the source of wisdom. In the ancient world goddesses were associated with wisdom and the earth; venerated as creators and spiritual guides, they were the source of blessings and well-being, and could be understood to be 'the cosmic forces that are the essential structure of the universe'. Long claims that these goddesses could also mediate between the earthly and the spiritual: they encompassed nature as a universal guide and source of wisdom. This 'widely-held religious system' was eventually extinguished by a 'volcanic uprush of history whose lava and dead ash enveloped all ideas of wisdom goddesses and of the deity of nature' (1992:181).[19] However, as Cynthia Eller has effectively demonstrated, the roots of Goddess worship lie in theology rather than any ancient matriarchy (see Eller 2000a, 2000b).

Goddess spirituality is at heart a mystery religion rather than an ecological spirituality. The Goddess as a political concept is non-ecological. The emphasis is on the mystery of uniting with the Goddess – discovering the Goddess within rather than relating to the non-human world, in the sense of seeing human beings as components in a wider web or network. Cynthia Eller has observed that genuinely polytheistic spiritual feminists – believing in a number of discrete goddesses – are a rarity (Eller, 1993:133, quoted in Raphael, 1999:59). Starhawk's view of the Goddess, while encompassing all, elevates the human female as the symbol of immanent unity. There are potentially ecological aspects of feminist witchcraft as developed by Starhawk, and these are found in the shamanic aspects of her writing – in particular that on the faery tradition. It is through fairies – as spirits of nature – that a more ecological dimension to feminist witchcraft may be experienced, although this is contradictory because Starhawk subsumes all to the Goddess. Inspired by Margaret Murray's thesis that fairies were descendants of Neolithic and Bronze Age peoples, those who inhabited Northern Europe ([1931] 1970), Starhawk, who was trained by Victor Anderson, a practitioner of his own interpretation of 'feri' magic derived largely from Gardnerian Wicca, claims that the warrior gods drove out the 'Goddess peoples' into the hills and mountains where they became known as the Faeries. It is through the Faeries that the 'Old Religion', one that worshipped the Goddess, has been preserved ([1979] 1978:4). It appears that Starhawk cannot let go of the symbol of the Goddess as a political metaphor and conflates it with Murray's writings on folklore. Here Starhawk parts company with Donna Haraway, a feminist political theorist and biologist, who argues that the Goddess as an imaginative organic body for political resistance and as an image of original unity with nature is inadequate as a political myth for a postmodern world (Haraway, 1990:190–192), an issue to which I shall return in the next chapter.

Anthropocentrism

A history of esotericism locates the human being in the centre of the cosmos. God, and increasingly Goddess, is experienced within as microcosm to macrocosm; the one is essentially a reflection of the other. This anthropocentric view is held co-determinously with neoplatonic pantheistic or animistic perspectives that see deity as sacred and immanent in nature. Some practitioners, as already discussed in the preceding section, may be regarded as panentheists who may also acknowledge a monotheistic unifying aspect (symbolized as the Goddess). Practitioners of nature religion tend to view all nature as alive and imbued with spirit, and many believe that communication is possible between humans and various aspects of the animated natural world (Carpenter, 1996:53–54). For Pagans such as Selena Fox and Jani-Farell Roberts, as well as New Agers like John Seed, the source of the problem that prevents people's real connection with nature is anthropocentrism – seeing nature from the human 'master' perspective. Despite the history of esotericism, which tends to foster an anthropocentric view, many approaches in nature religion do critique anthropocentrism and seek to replace it by either biocentrism – the idea that all living things take a central place – or eco-centrism – a standpoint from the environment as a whole – often symbolized as a web of connections, such as the web of wyrd, which I shall discuss below. Non-human nature has intrinsic value independent of human beings, and is not viewed as a resource to be consumed, or a lower order to be mastered or stewarded, even benignly.[20]

The anti-anthropocentrism debate is mainly located within Deep Ecology and ecophilosophical thought, as outlined in the discussion on identity in Chapter 3. The transpersonal ecophilosopher Warwick Fox points out that anthropocentric assumptions are associated with the Renaissance and medieval idea of the Great Chain of Being, and also with gnosticism (1995:200). Fox presents a cogent critique of anthropocentrism in his advocacy of an ecological connection with all beings, which he terms 'transpersonal ecology'. Fox's transpersonal ecology, which is a development of transpersonal psychology,[21] draws on Naess's Deep Ecology[22] and an expansive sense of self in which selves and things-in-the-world are conceived as processes (ibid.:197). This sense of self transcends ego and a personal sense of self in its relationship with the rest of nature. He argues that many people who are attracted to spiritual views see God as the Absolute, the Ultimate, or as 'pure consciousness', and as humans participate more in this ideal than other beings they are consequently superior – cosmic evolution equals human evolution. Taking a more ecological view, Fox argues that all life forms are products of distinct evolutionary pathways, and that at any given point in time are complete examples of their own kind rather than participating in some human spiritual ideal (ibid.:199–200). Fox cites Freya Mathews who claims that Deep Ecology, as a model for the basic metaphysical structure of the world, is concerned with the metaphysics of nature and of the relation of self to nature; it sees 'the identities of all things – whether at the level of elementary particles, organisms, or galaxies – as logically interconnected: all things are constituted by their relations with other things' (Mathews, quoted in Fox, 1995:236).

The influence of anthropocentrism in nature religion has resulted in a tendency to introspection. Steven Sutcliffe, in a study of the New Age, has pointed to a shift from a dualistic, apocalyptic, millennial, gnostic viewpoint that views the present world as corrupt, to an 'inward turn', an internal focus. This involves a movement away from the outside world to find the whole universe – the elemental kingdom, the angelic hierarchy, and also God – within. Through sleight of hand, writes Sutcliffe, the ontology of nature has significantly changed: the physical reality of nature has 'given way to an abstracted, introverted, quasi-solipsistic understanding' (1998:37). This inward turn has been termed 'self-spirituality' by Paul Heelas, who points out that many New Agers emphasize the spiritual natural order of a whole but see their initial task as making contact with the spirit within – to find the authenticity of nature within. To find 'ecological consciousness' it is therefore important to begin with the person – to work on individual consciousness and a sense of connection (1996:86).

Many Pagans find nature within through the confines of a magical circle in which the microcosm may connect with its reflection in the macrocosm. Anthropologist Lynne Hume says that like other modern Pagans, Wiccans practise a religious ecology that is founded on the belief that the natural world is part of the deities that created it, and that the physical world overlaps with the spiritual realm. The physical characteristics of sacred space need to be established to make connection and link to a metaphysical space. This, Hume argues, is based on the premise 'as above, so below' reflecting the Hermetic origins of the connection between the microcosm and the macrocosm, and the notion that the world is a mirror of the divine. Hume draws on Jonathan Smith (1978) to argue that place is sacralized as the result of the work of ritual and that a circle is sacred because it provides a link between this world and the next. It allows deities and spirits a passageway. A circle is sacred space that encapsulates participants in a protective sphere; it is a 'place between the worlds': 'The witch "conjures" the circle into existence and "rents the veil" between the two worlds to allow for communication.'

The circle is purified with salt and water, smoking, sweeping, and elementals guard the quarters. Hume notes that 'Once the circle is "dismantled", the power is dissipated, and the space returns to normal – it is no longer sacred.' She comments that witches move between 'landscapes of the earth and landscapes of the mind' (1998:311–318).

Starhawk sees the circle as a symbol of ecological interconnectedness, having a separating as well as an integrating function (Carpenter, 1996:60). The separation aspect has historical associations: the use of a ritual circle to create sacred space is derived from historical ritual magical practice. Originating, according to historian Norman Cohn, for the conjuration of demons and the coercion of spirits, it marked out a field of consecrated power that no demon could enter ([1975] 1993:100–110), and it was seen as a place to invoke universal powers according to the magical will. For Starhawk, the function of the circle is not so much to keep out negative influences but to keep in power so that it can rise to a peak (Starhawk, [1979] 1989:58) and be directed through magical intention. The notion of the will is central to magical practices deriving from the occultism influenced by the Hermetic esoteric tradition. I have argued that there are two gendered models of the will; the first derives from the work of Aleister Crowley, and is essentially a masculine individualistic 'will to power'; the second, which originates from the work of Dion Fortune, is concerned with psychological harmony, seeking a Jungian complementarity between femininity and masculinity. The former is non-ecological, giving human will precedence over the cosmos (see Greenwood 1996, 2000:171–175), and both are anthropocentric.

Monotheism and anthropocentrism are thus deeply embedded within the world-views and practices of many practitioners of nature religion. I now examine an alternative to the esoteric discourse – an organismic world-view that sees human beings as intrinsically a part of nature. It is partial and incomplete due to the historical factors in Western culture described earlier, but it is potentially more ecological than an esoteric approach.

An Organismic Discourse

Plato, writing in the *Timeaus*, has a creator-god bringing disorder into order. Morris makes five points about this creation: firstly, that the god did not create matter[23] but acted as a craftsman by ordering a pre-existing but disordered natural world and fashioning it into an eternal Ideal pattern; secondly, that the divine blueprint was based on a notion of an Ideal living creature with mind and reason, all parts of the universe were aspects contained within; thirdly, that nature – that aspect of a thing that made it behave the way it did – and natural things were in the process of becoming: of moving towards the realization of their essence or Ideal form; fourthly, that there was no distinction between nature and spirits, but rather between a world of necessity and the unchanging world of forms; and finally, that there were four elements – air, fire, earth and water – that were the basic constituents of nature, and these were linked to human experiences (Morris, 1996:27).

This kind of anthropomorphic cosmological attitude to the natural world was evident in Europe throughout the medieval period. The Roman Christian Boethius, in *The Consolation of Philosophy*, disseminated Plato's ideas, and Providence became the unchanging plan for the universe in the mind of God. This, Morris writes, implies three basic tenets: the first is that the world consists of a totality of interrelated things which are symbolically meaningful, and incorporates spirits, humans, and nature; the second involves the notion that nature is permeated with spirit or mind, and that it is a living entity, animate or vital; the third concerns the idea that there is no separation between human beings and nature, or between individual and society, and that all encompass a spiritual order (ibid.:27–28).

As already discussed, the development of certain forms of esoteric thinking, especially some mystic neoplatonism and positive gnosticism with their notions of spiritual evolution, has had the tendency to foster spiritual transcendence of the natural world. By contrast, the Renaissance magus Giordano Bruno (1548–1600), an ex-Dominican friar who was influenced by early Greek organismic ideas, saw God in panentheistic terms (through his presence in nature) and moved against the predominantly Christian esoteric thinking of other Renaissance magi, such as Ficino and Pico della Mirandola (as described earlier). By adopting a pagan world-view, Bruno tried to reach not a Christian Trinity (father, son and holy ghost) but a One within the world not above it. Giordano Bruno used the Kabbalah within a pagan philosophy to contact the celestial world. He sought to take magic back to what he saw as its purer pagan source in Egypt through the 'art of memory' – a technique for conveying the Hermetic religious message – for creating a unifying world-view in the mind (Yates, [1996] 1992).

Bruno was influenced by Agrippa's *De occulta philosophia* (1533), and in this work the universe was divided into three worlds: intellectual, celestial, and elemental, each in neoplatonic fashion being seen to receive influences from the one above. The virtue of the Creator was said to descend through angels in the intellectual world, to stars in the celestial world, and then to the elements in animals, plants, metals, stones, etc. Bruno followed Agrippa's system but replaced the Hebrew of the intellectual level with that of the Egyptian hieroglyphs as images taken from nature (ibid.:263). Humans could make progress upwards and draw virtues of the upper world by manipulating the lower (ibid.:131). As he outlined in the *Spaccio della bestia trionfante*, God communicates by the effects of nature:

So that God, considered absolutely, has nothing to do with us, but only as He communicates Himself by the effects of nature, to which He is more nearly allied than nature itself; so that if He is not nature itself, certainly He is the nature of nature, and the soul of the soul of the world, if He is not the very soul itself (quoted in Yates, [1964] 1991:269).

Being a monist, an anti-dualistic thinker, Bruno did not create a split between the spiritual and material world: the world was not created by a God who stood outside of his creation but was organized by a dynamic principle within. Bruno was influenced by the pre-Socratic philosopher Anaximander, who saw in *apeiron* the source of everything, the ultimate principle (Mendoza, 1995:124) that contained the principle of separation – the *nous* or 'mind' (not as modern concept of intelligence but as the origin of the 'other'). Bruno synthesized *apeiron* and *nous* as a clash of dialectical opposites in the cosmic mind. He was also influenced by Heracleitus' notion of *panta rei* as the unity of the world, the unification of opposites – fire, sea, earth, etc. – the incessant, universal and eternal becoming. From the Stoics he got the idea that matter was alive, not inert and passive; everything was animated by the 'soul of the universe'. Nature is an organism – a whole whose parts are in harmony.

In some respects Carl Jung is an inheritor of this organismic psychic world-view. The collective unconscious, Jung argued, was the link between the human psyche and organic nature, not something mystical like a 'group mind'; he sought to reconcile biology with spirit (Stevens, 1990:36–37, 40):

The psyche, if you understand it as a phenomenon occurring in living bodies, is a quality of matter, just as our body consists of matter. We discover that this matter has another aspect, namely, a psychic aspect. It is simply the world seen from within (quoted in Sabini, 2002:82).

Jung claims that phylogenetically as well as ontogenetically human beings have grown up out of the 'dark confines of the earth'; the factors that affect us most closely became archetypes, and it is these 'primordial images which influence us most directly, and therefore seem to be the most powerful' (quoted in Sabini, 2002:69). Archetypes – as active biological living dispositions, inherited modes of functioning – are patterns of behaviour not ideas. For Jung archetypal experiences are part of the psychic constitution; they are propensities that, through repeated selection and mutation occurring over hundreds of thousands of years, have resulted in the present archetypal structure of the human species. Archetypes predispose a certain approach to life; they organize perception and experience and are expressed in myths and dreams, etc. (Stevens, 1990:35–39; Sabini, 2002:18).

Ecological Spirituality?

Murray Bookchin argues that a line of organismic thought, a 'legacy of freedom', has run like an undercurrent within Western civilization and other parts of the world. It appears in the 'organic society' of prehistoric Europe but was destroyed by the rise of hierarchy and the domination of the emergence of states and capitalism (Biehl, 1997:9). This legacy is to be found in ecology, but for Bookchin this excludes a spiritual component for he separates spirit from matter. Viewing the world in terms of gods and spirits is for Bookchin a crude form of anthropocentrism – the projection of the human world onto nature – and contrary to any genuine ecology. Against collapsing distinctions into a spiritual 'oneness', Bookchin sees a naturalistic outlook being supplanted by a supernatural tendency that is inherently alien to nature's own fecundity and self-creativity (ibid.:137).

Bookchin attempts to heal the split between human beings and nature through ecology, the goal of which, he says, is wholeness. This is not an immutable homogeneity but a 'dynamic unity of diversity', and he notes that '[i]n nature, balance and harmony are achieved by ever-changing differentiation, by ever-expanding diversity'. Most importantly, it does not involve a 'surrendering to mystical 'Nature', a nature that is beyond human comprehension, a nature that demands awe and subservience'. Drawing on Charles Elton's observation that the world's future has to be managed, Bookchin asserts that this management is like steering a boat: ecology teaches how to find the current and understand the direction of the stream (Bookchin, 1997:32–35).

Bookchin's vitriolic attack against supernaturalism – as a mystification that separates human beings from the rest of nature – is a more extreme form of the critique of esotericism made in this chapter. However, as we have seen, esotericism is not the only aspect or feature of nature religion. While there are 'mystical tendencies' that seek in the aspirant practitioner a union with a divine presence separate from the material world, there are also moves to relate more directly with nature. Gordon MacLellan and Adrian Harris, for example, unite ecology with a spiritual dimension. Gordon told me that he sees ecology as 'the engine that drives the patterns of life', and magic and spirituality as the 'mechanisms by which it manifests'.[24] Adrian, as noted in Chapter 3, likens spirituality to an ecosystem; it weaves people into a pattern of the universe through nature. A spiritual interpretation is compatible with a scientific approach, as Gordon's work in environmental education shows (see Chapter 6). Practitioners do seek to relate to nature in more complex ways than Bookchin's stereotyping portrays, even if it is not always ecologically. His objection to nature worship as a form of self-subjugation and servitude is a crude view of religion and demonstrates a simplistic understanding of 'mystical ecologies' (Bookchin, 1997:66).

As I have shown in earlier chapters, practitioners of nature religion do recreate something of an interconnected view of the world. Many incorporate elements of New Age philosophy, much of which is based on the idea that the world is animate, consisting of a totality of interrelated beings. Drawing on systems thinking, pioneered in the early twentieth century by biologists, with later additions of Gestalt psychology, ecology and quantum physics, this is concerned with web-like connections, relationships and context; and the essential properties of an organism or a living system are properties of the whole (Capra, 1996:29). Living systems are viewed as part of a web that interacts in a network fashion as an ecosystem.

This view of nature as a system is associated with the views of Gregory Bateson who, as already discussed in Chapter 5, challenged the assumptions and methods of science by looking for patterns behind patterns and processes beneath structure, seeking relationship as the basis for all definition (Bateson, 1985; Capra, 1989:74–75). It is also associated with the work of physicists David Bohm, author of *Wholeness and the Implicate Order* and proponent of an organic point of view for the universe (Bohm, 1999:59), and Fritjof Capra who advocates the need for systems thinking as an interdisciplinary conceptual framework for a basic pattern of organization for ecological sustainability.[25] The systems thinking approach is increasingly being analysed in terms of cybernetics, a branch of study concerned with self-regulating systems of communication and control in living organisms and machines (Lovelock, [1979] 1995:44; see p.118n6). The ecology dynamic draws on the work of the British scientist James Lovelock who in 1969 formulated the 'Gaia hypothesis', the notion that the entire range of living matter on earth could be regarded as constituting a single living entity 'capable of manipulating the Earth's atmosphere to suit its overall needs and endowed with faculties and powers far beyond those of its constituent parts' (Lovelock, [1979] 1995:9). Lovelock later modified this to the 'Gaia theory' that explained how regulation is the property of the whole evolving system of life – air, ocean, and rocks ([1979] 1995:144). Lovelock's work helped promote a new holistic understanding of life at all levels of living systems of organisms, social systems and ecosystems.

Many practitioners of nature religion, particularly shamanic practitioners, look to small-scale shamanic societies, as outlined in Chapter 2. Others seek to 'rediscover' Celtic or Anglo-Saxon holistic world-views; this is not unproblematic for the academics studying them and raises questions about the political dimensions of knowledge (Greenwood, 2003). These world-views are based in mythology and speaking to the mind as a part of nature they demonstrate magical consciousness. Perhaps one of the most influential of these 'indigenous' world-views to Pagans, particularly those of the Heathen or 'Northern' traditions, is Brian Bates's 'psychological archaelogy' on wyrd as an animistic and ecological model for relating to the world ([1983], 1996, 2002; and see Chapter 1). Bates's reconstruction of a shamanistic Anglo-Saxon view of the cosmos as connected by an enormous all-reaching system of fibres like a three-dimensional spider's web – where any event, anywhere, resulted in reverberations and repercussions throughout the web – is a model that encompasses individual life events, general physical and biological phenomena, and non-material and material events (1996:6). The web is wyrd, a magico-spiritual pattern of fate or destiny that offers a holistic pattern of interconnections; one that accommodates ecology.

Bates draws on the work of Brian Branston, who, in *The Lost Gods of England* ([1957] 1984), wrote about his search for a pagan mythology that had not been completely suppressed by the English conversion to Christianity, which started when Augustine landed in Thanet in 597 CE a hundred years after the first Angles, Saxons and Jutes had begun to settle ([1957] 1984: 57). Taking a role of detective, Branston tried to piece together an older pagan mythology in the Anglo-Saxon epic poem *Beowulf,* a poem composed in either the north of England or East Anglia around 650 CE. Branston notes that the conscious intention of *Beowulf* is Christian but that the setting is pagan and gives a number of clues about Old English mythology and the idea of an all-powerful fate or destiny termed 'wyrd'. Branston claims that wyrd was originally conceived as an omnipotent old woman to whom even the gods were subject (ibid.:57–66). Wyrd was originally one of three Fatal Sisters who spun threads or wove cloth representing human lives.[26] As the Christian religion was gaining the upper hand, Branston claims that God and wyrd were identified with each other, wyrd becoming an attribute of God as his Providence. However, in written works of the Old English period 'the thought of wyrd as a goddess was consciously played down by monkish writers and copyists'. Nevertheless, the idea was kept alive after the conversion to Christianity in notions of three pagan Fates;[27] this lived on in the oral tradition for centuries, reaching what Branston describes as its most dramatic representation in 1605 as the three 'Weird Sisters' in Shakespeare's *Macbeth*. Shakespeare transformed these sisters into witches ([1957] 1984:66–67).

Bates's work in the novel *The Way of Wyrd* is based on psychological analysis developed from a 'major research project into the nature of Anglo-Saxon sorcery' in order to reconstruct a pagan way of seeing the world ([1983] 1996:10). However, the view of wyrd as 'fate' or 'destiny' is not widely accepted amongst academics (Wallis, 2003:131). Historian Ronald Hutton, for example, comments that due to the mix of north European and Graeco-Roman cultural influences in early medieval Britain it is difficult to separate out different elements. Hutton writes that it is not clear whether the Anglo-Saxon notion of wyrd was actually a part of a pagan world-view or a result of the medieval writings of the Christian Boethius, who propounded an identical philosophy. In addition, he notes that it now seems generally accepted among scholars that the three Norns or Wyrd Sisters in Norse and Germanic mythology are borrowed from the Three Fates in Greek mythology (Hutton 1991:296).

Archaeologist Robert Wallis, in his study of what he terms 'neo-shamanisms', takes issue with Bates's view of Anglo-Saxon shamanism in *The Way of Wyrd* – which he calls an ingenious integration of 'shamanic metaphors and a specific vision of early Anglo-Saxon England' (Wallis, 2003:130) – on a number of points. Firstly, he claims that Bates's views are speculative and heavily influenced by the fictional work of Carlos Castaneda (which is problematic in terms of authenticity, as I have already mentioned in Chapter 2). Secondly, that evidence for paganism and the use of magic – as found in certain Anglo-Saxon manuscripts such as the *Lacnunga* (from which Bates gets much of his evidence, and terms a 'spellbook') and healing rituals (Bates gives a 'wonderfully evocative narrative' of a horse being cured of elf shot) – is not evidence for shamanism. Thirdly, Wallis claims that Bates uses 'universal' features of shamanism in a similar way to that of Michael Harner in his Core Shamanism; this is primarily for a neo-shamanic audience rather than as an explanation of Anglo-Saxon shamanism. Lastly, Wallis accuses Bates, in his later work *The Wisdom of the Wyrd: teachings for today from our ancient past* (1996), of reconstructing 'Anglo-Saxon shamanism' from a wide range of northern European sources – using material from Celtic, Nordic, Anglo-Saxon and the Bronze Age, among others. Wallis says that Bates's use of evidence is too sweeping and generalist for archaeologists and historians – 'a myriad of hitherto unrelated data is employed to support the case for an Anglo-Saxon shamanism' (2003:132–134).

Wallis's work shows the chasm that can sometimes appear between academic and practitioner understandings – for the latter wyrd appears to be a powerful 'symbolic system' for connecting the self to an organismic ecological world-view. Indeed, Wallis is ultimately ambivalent about Bates's work: although he points out that there is no singular 'truth' about the past, he also acknowledges that – as academic and neo-shamanic approaches are not commensurable – it is not 'wholly correct' to deconstruct Bates's neo-shamanistic writing approach academically, calling it a bold, new approach to 'old' evidence (ibid.:136). How is it possible to resolve this ambivalence between accepted academic views, on the one hand, and those that practitioners relate to, on the other, in this dilemma of different approaches to understanding shamanism? My argument – and the argument that I have taken in this book – is that taking a cognitive approach to this material is a solution: it gives insight into magic as a form of knowledge common to all human beings. Wallis is surely right when he accuses Bates of universalizing and psychologizing to make a specific vision of early Anglo-Saxon England consumable for the Western mind (ibid.:130–131), but what he does not appreciate is that if shamanism is viewed, along with paganism and magic, as employing an animistic world-view – one that creates spirit connections between things – then all the distinctions that he employs to determine exactly what is, or what is not, neo-shamanism (which interestingly he does not define) disappear.

The similarities, rather than differences, between contemporary nature religion practices and other cultural expressions, which may be separated historically or geographically, become clear when shamanism – Western or non-Western – is viewed as a type of magical thinking that orders a certain world-view (and a comparison may be made with Evans-Pritchard's classic study of the Azande). We can be relatively confident that the Anglo-Saxons, during the historical period that Bates writes about, had an organismic cosmological attitude to the natural world common to pre-literate peoples the world over; there is much evidence for this amongst many small-scale societies today. Whether we call it 'wyrd' or not does not really matter practically, but it is of importance to historians and archaeologists. As with so much concerning culture of the past, it may remain an unanswerable question as to whether wyrd, as fate or destiny, was indeed a widely held Anglo-Saxon world-view. We will never really know specifically what the people who created the cave paintings in the Stone Age – so often held up to be the first shamans – really thought; likewise, we will never know exactly in which ways Anglo-Saxons understood their universe. Much of what we think we know is derived from those who wrote about the Anglo-Saxons; and in addition, our interpretations of evidence always remain our interpretations. Importantly, these interpretations are usually made from the standpoint of looking back to the past to understand the present. Notwithstanding, we may make educated and imaginative guesses drawing on deep levels of magical consciousness, as well as contemporary small-scale people's world-views as possible illuminating parallels.

More importantly, for practitioners anyway, the model of wyrd offers a way to make sense of their lives in a holistic way; it also offers a framework for combining ecology with a spiritual dynamic. Notions of spirituality do not have to be cut off from ecology, as in Bookchin's view; they are part and parcel of human life. This has practical implications not only for practitioners but also for academics, and increasingly for academic/practitioners (such as Wallis). When analysing this type of material there is a real need for social scientists to choose their theoretical models according to the world-views of those they study; it is vital to use theories that resonate with practitioners' own understandings of magic, otherwise chasms of misunderstanding appear and communication becomes difficult, if not impossible, between researcher and those researched, as well as between the social sciences and mainstream society. I have written on the central issue concerning the politics of knowledge in relation to the morality and ethics of anthropological fieldwork elsewhere (see Greenwood, 2003:203).

Thus Bates's universalizing, like Lévi-Strauss's cognitive approach to anthropology, speaks more about the mind that thinks rather than the specific historical data. It is a way of thinking that we all have access to; it is an aspect of mind that I have here described as magical consciousness. As such it 'speaks' to practitioners in a symbolic and mythological language of connections, a symbolic system of meanings. It is a notion of mind, unlike Lévi-Strauss's, that is located within nature and an ecological perspective. This is very much in accord with Lévy-Bruhl's 'law of participation' as a type of thinking based on the association of persons and things, and also with Frazer's notion of sympathetic magic, the psychological association of ideas. If wyrd is viewed as a symbolic system for analogical thought it can aid understanding of an animistic and magical cognition potentially common to all humans; this cognition is part of the process of consciousness, experienced in varying degrees by the majority of the human species and apparently evident throughout prehistory and history, as well as through wide geographical location. It creates organismic conceptions of the cosmos that Europeans had in the past but that, for the reasons already given, have become marginalized and with which Westerners have now become deeply unfamiliar. In my view, academics, such as Wallis, need to include this aspect of knowledge into their analyses and then bridges may be made between academic and practitioner understandings. The value of Bates's work is that it is, as he claims, a 'psychological archaeology' (Bates, [1983] 1996:13), and this is how it should be evaluated. For practitioners, this type of thinking offers a coherent way to think spiritually and ecologically within a subculture that consists of a confusing multiplicity of fragmented histories, cosmologies and practices.

Magical consciousness can facilitate an ecological awareness when spirit is located in nature rather than in some ultimately transcendent being. Rupert Sheldrake has pointed to the vital point in Western history when Cartesian mechanistic science expelled soul from nature leaving a passive and inanimate *natura naturata* opposed to the invisible divine power of *natura naturans* (1990:61–62). Sheldrake – who, along with other scholars such as Carl Jung, who connected human beings with nature through the collective unconscious (the psyche occurred within inspirited matter as well as living bodies) (Sabini, 2002:14, 72, 82); Gregory Bateson (1985), who claimed that there was no separation between mind and nature; Tim Ingold (2001), with his whole organism in its environment approach; and David Abram (1997), who talks about deep participatory perception with a world of multiple intelligences – seeks to restore spirit to matter. This process calls for another way of thinking, one that does not deny causality but works on the altogether different principle of participation. Magical consciousness is a way of such thinking that connects with nature; is not essentially mystical but it may be interpreted as such according to magico-religious tradition.

Returning to the original question of whether nature religion is ecological, the extent to which people choose to focus on esoteric and/or organismic elements determines the answer. The paradoxes and contradictions highlighted here in this chapter are part and parcel of contemporary thought and practice among practitioners. The jury is out as to whether the balance amongst practitioners will swing in favour of an ecological approach. Annie, the feminist witch, told me that she thought that people either had a strong internal imaginative life or a strong interest in natural history. Either way, moving from one to the other was problematic – 'people are not connected', she said. Time will tell whether people will 'connect' and whether nature religion can, in the main, be considered ecological.

In the next chapter I widen the analysis of nature spiritualities by a consideration of postmodernity and globalization to consider how magical consciousness operates in the city.

Notes

1. As I have noted previously, magical practices have a complex relationship with Christianity (which is the dominant religion in most countries where they are practised); they are often not as different from Christianity as they claim to be (Greenwood, 2000:4–5).
2. Murray Bookchin is critical of all theories that seem to inhibit the 'self-realization' of nature and ecological thinking, especially Marxism, Deep Ecology, systems theory and religious mysticism (Morris, 1996:133–134). Brian Morris points out three of Bookchin's objections to Deep Ecology: the first is that Deep Ecology's priority of nature over human beings seeks to reverse the historical aspect of human domination, thereby deflecting other human relationships (such as empathy or kinship with nature); the second objection is that Deep Ecology obscures the social origins of ecological problems; and the third is that human beings are intrinsically a part of nature but that they are unique due to the capacity for self-consciousness. Consequently, biocentrism and anthropocentrism are equally misplaced (the former is advocated by Deep Ecologists, while the latter is condemned). Bookchin's critique of systems theory, according to Morris, is based on what he sees as writers such as Bateson, Prigogine and Capra appropriating ideas from diverse traditions and uncritically accepting the essential tenets of mechanism when they talk about abstract life forms (ibid.).
3. The protest was against a possible US attack on Iraq and was held on 28 September 2002. Several groups of Pagans were present: Pagans for Peace, a Gaia group, Dragon Environmental Network, and Reclaiming.
4. A Modron is an officer responsible for the interests and concerns of the members.
5. The eco-warrior myth was allegedly created by the media: 'Eco-Warriors should not be confused with pixies who are real, and magical and really do live in the woods' (Evans, 1998:83).

6. Personal communication, 18 March 1999.
7. According to the the Order of Bards, Ovates and Druids' announcement in *Pagan Dawn*, in ancient times Sacred Groves were places of sanctuary and worship for the Celts and their spiritual elders, the Druids (1999:17).
8. William James cites the experience of the German idealist Malwida von Meysenburg:

> I was alone upon the seashore as all these thoughts flowed over me, liberating and reconciling; and now again, as once before in distant days in the Alps of Dauphine, I was impelled to kneel down, this time before the illimitable ocean, symbol of the Infinite. I felt that I prayed as I had never prayed before, and knew now what prayer really is: to return from the solitude of individuation into the consciousness of unity with all that is, to kneel down as one that passes away, and to rise up as one imperishable. Earth, heaven, and sea resounded as in one vast world-encircling harmony. (James, [1902] 1977:381).

9. The word 'mystery' (*mysterion*) derives from the Greek verb *muo*, meaning 'to shut or close the lips or eyes' (Happold, 1979:18).
10. 'Panentheism' describes the doctrine that God is immament in all things, but also transcendent; He is more than the sum total of all the parts of the universe. This is different to 'pantheism': the doctrine that God is identifiable with the forces of nature and with all natural substances.
11. Frances Yates writes that the forward impulse of the Renaissance was derived from looking backwards to a pure golden age of purity and truth in antiquity. Progress was seen in terms of a rebirth of antiquity not in terms of evolution. The return to a golden age was, however, based upon an error of dating. The work most influential to Renaissance magi – the *Corpus Hermeticum* – was not of profound antiquity but written in the second to third centuries CE. This work, which is in fact a composite of individual treatises, offering no coherent system, was written by various unknown authors, was probably Greek, and was not, as believed in the Renaissance, the work of an Egyptian priest Hermes Trismegistus. The works have a philosophical nature and concern sympathetic magic and astrological and occult secret virtues of making talismans for drawing down the powers of the stars. They describe the religion of the Egyptians and how they drew down the powers of the cosmos into the statues of their gods. They also record individual souls seeking revelation and divine gnosis without the aid of a personal God or Saviour but through a religious approach to the universe ([1964] 1991:1).
12. Various systems of thought – from Jungian psychology, modern Wicca, to the worship of nature through the Greek god Pan – have been overlaid onto this basic schema.
13. The term 'theosophy' comes from the Greek *theos*, god, and *sophia*, wisdom; it is a philosophical-religious system which claims knowledge of the existence

and nature of diety obtained by individual revelation or through the operation of a higher faculty.

14. Although the stated aim was the promotion of the idea that all religions contained the same essence, the Theosophical Society was biased against Christianity and took little account of either Islam or Judaism (Washington, 1993:57).

15. These were 'Mahatmas', adepts or initiates, 'beings whose rigorous esoteric training and absolute purity have invested them with supernatural powers' (Washington, 1993:34).

16. Blavatsky's theories were based on a racial theory of human evolution:

> She extended her cyclical doctrine with the assertion that each round witnessed the rise and fall of seven consecutive root-races which descended on the scale of spiritual development from the first to the fourth, becoming increasingly enmeshed in the material world (the Gnostic notion of a Fall from Light into Darkness was quite explicit), before ascending through progressively superior root-races from the fifth to the seventh. According to Blavatsky, present humanity constituted the fifth root-race upon a planet that was passing through the fourth cosmic round, so that a process of spiritual advance lay before the species. The fifth root-race was called the Aryan race and had been preceded by the fourth root-race of the Atlanteans, which had largely perished in a flood that submerged their mid-Atlantean continent. (Goodrick-Clarke, 1992:20)

17. Dion Fortune had been initiated into the Hermetic Order of the Golden Dawn's London temple of Alpha and Omega in 1919. Fortune disliked the idea of pouring the regenerative spiritual force of the East into the group-soul of the British Empire (Richardson 1987:130).

18. An emphasis on the Goddess is, to some extent, a reaction to patriarchal interpretations of Christianity on the one part, and a New Age emphasis on the light, on the other. Feminist artist and writer Monica Sjöö has launched an attack on the New Age, calling it patriarchal. She claims that New Age embraces reactionary, anti-life and fascist views; it cannot come to terms with women's powers – symbolized as the Goddess: 'They deny consciousness and divine powers to the Earth Mother, even when they call Her "Gaia." She argues that by creating a God who is all light and transcendent, the rest of creation is demonized (1992:8–11). Sjöö's view is that the New Age does not engage with the dark, destructive aspects of nature. Wouter Hanegraaff also claims that the New Age tends to ignore the dark. Finding evidence of an attitude to nature which denies an experience of the sacred as mystery, he asserts that there is a gulf between traditional pre-Enlightenment esotericism, within which New Age has its roots, and a later secularized reinterpretation which attempts to resacralize nature as harmonious and benevolent, without making room for nature's association with death and the supernatural. New

Age has, he argues, thus come to be shaped by secular naturalism with its universal natural laws, rather than an experience of the sacred as *mysterium tremendum ac fascinans* (1998:26).

19. Interpretations of prehistoric data are overburdened by the desires and assumptions stemming from the attempt to redefine female aspects of deity that have been deliberately repressed by patriarchal institutional religions. In seeking to uncover the roots of the male domination of women in the overthrow of matriarchy, feminist witches found answers to why and how the gender hierarchy had developed (Eller, 2000b:182). As Cynthia Eller points out, the problem is that origin stories reduce historically specific facts to timeless archetypes not tailored to specific cultural environments but to a totalizing image of 'patriarchy'. Eller argues that ancient matriarchies should be viewed as a myth which stems from a nostalgia for a lost past. Feminist matriarchalists begin with a vision of the world as they would like it to be, project it into the past, and then try to make the present emerge from the ideal (ibid.:185). The myth rests on the notion of 'the natural' as a way of being in harmony with a nature uncontaminated by alienating patriarchal culture.

20. It is not clear how the notion of intrinsic value is determined. Does it mean that the natural world has value or just some parts? In the former case, this would mean that viruses had equal value with whales, for example. It is part of the nature of all species to interact with the rest of the natural world – as hunter to prey through food chains, for example – and it follows that the idea of non-interference with other species would involve a denial of the nature of all species, human and non-human. So, what is the basis of interconnection? Arne Naess was aware of the limitations of biocentrism and ecocentrism and advocated using interconnection as a guideline for not inflicting unnecessary harm upon living beings, and treating all aspects of nature as having value. It is inevitable that there has to be some killing and exploitation of non-human life, but the uniqueness of human beings must not be used as a premise for the domination of nature. Naess also has strong views on social justice and is against the domination of human beings by other human beings; but he employs a rather abstract normative schema (Morris 1996:150), and Deep Ecology does not address social problems, allegedly due to an emphasis on providing a rationale for a 'deep and joyful concern for all nature' (McLaughlin, 1995:267). The need has been to motivate an unrealized potential in human beings to have varied experiences in nature and thus to transcend isolation and identify with other beings, thereby changing consciousness. Ritual is seen to be a central tool for learning to think logically, analogically and ecologically: 'during rituals we have the experience, unique in our culture, of neither *opposing* nature nor *trying* to be in communication with nature, but of *finding* ourselves within nature' (LaChapelle, 1995:225).

21. Transpersonal ecology developed out of transpersonal psychology, which in turn was a response to behavourist and Freudian psychology's perceived deterministic view of human nature. The work of founder transpersonal psychologists Abraham Maslow (1908–1970) and Anthony Sutich (1907–1976) was influenced by Spinoza and the ideal of living under the aspect of eternity, and the Taoist notion of living in harmony with the nature of things (Fox, 1995:295). Subsequent transpersonal psychologists include Stanilav Grof, Charles Tart, Roger Walsh, John Welwood and Ken Wilber, among others (ibid.:298).

22. Brian Morris takes a more critical approach to Naess's work, and while noting that he has important things to say – including the need for a 'gestalt' or relational way of thinking, and the need to reflect on and articulate an alternative ontology (1996:148) – he points out that Naess does not locate the environmental problem with its source – namely, the capitalist economic system (ibid.:149, 152). Naess, who follows Spinoza in suggesting a 'philosophy of oneness' in identification with the natural world, argues for a biocentric approach towards nature: all life forms should be seen as having intrinsic value. This is the principle of 'biospherical egalitarianism' and, according to Morris, this is positive because it 'never lapses into misanthropy' but functions as a guideline for humans not to inflict unnecessary suffering upon other living beings. In his favour, Naess does not take a romantic view towards nature and recognizes that some killing and exploitation of animals is unavoidable; he is aware that tribal communities with hunting cultures have a sense of kinship or identification with nature. Human beings are unique, but this uniqueness is not the basis for the domination of nature or other other human beings. However, Morris questions how 'deep' or radical Naess's views really are: the stress he puts on changing lifestyle and on 'self-realization' might be important for the white affluent middle classes of Europe and North America, but they 'can all too easily lead to a politics of 'survivalism' rather than addressing the real political issue of confronting capitalism. Although he stresses the importance of community, autonomy, local self-sufficiency, decentralization, cooperation, etc. his discussion tends to be abstract and normative (ibid.:150–52).

23. For a comparable cosmology see Carlo Ginzburg's *The Cheese and the Worms: the cosmos of a sixteenth-century miller* ([1976] 1992b). Ginzburg, uses trial accounts to show the heretical views of Menocchio in which he proclaims that life spontaneously generated from inanimate matter: God did not create the world but rather it is produced by nature 'just as worms are produced from cheese'. He used the experience of maggots appearing in decomposed cheese to elucidate the birth of living things from chaos. From chaos came the angels, as the first living beings, and then God, who was the greatest among them (ibid.:57).

24. Personal communication, 15 October 2002.
25. Fritjof Capra, in a talk at Alternatives, St James's Church, Piccadilly, London on 22 July 2002 concerning the ideas behind his new book *Hidden Connections: a science for sustainable living,* pointed out that the global capitalistic economy needed reshaping. He argued that technological networks could be used for other means than producing profit. An alternative network compatible with human dignity and ecological sustainability could be developed with a different set of values and beliefs based on a spiritual view of the world, one that sees the part and the larger whole.
26. In Iceland, which did not convert to Christianity until much later, the Sisters were called the Nornir and are said to live by the side of one of the roots of the mythological world tree Yggradsil; they were originally thought of as spinners (Branston, [1957] 1984:68).
27. The Greek Fates were Clotho, who spun; Lachesis, who measured the thread; and Atropos, who snapped or cut it, thus ending a person's life. The Romans called the Fates 'Parcae', a word associated with the Latin verb *parere* 'to bring forth'. These basic ideas concerning the Fates go back, according to Brian Branston, to Indo-European times of at least 6,000 years ago ([1957] 1984:70).

–9–

Nature in the City: A Globalizing Postmodern World?

The central theme of this book has been to demonstrate how some people connect with nature and come to feel a part of it through magical consciousness. As I have already indicated in Chapter 3, a sense of finding the sacred in nature is sometimes not just in the romantic sense of seeing the spiritual in a beautiful landscape and special sites – such as Cae Mabon in Wales or Seahenge in North Norfolk – but also in the ordinary, the everyday, and in the city. Nature religion is primarily, although not exclusively, practised by urban dwellers. Books with titles such as *City Magick: urban rituals, spells, and shamanism* by Christopher Penczak (2001), *Witchcraft and the Web: weaving Pagan traditions* by M. Macha Nightmare (2001), *The Urban Primitive: Paganism in the concrete jungle* (Kaldera and Schwartzstein, 2002) and *Spirit in the City: the search for the sacred in everyday life* (Heaven, 2002), as well as Eric Davis's *Techgnosis: myth, magic, and mysticism in the age of information* (1999), express the need to make nature religion relevant for urban dwelling in an age of rapid and seemingly ever-changing technological development.

A discourse of romanticism sets machines and the process of city industrialization against a view of organic nature (Davis, 1999:325–326); practitioners may prefer to invoke spirits of forests, wolves and ravens rather than spirits of pigeons, cockroaches and rats, but they do not generally reject city living or technology. Indeed many, if not most, work using computers, the Internet, and the latest in technological innovation; email discussion lists are an important means of sharing information, as well as organizing events and demonstrations. Practitioners incorporate the facilities of the contemporary world into their magical practices and world-views; connections are made between places in the everyday city as well as during the more explicitly magical rituals at high-profile sacred sites or in the countryside. Magic is indeed in the mind. This is something akin to the manner portrayed by Jonathan Raban's *Soft City* (1974). Running counter to Weber's notion that the world was disenchanted (Gerth and Wright Mills [1948] 1970:155), Raban's view of the city was as a new kind of 'enchanted' discourse. It was written, according to geographer David Harvey, at 'that cusp in intellectual and cultural history when something called "postmodernism" emerged from its chrysalis of the anti-modern to establish itself as a cultural aesthetic in its own right' (Harvey, 1991:3). Raban's conception of the 'soft city' gives an insight into a magical consciousness of the day to day, the everyday, as I shall show.

I have examined magical consciousness as a type of holistic cognition; arguing that magic must be understood as in the mind, and that the mind is in nature as a certain type of relational thinking. It has been claimed by some writers that nature religion is a response to the rapid social change and fragmentation associated with postmodernity and globalization (Beyer, 1998; Ivakhiv, 2001; Vitebsky, 2003). Adrian Ivakhiv, for example, argues that nature religion can be understood as a condition of postmodernity (2001:1–11), while Piers Vitebsky claims that shamanic indigenous knowledge cannot be transported to the West in its 'true' holistic form, and that it is used to perpetuate a superior type of global knowledge (2003:296). Whilst acknowledging that both these authors make important observations, my aim in this chapter is to further emphasize the point that magical consciousness – as a type of thinking that is explained and defined in different ways cross-culturally – is potentially innate to human beings. When studied as such, it can add another dimension to the analysis of nature spiritualities, one that, amongst other things, avoids dualisms between non-Western and Western modes of thought. In this chapter I reflect on nature religion in the light of some thinking on globalization and postmodernism.

A Globalized Postmodern World?

Adrian Ivakhiv (2001) points out that New Agers who are 'ecologically adrift' may be seeking to retrieve connections to landscapes and the earth, but they do so from a point of privilege within a postmodern marketplace and they 'arguably, remain incapable of establishing genuine connections to a landscape or to a cultural tradition'. The postmodern marketplace refashions and appropriates places, and the wealthy can 'shop around drifting touristically from one setting to another, while the less well-off are forced to drift in the less romantic quest for wage labor subsistence' (ibid.:230–231).

Feeling compelled to look beyond the images and commodities of popular culture, New Agers seek the real nature, but these hoped-for new foundations are, for Ivakhiv, proposed in the arena of the marketplace, a 'realm in which "tradition", the "sacred", "nature", and the "good life" have all become signs in a play of "staged authenticities" (MacCannell, 1992). Privileged tourists may explore the world in a search for authenticity. Postmodernity acts like a mirror reflecting images and desires onto a fragmented and de-territorialized landscape onto which new identities and places are being constructed and contested (Ivakhiv, 2001:10–11). New Agers live within a scientific society that they see as characterized by linear time, social divisiveness, materialism and spiritual forgetfulness; it is also seen as being short-sighted, greedy and indulgent. New Age and ecospirituality discourses, by contrast, offer a sense of empowerment for personal life choices and practice; there is less dependence on consumer materialist values and conformity with mainstream culture, and a corresponding greater reliance on intuition, inner guidance, and on finding personal answers through a variety of contemplative and divinatory practices. The aim is to reawaken personal capacities for creativity, wisdom, and inner guidance (ibid.:227–228).

Ivakhiv has put his finger on some of the ambiguities within the New Age, and nature religion in general. The capitalist marketplace, where there is a profusion of different spiritualities available, sometimes leads to a superficial 'pick and mix' engagement on the part of the consumer who is looking for enlightenment. However, this is not the whole story. While the New Age is prone to a great deal of commercialization, it is not necessarily ecologically adrift, as John Seed's work on Deep Ecology shows, particularly in his participation in an anti-Burger King demonstration (see Chapter 3). Neither is it incapable of establishing 'genuine' connections to landscape or tradition (as Ruth's experience at Findhorn showed in Chapter 5). The increasing commodification and consumerism of many nature spiritualities is only one aspect of nature religion. Most practices offer techniques and social and psychological frameworks for experiencing alternative ways of being in the world that are, as Ivakhiv points out, anti-materialistic. The alternative lifestyles promoted may be experienced as coming from a source of inner spiritual wisdom and authenticity. However, the idea of an authentic spirit within is not new and so it is not specifically postmodern. There was a pantheism inherent in neoplatonism whereby a distinction between God and creation was lost, God was naturalized, conceived in human terms and deified (Leff, [1967] 1999:400–401). This view, which was judged as heresy in the later Middle Ages, was nonetheless influential amongst mystics from the thirteenth century onwards. The search for God in the soul, with its emphasis on inner experience, encouraged a rejection of the institutional authority of the Church in favour of the authority found within (ibid.:310).

There are aspects of nature religion that may, however, be termed postmodern. The Goddess can be seen as a reaction to a patriarchal God. Indeed, the contemporary search for the free spirit is more likely to be found through a Goddess who is immanent within the world rather than through a God. Participation is shaped through a number of esoteric practices as well as a variety of ideological orientations – from animism, pantheism, and polytheism to monotheism as the Goddess. But is the Goddess a useful metaphor for this free spirit in contemporary Western societies? There are inherent problems with this approach, as I have discussed in the previous chapter. Are postmodern cyborgs a more appropriate model for the twenty-first century?

Donna Haraway, a feminist political theorist and biologist,[1] has attempted to find a way of connected thinking and acting in what she describes as 'profoundly contradictory worlds', not as a goddess but as cyborg (Haraway, 1990:190). In postmodernity new cyborg technologies are said to erode the boundaries set up between human being, machine and nature: 'a cyborg world might be about lived social and bodily realities in which people are not afraid of their joint kinship with animals and machines' (ibid.:196). Ideas expressing the essential natural self are questioned through the notion of a cybernetic organism which is a hybrid of animal and machine; and also in the notion that technology transcends status as a thing and allows for 'incorporeal encoding and transmission of mind and meaning' (Davis, 1999:4). She notes that Western science and politics has a tradition of appropriating nature as a resource for the productions of culture (Haraway, 1990:191); this has the effect of creating a breach between human and animal. There is also ambiguity between natural and artificial, mind and body, and 'the certainty of what counts as nature'. The boundary between the physical and the non-physical is very imprecise, but for Haraway there must be no recall to an imagined organic body for political resistance. Cyborgs are about breaching boundaries that confuse specific historical people's stories of distinct categories (Haraway, 2000:125).

A cyborg is a political myth, a science fiction, a creature of a postmodern, post-gender world with 'no truck with organic wholeness' nor original unity with nature (Haraway, 1990:192). Being a disassembled and reassembled postmodern collective and personal self, the cyborg is a mode of interacting with the world that is relentlessly historically specific (Haraway, 2000:133). Cyborg imagery refuses the demonization of technology and embraces the task of reconstructing non-dualistic and relational world-views; it is, for Haraway, a 'dream not of a common language, but of a powerful infidel heteroglossia' and it means 'both building and destroying machines, identities, categories, relationships, spaces, stories' (ibid.:223). Calling for a new 'historicization of the unconscious' constructed from our merging with the non-human to create a new kinship structure (ibid.:125), Haraway is concerned with building alternative ontologies using the imagination (ibid.:120). As a child she was fascinated by 'imagining elaborate miniature people's worlds and playing with tiny figures in the grass' (Haraway, 2000:132), and it is perhaps this imaginative faculty which aids the process of building alternative ontologies: 'Understanding the world is about living inside stories' (ibid.:107).

Using relational metaphors, Haraway seeks to focus on whole systems rather than parts. Her notion of a cyborg as a postmodern science fiction, a political myth, could be said to allow for an environmentalist accommodation, in the sense of creating connection between humans and other animals, as well as technology, but it is certainly not ecological in terms of being based in nature and probably would not appeal much to practitioners of nature spiritualities.

Is nature religion a response to postmodernism? Well, partly, in terms of a reaction to an increasingly fragmented and rapidly changing society where there are more options open to the individual. Practitioners might seek stability in the diversity of nature in the form of a goddess as a source of identity and explanation of life, much as Jews, Christians and Muslims do in God. However, an important part of most practices is the expansion of consciousness and its accompanying holistic world-view, and this, as I have argued, is part of what it is to be human; it cannot, therefore, be totally explained as a reaction to the insecurities of postmodernity. Can nature religion be explained in terms of globalization? Not wholly, I would suggest. Vitebsky claims that holism, other than as an ideal, does not exist in a globalized world. He asserts that holistic indigenous knowledge cannot be successfully transplanted to a fragmented society. A holistic ideal in Western societies is unattainable due to a lack of appropriate context; he laments: 'Even as astronomy sees ever further into space, the arena of human consciousness has shrunk from the cosmos to a mere globe. So ironically, the more global things become, the less holistic they are since they pertain *only to this globe*' (2003:296). Like Ivakhiv, who notes the economic difference between privileged New Agers and those seeking wage labour subsistence, Vitebsky is concerned with the imbalance of power on a global level:

> the coercive nature of interaction between the components of this globe requires, not the homogenisation of the Coca-Cola model, but the perpetuation of some kinds of difference. These differences are ones of relative power and involve a sort of class structure of epistemologies in which global knowledge can rest assured of its superiority only if it can point to other, inferior knowledges (Vitebsky, 2003:296).

These are important political aspects that contribute to our understanding of nature religion; however, there are other dimensions that are not immediately apparent within such an analysis. Vitebsky's notion of a 'class structure of epistemologies' is static and too simplistic. As I have argued, using the work of anthropologists Evans-Pritchard and Tambiah in Chapter 5, there are different ways that human beings think in all cultures; the only essential difference is one of context. Vitebsky creates a dualism between 'indigenous' and 'global' knowledge; he does not account for the fact that there are many ways of knowing in one society, and indeed globally. It is the capitalist economic system that plays an important role in a hegemony of knowledges in creating a market place for spiritualities. Non-Western indigenous knowledge is holistic, as Vitebsky claims, but potentially so too is the knowledge derived from magical consciousness in Western societies. Human consciousness the world over tends to be concerned with cognitive map-making, and creating meanings between things. One can think holistically and magically in the city as well as in some small out-of-the-way village, as I shall show in the following section using the work of Jonathan Raban.

Magic in the City

Jonathan Raban saw the city as a place for the expression of personal identity – an identity that is soft, fluid and open to the will and to the imagination. The city is a theatre: a series of stages upon which individuals can 'work their own distinctive magic while performing a multiplicity of roles'. Cities, unlike villages and small towns, he argues, are plastic by nature: 'We mould them in our images: they, in turn, shape us by the resistance they offer when we try to impose our own personal form on them' (Raban, 1974:9). Living in a city, a person slips unconsciously into 'magical habits of mind'. The city is mapped by private benchmarks that are meaningful only to that individual; 'Like any tribesman hedging himself in behind a stockade of taboos, I mark my boundaries with graveyards, terminal transportation points and wildernesses. Beyond them, nothing is to be trusted and anything might happen' (ibid.:166).

Inside this private city there is a grid of reference points of personal attribution of meaning: 'A black-fronted bookshop in South Kensington, a line of gothic balconies on the Cromwell Road...' Symbols denote a particular quarter – the underground may, for example, turn into an object of superstition, an irrational way of imposing order on the city: 'the Piccadilly Line is full of fly-by-nights and stripe-shirted young men who run dubious agencies'. Raban suggests that there is more than a merely vestigial magicality in the way people live in cities – magic is a way of surviving living in the city:

> Magic may be a major alternative to rejection of the city as a bad unmanageable place; it offers a real way of surviving in an environment whose rationale has, like a dead language, become so obscure that only a handful of specialists (alas, they are all too frequently sociologists, urban economists and town planners) can remember or understand it. The rest of us make do with an improvised day-to-day magic, which, like shamanism, works because we conspire that it shall work (Raban, 1974:169).

While Raban's language reflects a Western sense that magic is irrational, it does make the important point that it is possible to live in the city with a magical frame of mind: it is possible to create meaningful connections with place through the creation of conceptual maps – an 'improvised day-to-day magic'.

In the 'private city' these maps may be exclusively individual for the people who live and work there. They may be specific to the individual as he or she commutes to and from work, or the symbolic frameworks may be collectively shared by a group of people. The basic premise is the same: it concerns the creation and establishment of connections and relationships with the environment, whether town, city or countryside. Meanings build up over time and are constantly open to renegotiation according to experience. Anywhere can become 'sacred', and according to magical ideology all is interconnected within synchronistic maps of meaning. Syncronicity and analogical thinking feature heavily within this frame of mind; and connections between otherwise disparate events, places and things become meaningfully encoded within their own particular logic and are framed within a wider ideological map, as in Bateson's notion of ideation.

The city, as witch Christopher Penczak observes, is a 'powerful landscape of magick' (2001:3); it has a hidden side, a non-physical realm that exists side by side with normal reality (ibid.:16). Raban claimed that the underground was a way of imposing order on the city; Penczak also imbues it with magical power. Mechanical spirits may manifest physically in the form of subways, which are 'great electric serpents running through the city. They are akin to underworld gods, like the great king worm burrowing under us. They already work with us, taking us to destinations all over the city, but their subtle power is not often recognized' (ibid:.63). The underground and subways are infrastructure for the processes of thinking, or journeying to other dimensions. Tall buildings like skyscrapers, says Penczak, may function as cosmic axes for interconnecting realms, just as the Norse World Tree formed a link between the deities, human beings, giants and the dead. Forming a ladder between realms, skyscrapers stretch up to the sky and down to underground maintenance systems and sewers (ibid.:76, 93). Graffiti becomes magical sigils, written symbols that evoke power and which, when meditated upon, reveal their inner meanings (ibid.:176–177). The streets of the city are pathways of power that may be used creatively and mapped to manifest desires and intentions, as well as connecting individual to place. 'What could be more in harmony with your environment than that?' asks Christopher Penczak?

The point is that this appears to be a common human way of thinking – a holistic way of imposing order – and it matters little whether it is private and individual, as proposed by Raban, or shaped by a social group with certain common assumptions and ideals, whether it is contemporary Western and based in the city, or age-old and located among Sakha (Yakut) shamans of the Viliuisk area of north-east Siberia. Magical consciousness – in one form or another – appears to be pervasive.

The only real difference between the Western magical cognition and so-called indigenous thinking is the context. The specificities of living as a reindeer herder in Siberia or in a modern Western city may be different – very different – but the human *attitude* of mind – in the ability to create cosmological maps – is the same. The assertion that there is a lack of an appropriate context for holistic knowledge in Western societies belies the potential for Westerners to re-create magical ways of mind wherever they are, as the profusion of books on magic in the city, some of which have been mentioned at the beginning of this chapter, demonstrate. In terms of Vitebsky's notion of a class structure of epistemologies, power and knowledge are never absolute and some of the practices that practitioners of nature spiritualities engage in – such as anti-globalization protest – challenge the superiority of so-called 'global knowledge'.

Magical thinking is not usually associated with modern Westerners. Murray Bookchin, for example, thought that animism was infantile and represented a false image of the world, 'understandable as the beliefs of preliterate peoples' but not in modern people (Morris, 1992:73–74; see also Nemeroff and Rozin, 2000). This creates a bleak picture for any form of ecospirituality; it also ignores an important part of what it is to be human. Rather than seeing animism as a false world-view, as Bookchin does, it is better, in my view, to see it as part of the process of consciousness that forms a certain conception of the world, one that was probably experienced by early *Homo sapiens*. It seems likely that our early human ancestors would have thought animistically; rock art depicting animal/human relationships appears to have had a spiritual significance, making this conception of the world innate to our species. If contemporary hunting and gathering cultures are used as an example, we can suppose that our earliest human ancestors had a similar relationship with the world around them. If in following an animal the hunters think as the animal, they are more likely to know what the animal will do, and thus be more successful in making a kill.

Contemporary practitioners of nature spiritualities have to create meaningful relationships with place; they are not like hunter-gatherers, nor do they have an already established culture like the Australian Aborigine's Dreamtime, for example. Most have no established tradition and so they have to create it, even as Jasper has done in relation to Romany gypsy practices. There are multiple interpretations of the land, and the stories that emerge from the human imagination about the land are not 'fiction'; they may be better understood as a form of ideation or world-view. Again, they unify perceptions and experiences, as Ernest Thompson Seton, for example, has shown in the way he has utilized his knowledge about ecology to tell stories about animals. Thinking with wildlife enables an experiential familiarity with the landscape. What is needed, as Wendell Berry suggests, is a community-based ecology with a language to speak of the particularities of place, a language of folktales and mythology but one rooted in ecology.

All, in their various ways, give a sense of identity and connection through an *emotional* relationship with place through notions of ancestors, folk beliefs and myths. Is this a prerequisite for environmental or ecological awareness? One environmental educator, a colleague of Gordon MacLellan's, told me how she had been involved in environmental education for a long time. As we walked back to the car park from Tegg's Nose, a country park in Cheshire created from a disused quarry, where she and Gordon had been creating a drama with local schoolchildren on the 'life of stone',[2] she said that she had been passionate about environmental issues as a child but had only recently come to realize that it was no good telling people to recycle, or preaching about environmental issues. She told me how she used to be very militant but then realized that 'you can't lecture people, you have to let them connect spiritually so they want to care for the environment'.

Working with Gordon had brought previously separate areas of her life together: her love of art, her spirituality, and also her passion for the environment. She had learnt from Gordon's approach that it was important to get people emotionally involved with places by creating situations where they came together with other people in feeling passionate about where they lived, and then, hopefully, she said, environmental awareness would follow.

I have sought to demonstrate in this work how nature spiritualities have occurred at a specific point in time; their practices and effects are varied and contradictory but there is an underlying theme that does unite the multiplicity of views and ways of being in the world. This theme is based on that aspect of consciousness that allows for creative participation between human beings and spiritual worlds of ancestors, deities, hedgehogs, crabs and all manner of other-than-human people. Magical consciousness is not primarily supernatural or mystical (although it may be expressed in these idioms), nor is it a response to the 'postmodern condition' or to globalization; rather, it is a context-specific expression of one aspect of what it is to be human.

Notes

1. Haraway writes within a postmodern discourse that celebrates difference, otherness, and plurality. A politics of difference valorizes oppositional traditions such as witchcraft, as well as being a woman, Welsh, black, Aboriginal, etc. in a renegotiation of existing terms (Jordan and Weedon, 1995:562).
2. This project was conducted in local schools in mid-June 2002. The children in the two oldest year groups put on performances for the rest of the school as well as for parents, grandparents and brothers and sisters. The first was held in the school hall during the normal working day; the second was performed at Tegg's Nose. A sense of animation was shared by the children and the audience, linking the school community, relatives, and assorted onlookers with their location and each other.

Bibliography

Abram, D. (1997) *The Spell of the Sensuous*, New York: Vintage Books.

Adler, M. ([1979] 1986) *Drawing Down the Moon*, Boston: Beacon Press.

Albanese, C. (1991) *Nature Religion in America: from the Algonkian Indians to the New Age*, Chicago: Chicago University Press.

Anderson, C. (1994) *Fifty Years in the Feri Tradition*, Private publication.

Andrews, T. (1998) *A Dictionary of Nature Myths*, Oxford: Oxford University Press.

Ankarloo, B. and S. Clark (eds) (2002) *Witchcraft and Magic in Europe*, Volume 3, *The Middle Ages*, London: The Athlone Press.

Ankarloo, B. and G. Henningsen (eds) (1993) *Early Modern European Witchcraft*, Oxford: Clarendon Press.

Annett, S. (1976) *The Many Ways of Being: A Guide to Spiritual Groups and Growth Centres in Britain*, London: Abacus.

Armitt, L. (1996) *Theorizing the Fantastic*, London: Arnold.

Arrowsmith, N. with G. Moorse (1977) *A Field Guide to the Little People*, London: Macmillan.

Bailey, A. ([1951] 1973) *The Unfinished Autobiography*, New York: Lucis Publishing Co.

Bailey, A. (1955) *Discipleship in the New Age (vol. 2)*, New York: Lucis.

Banks, J.T. (ed.) (1989) *The Selected Letters of Virgina Woolf*, New York: Harcourt Brace Jovanovich.

Baring, A. and J. Cashford (1993) *The Myth of the Goddess*, London: Arkana.

Basilov, V. (1984) *Izbranniki dukhov*, Moskow: Nauka, cited in the Introduction to Marjorie Mandelstam Balzer (ed.) (1997) *Shamanic Worlds: rituals and lore of Siberia and Central Asia*, New York: New Castle Books.

Bates, B. ([1983] 1996) *The Way of Wyrd*, London: Arrow.

Bates, B. (1996) *The Wisdom of the Wyrd*, London: Rider.

Bates, B. (2002) *The Real Middle-Earth: magic and mystery in the Dark Ages*, London: Sidgwick and Jackson.

Bateson, G. (with J. Ruesch) (1951) *Communication*, New York: Norton.

Bateson, G. ([1972] 2000) *Steps To an Ecology of Mind*, Chicago: University of Chicago Press.

Bateson, G. (1985) *Mind and Nature: a necessary unity*, London: Fontana.

Bender, B. (1998) *Stonehenge: making space*, Oxford: Berg.

Bender, B.and M. Winer (2001) *Contested Landscapes: movement, exile and place*, Oxford: Berg.

Benham, P. (1993) *The Avalonians*, Glastonbury: Gothic Images Publications.

Berry, W. (2000) 'Life is a Miracle: What Kind of a Culture will Honor the Preciousness of individual lives and places?', *Orion*, Spring: 29–39.

Beth, R. (1996) *Hedgewitch: a guide to solitary witchcraft*, London: Robert Hale.

Bettelheim, B. ([1976] 1991) *The Uses of Enchantment: the meaning and importance of fairy tales*, London: Penguin.

Beyer, P. (1998) 'Globalisation and the Religion of Nature', in J. Pearson, R.H. Roberts and G. Samuel (eds) *Nature Religion Today: paganism in the modern world*, Edinburgh: Edinburgh University Press.

Biehl, J. (ed.) (1997) *The Murray Bookchin Reader*, London: Cassell.

Blackmore, S. (2002) 'The Grand Illusion', *New Scientist*, 22 June.

Blain, J. (2000) *Wights and Ancestors*, Devizes: Wyrd's Well.

Blain, J. (2002a) 'Seeking the Ancestors: one heathen's view', *Pagan Dawn*, Lammas.

Blain, J. (2002b) *Nine Worlds of Seid-Magic: ecstasy and neo-shamanism in North European paganism*, London: Routledge.

Blake, W. (1970) *Songs of Innocence and of Experience*, Oxford: Oxford University Press.

Blake, W. (1975) *The Marriage of Heaven and Hell*, Oxford: Oxford University Press.

Blavatsky, H. (1888) *The Secret Doctrine*, London: Theosophical Publishing House.

Blavatsky, H. ([1877] 1988) *Isis Unveiled*, Volume 1, London: W.J. Bouton.

Bloch, M. (1986) *From Blessing to Violence: history and ideology in the circumcision ritual of the Merina of Madagascar*, Cambridge: Cambridge University Press.

Bloch, M. (1992) *Prey into Hunter: the politics of religious experience*, Cambridge: Cambridge University Press.

Bloom, W. (1991) *The New Age*, London: Rider.

Bloom, W. (1999) *Working with Angels, Fairies and Nature Spirits*, London: Piatkus.

Bohm, D. (1999) 'Cosmos, Matter, Life and Consciousness', in David Lorimer (ed.) *The Spirit of Science: from experiment to experience*, New York: Continuum.

Bol, M. (ed.) 1998: *Stars Above, Earth Below: American Indians and nature*, Niwot, Colo.: Roberts Rinehart Publishers.

Bookchin, M. (1997) 'Social Ecology', from *The Ecology of Freedom* (1982) in Janet Biehl (ed.), *The Murray Bookchin Reader*, London: Cassell.

Borrow, G. ([1914] 1935) *The Zincali: an account of the gypsies of Spain*, London: Dent.

Bourguignon, E. (1979) *Psychological Anthropology: an introduction to human nature and cultural differences*, New York: Holt, Rinehart and Winston.

Bowman, M. (1995) 'The Noble Savage and the Global Village: cultural evolution in the New Age and neo-pagan thought', *Journal of Contemporary Religion*, 10 (2).

Bradley, M. (1984) *The Mists of Avalon*, London: Sphere.

Bradley, R. (2000) *An Archaeology of Natural Places*, London: Routledge.

Branston, B. ([1957] 1984) *The Lost Gods of England*, London: Thames and Hudson.

Briggs, K. (1976) *A Dictionary of Fairies*, London: Routledge.

Brightman, R. (1993) *Grateful Prey: Rock Cree Human–Animal Relationships*, Berkeley: University of California Press.

Brody, H. ([1981] 2002) *Maps and Dreams*, London: Faber and Faber.

Brooke, J.H. (1991) *Science and Religion: some historical perspectives*, Cambridge: Cambridge University Press.

Buckland, R. (1998) *Gypsy Witchcraft and Magic*, St. Paul, Minn.: Llewellyn.

Budapest, Z. ([1980] 1990) *The Holy Book of Woman's Mysteries*, London: Hale.

Burch, E. and L. Ellanna, (1996) *Key Issues in Hunter-Gatherer Research*, Oxford: Berg.

Butter, R. (1999) *Kilmartin: an introduction and guide*, Kilmartin, Argyll: Kilmartin House Trust.

Caplan, P. (ed.) (2003) *The Ethics of Anthropology: debates and dilemmas*, London: Routledge.

Capra, F. (1989) *Uncommon Wisdom: conversations with remarkable people*, London: Flamingo.

Capra, F. (1996) *The Web of Life: a new scientific understanding of living systems*, New York: Anchor Books.

Capra, F. (2002) *The Hidden Connections: a science for sustainable living*, London: HarperCollins.

Carpenter, D. (1996) 'Emergent Nature Spirituality: an examination of the major spiritual contours of the contemporary pagan world-view', in J.R. Lewis (ed.) *Magical Religion and Modern Witchcraft*, Albany: State University of New York Press.

Carr-Gomm, P: ([1991] 1995) *The Druid Tradition*, Shaftesbury, Dorset: Element.

Carroll, J. (1987) *Liber Null and Psychonaut* York Beach, Me.: Samuel Weiser.

Carroll, J. (1992) *Liber Kaos and the Psychonomicon*, London: BM – Dazzle.

Carson, R. (1962) *Silent Spring*, Boston: Houghton Mifflin.

Carter, A. (1992) *The Virago Book of Fairy Tales*, London: Virago.

Castaneda, C. (1970) *The Teachings of Don Juan: a Yaqui way of knowledge*, Harmondsworth: Penguin.

Castaneda, C. (1973) *A Separate Reality: further conversations with Don Juan*, Harmondsworth: Penguin.

Castaneda, C. (1975) *Tales of Power*, London: Hodder and Stoughton.

Castleden, R. (1998) *The Stonehenge People: an exploration of life in neolithic Britain 4700–2000 BC*, London: Routledge.

Cavendish, R. (1975) *The Powers of Evil*, London: Routledge and Kegan Paul.

Cavendish, R. ([1967] 1984) *The Magical Arts*, London: Arkana.

Cavendish, R. (1990) *A History of Magic*, London: Arkana.

Champion, M. (2000) *Seahenge: a contemporary chronicle*, Aylsham, Norfolk: Barnwell's Timescape Publishing.

Chapman, J. (1993) *Quest for Dion Fortune*, York Beach, Me.: Samuel Weiser.

Chapman, M. (1992) *The Celts: the construction of myth*, New York: St Martin's Press.

Christ, C. (1997) *Rebirth of the Goddess: finding meaning in feminist spirituality*, Reading, Mass.: Addison-Wesley.

Churchill, W. (2003) 'Spiritual Hucksterism: the rise of the plastic medicine men' in Graham Harvey (ed.), *Shamanism: a reader*, London: Routledge.

Cohen, A. and N. Rapport (eds) (1995) *Questions of Consciousness*, London: Routledge.

Cohn, N. (1970) 'The Myth of Satan and His Human Servants', in M. Douglas (ed.), *Witchcraft Confessions and Accusations*, London: Tavistock.

Cohn, N. ([1975] 1993) *Europe's Inner Demons*, London: Pimlico.

Comaroff, J.and Comaroff, J. (1992) *Ethnography and the Historical Imagination*, Boulder, and San Francisco: Westview Press.

Cooper, J. (1972) *Taoism: the way of the mystic*,Wellingborough: Aquarian.

Corbin, H. ([1955,1956] 1997) *Alone with the Alone: creative imagination in the Sufism of Ibn 'Arabi*, Princeton: Princeton University Press.

Cranston, M. (1995) *The Romantic Movement*, Oxford: Blackwell.

Crapanzano, V. (1980) *Tuhami: portrait of a Moroccan*, Chicago: University of Chicago Press.

Crapanzano, V. and V. Garrison (eds) (1977) *Case Studies in Spirit Possession*, New York: John Wiley.

Crowley, A. ([1922] 1979) *Diary of a Drug Fiend*, London: Abacus.

Crowley, A. ([1976] 1991) *Magick in Theory and Practice*, Secaucus, N.J.: Castle. (Originally printed as *Magick by the Master*, Therion, Paris, 1929.)

Crowley, V. (1989) *Wicca: the old religion in the New Age*, London: Aquarian.

Crowley, V. (1993) 'Women and Power in Modern Paganism', in E. Puttick and P. Clarke (eds), *Women as Teachers and Disciples in Traditional and New Religions*, Lampeter: Edwin Mellin Press.

Crowley, V. (1998) 'Wicca as Nature Religion', in J. Pearson, R.H. Roberts and G. Samuel (eds) *Nature Religion Today: paganism in the modern world*, Edinburgh: Edinburgh University Press.

Bibliography

D'Alviella, G. (1981) *The Mysteries of Eleusis: the secret rites and rituals of the classical Greek Mystery tradition*, Wellingborough: Aquarian.

Daly, M. ([1973] 1986]) *Beyond God the Father*, London: Women's Press.

Darier, É. (ed.) (1999) *Discourses of the Environment*, Oxford: Blackwell.

Davidson, J. and R. Davidson (eds.) (1980) *The Psychobiology of Consciousness*, New York: Plenum Press.

Davis, E. (1999) *Techgnosis: myth, magic and mysticism in the age of information*, London: Serpent's Tail.

Deacon, R. (1976) *Matthew Hopkins: witch finder general*, London: Frederick Muller Ltd.

Deleuze, G. and F. Guattari (1988) *A Thousand Plateaus: Capitalism and Schizophrenia* (trans. B. Massumi), London: Athlone Press.

Deloria, P. (1998) *Playing Indian*, New Haven: Yale University Press.

Devall, B. (1995) 'The Ecological Self', in A. Drengson and Y. Inoue (eds), *The Deep Ecology Movement: an introductory anthology*, Berkeley, Calif.: North Atlantic Books.

Devereux, P. (2000) *The Illustrated Encyclopedia of Ancient Earth Mysteries*, London: Cassell and Co.

Devereux, P., J. Steele and D. Kubrin (1992) *Earthmind: communicating with the living world of Gaia*, Rochester, Vt.: Destiny Books.

Dodds, E.R. (1990) *Pagan and Christian in an Age of Anxiety*, Cambridge: Cambridge University Press.

Drengson, A. and Y. Inoue (eds) (1995) *The Deep Ecology Movement: an introductory anthology*, Berkeley, Calif.: North Atlantic Books.

Duerr, P.H. (1985) *Dreamtime: concerning the boundary between wilderness and civilization* (trans.by Felicitas Goodman), Oxford: Blackwell.

Dumont, L. (1985) 'A Modified View of Our Origins: the Christian beginnings of modern individualism', in M. Carrithers, S. Collins, and S. Lukes (eds), *The Category of the Person*, Cambridge: Cambridge University Press.

Edelman, G. (1992) *Bright Air, Brilliant Fire: on the matter of the mind*, London: Penguin.

Edgar, I. (1995) *Dreamwork, Anthropology and the Caring Professions: a cultural approach to dreamwork*, Aldershot: Avebury.

Edgar, I. (1999) 'The Imagework Method in Health and Social Science Research', *Qualitative Health Research*, 9 (2), March:198–211.

Eliade, M. ([1954] 1972) *The Myth of the Eternal Return: cosmos and history*, London: Arkana.

Eliade, M. ([1964] 1989) *Shamanism: archaic techniques of ecstasy*, London: Arkana.

Eliade, M. (1975) 'Some Observations on European Witchcraft', *History of Religions*, 14.

Eller, C. (2000a) 'The Roots of Feminist Spirituality', in Wendy Griffin (ed.), *Daughters of the Goddess*, Walnut Creek, Calif.: Altamira.

Eller, C. (2000b) *The Myth of Matriarchal Prehistory*, Boston: Beacon.

Ellingson, T. (2001) *The Myth of the Noble Savage*, Berkeley: University of California Press.

Ellis Davidson, H. (1964) *Gods and Myths of Northern Europe*, Harmondsworth: Penguin.

Evans, K. (1998) *Copse: the cartoon book of tree protesting*, Wiltshire: Orange Dog Productions.

Evans-Pritchard, E. ([1965] 1990) *Theories of Primitive Religion*, Oxford: Clarendon.

Evans-Pritchard, E. ([1937] 1985) *Witchcraft Oracles and Magic Among the Azande*, Oxford: Clarendon.

Evert Hopman, E. and L. Bond (1996) *People of the Earth: the new Pagans speak out*, Rochester, Vt.: Destiny Books.

Faivre, A. (1989a) 'Esotericism', in L. Sullivan (ed.), *Hidden Truths: magic, alchemy, and the occult*, L. Sullivan. New York: Macmillan.

Faivre, A. (1989b) 'Hermetism', in L. Sullivan (ed.), *Hidden Truths: magic, alchemy, and the occult*, New York: Macmillan.

Faivre, A. (1989c) 'Speculations About Nature', in L. Sullivan (ed.), *Hidden Truths: magic, alchemy, and the occult*, New York: Macmillan.

Faivre, A. (1989d) 'What is Occultism?', in L.E. Sullivan (ed.) *Hidden Truths: magic, alchemy, and the occult*, New York: Macmillan.

Faivre, A. (1994) *Access to Western Esotericism*, New York: State University of New York Press.

Farell-Roberts and Motherwort (1997) 'Protest at Lyminge Wood', *Pagan Dawn* No. 125 (Samhain), p.24.

Farrar, S. and J. Farrar (1991) *A Witches Bible Compleat*, New York: Magickal Childe Publishing.

Favret-Saada, J. (1980) *Deadly Words: witchcraft in the Bocage*, Cambridge: Cambridge University Press.

Ferguson, J. (1976) *An Illustrated Encyclopaedia of Mysticism and the Mystery Religions*, London: Thames and Hudson.

Ferguson, M. (1982) *The Aquarian Conspiracy: personal and social transformation in the 1980s*, London: Paladin.

Findhorn Community (1975) *The Findhorn Garden: pioneering a new vision of man and nature in cooperation*, New York: Harper and Row.

Flaherty, G. (1992) *Shamanism and the Eighteenth Century*, Princeton, N.J.: Princeton University Press.

Flint, V. (1993) *The Rise of Magic in Early Medieval Europe*, Oxford: Clarendon.

Fortune, D. ([1927] 1976) *The Cosmic Doctrine*, Wellinborough: Aquarian.

Fortune, D. ([1935] 1987) *The Mystical Qabalah*, London: Aquarian.

Fortune, D. (1987) *Applied Magic and Aspects of Occultism*, Wellingborough: Aquarian.

Fortune, D. (1988) *Psychic Self-Defence*, London: Aquarian.

Fortune, D. ([1959] 1989) *The Sea Priestess*,Wellingborough: Aquarian.

Fox, W. (1995) *Toward a Transpersonal Ecology: developing new foundations for Environmentalism*, Totnes: Green Books Ltd.

Fraser, A. (1999) *The Gypsies*, Oxford: Blackwell.

Frazer, J. ([1921] 1993): *The Golden Bough*, Ware, Herts.: Wordsworth.

Gadon, E. (1990) *The Once and Future Goddess*, Wellingborough: Aquarian.

Gage, M. ([1893] 1982) *Woman, Church and State: a historical account of the status of woman through the Christian ages*, New York: Arno Press.

Gardner, G. (1949) *High Magik's Aid*, London: Houghton.

Gardner, G. ([1954] 1988) *Witchcraft Today*, New York: Magickal Childe.

Garner, A. (1963) *The Moon of Gomrath*, London: Collins.

Geertz, C. (1973) *The Interpretation of Cultures*, New York: Basic Books.

Geertz, C. (2000) *Available Light: anthropological reflections on philosophical topics*, Princeton: Princeton University Press.

Gellner, E. ([1985] 1996) *The Psychoanalytic Movement: the cunning of unreason*, Evanstown, Ill.: Northwestern University Press.

Gerth H. and C. Wright Mills (eds) ([1948] 1970) *From Max Weber: essays in sociology*, London: Routledge and Kegan Paul.

Giddens, A. (1991) *Modernity and Self Identity*, Cambridge: Polity Press.

Gimbutas, M. (1982) *The Goddesses and Gods of Old Europe: myths and cultural images*, Berkeley: University of California Press.

Gimbutas, M. (1989) *The Language of the Goddess*, San Francisco: Harper and Row.

Ginzburg, C. (1992a) *Ecstasies: deciphering the witches' sabbath*, New York: Penguin.

Ginzburg, C. (1992b) *The Cheese and the Worms: the cosmos of a sixteenth-century miller*, London: Penguin.

Ginzburg, C. (1993) 'Deciphering the Sabbath', in B. Ankarloo and G. Henningsen (eds), *Early Modern European Witchcraft*, Oxford: Clarendon Press.

Glucklich, A. (1997) *The End of Magic*, New York: Oxford University Press.

Goodrick-Clarke, N. (1990) *Paracelsus: essential readings*, Wellingborough: Aquarian.

Goodrick-Clarke, N. (1992) *The Occult Roots of Nazism: secret Aryan cults and their influence on Nazi ideology*, London: I.B Tauris.

Gottlieb, R. (ed.) (1996) *This Sacred Earth: religion, nature, environment*, New York: Routledge.

Graves, R. ([1961] 1981) *The White Goddess: a historical grammar of poetic myth*, London: Faber and Faber.

Gray, W. (1989) *Between Good and Evil*, St Paul, Minn.: Llewellyn.

Gray, W. ([1975] 1992) 'Patterns of Western Magic: a psychological appreciation', in C. Tart (ed.), *Transpersonal Psychologies*, San Francisco: Harper.

Green, M. (1991) *A Witch Alone: thirteen moons to master natural magic*, London: Aquarian.

Greenwood, S. (1995) 'Feminist Witchcraft: a transformatory politics', in F. Hughes-Freeland and N. Charles (eds), *Practising Feminism: identity, difference and power*, London: Routledge.

Greenwood, S. (1996) 'The Magical Will, Gender and Power in Magical Practices', in G. Harvey and C. Hardman (eds), *Paganism Today*, London: Thorsons.

Greenwood, S. (1998) 'The Nature of the Goddess: sexual identities and power in contemporary witchcraft', in Joanne Pearson, Richard Roberts and Geoffrey Samuel (eds), *Nature Religion Today: paganism in the modern world*, Edinburgh: Edinburgh University Press.

Greenwood, S. (2000) *Magic, Witchcraft and the Otherworld*, Oxford: Berg.

Greenwood, S. (2001) *The Encyclopedia of Magic and Witchcraft: an illustrated historical reference to spiritual worlds*, London: Lorenz Books.

Greenwood, S. (2003) 'British Paganism, Morality, and the Politics of Knowledge', in Pat Caplan (ed.), *Anthropology and Ethics*, London: Routledge.

Griffin, S. ([1978] 1984) *Woman and Nature: the roaring inside her*, London: Women's Press.

Griffiths, J. (1998) 'Foreword' to *Copse: the cartoon book of tree protesting*, Kate Evans, Wiltshire: Orange Dog Productions.

Grof, S. (1993) *The Holotropic Mind: the three levels of human consciousness and how they shape our lives*, New York: HarperCollins.

Hanegraaff, W. (1998) 'Reflections on New Age and the Secularization of Nature' in Joanne Pearson, Richard Roberts and Geoffrey Samuel (eds), *Nature Religion Today*, Edinburgh: Edinburgh University Press.

Happold, F.C. (1979) *Mysticism: a study and an anthology*, Harmondsworth: Penguin.

Haraway, D. (1990) 'A Manifesto for Cyborgs: science, technology, and socialist feminism in the 1980s', in L. Nicholson (ed.), *Feminism/Postmodernism*, New York: Routledge.

Haraway, D. (2000) *How Like a Leaf: an interview with Thyrza Nichols Goodeve*, New York: Routledge.

Harner, Michael ([1980] 1990) *The Way of the Shaman*, San Francisco: Harper.

Harris, A. (1996) 'Sacred Ecology', in Graham Harvey and Charlotte Hardman (eds), *Paganism Today*, London: Thorsons.

Harvey, D. (1991) *The Condition of Postmodernity*, Oxford: Blackwell.

Harvey, G. (1993) 'Avalon from the Mists: the contemporary teaching of Goddess Spirituality', *Religion Today*, 8(2):10–13.

Harvey, G. (1994) 'The Roots of Pagan Ecology', *Religion Today*, 9(3).

Harvey, G. (1997) *Listening People, Speaking Earth*, London: Hurst and Co.

Harvey, G. (2000) 'Fantasy in the Study of Religions: paganism as observed and enhanced by Terry Pratchett', DISKUS, Vol. 6. http://www.uni-marburg.de/religionswissenschaft/journal/diskus

Harvey, G. (ed.) (2003) *Shamanism: a reader*, London: Routledge.

Hawken, P. (1976) *The Magic of Findhorn*, Glasgow: Fontana.

Heaven, R. (2002) *Spirit in the City: the search for the sacred in everyday life*, London: Hambledon and London.

Hedley Brooke, J. (1991) *Science and Religion: some historical perspectives*, Cambridge: Cambridge University Press.

Heelas, P. (1996) *The New Age Movement: the celebration of the self and the sacralization of modernity*, Oxford: Blackwell.

Heims, S.P. (1977) 'Gregory Bateson and the Mathematicians: from Interdisciplinary Interaction to Societal Functions'. *Journal of the History of the Behavioral Sciences* 13, p.150.

Herzfeld, M. (1991) *A Place in History: social and monumental time in a Cretan town*, Oxford: Princeton University Press.

Higton, T. (1990) 'The Environment as Religion', in Michael Cole, Tony Higton, Jim Graham and David C. Lewis (eds), *What is the New Age?*, London: Hodder and Stoughton.

Hine, P. (1992) *Condensed Chaos*, London: Phoenix Publications.

Hine, P. (1994) *The Pseudonomicon*, Irvine, Calif.: Dagon Productions.

Hine, P. (1999) 'Magic in the Great Outdoors', in *The Right Times: exploring and experiencing ancient sites in the 21st Century*, July–September edition.

Hobsbawn, E. and T. Ranger (eds) (1983) *The Invention of Tradition*, Cambridge: Cambridge University Press.

Hooykaas, R. (1977) *Religion and the Rise of Modern Science*, Edinburgh: Scottish Academic Press.

Hopman, E.E. and L. Bond (eds) (1996) *People of the Earth: the new pagans speak out*, Rochester, Vt.: Destiny Books.

Hultkrantz Å (1982) 'Introduction: the culture of the hunters – man's oldest culture', in Å. Hultkrantz and Ø. Vorrens (eds) *The Hunters: their culture and way of life*, Tromsø Museum Skrifter Vol. xviii. Tromsø: Universitetsforlaget.

Hultkrantz, Å. and Ø. Vorrens (eds) (1982) *The Hunters: their culture and way of life*, Tromsø Museum Skrifter (Vol. xviii), Tromsø: Universitetsforlaget.

Hume, L. (1997) *Witchcraft and Paganism in Australia*, Melbourne: Melbourne University Press.

Hume, L. (1998) 'Creating Sacred Space: outer expression of inner worlds in modern Wicca', *Journal of Contemporary Religion*, 13(3):309–319.

Humphrey, C. (with Urgunge Onon) (1996) *Shamans and Elders*, Oxford: Clarendon.

Hutton, R. (1991) *The Pagan Religions of the Ancient British Isles*, London: BCA.

Hutton, R. (1993) *The Shamans of Siberia*, Glastonbury: Isle of Avalon Press.

Hutton, R. (1994) 'Neo-Paganism, Paganism and Christianity', *Religion Today*, 9(3): 29–32.

Hutton, R. (1996) 'Who Possesses the Past?', in Philip Carr-Gomm (ed.), *The Druid Renaissance*, London: Thorsons.

Hutton, R. (1998) 'The Discovery of the Modern Goddess', in Joanne Pearson, Richard Roberts and Geoffrey Samuel (eds), *Nature Religion Today*, Edinburgh: Edinburgh University Press.

Hutton, R. (1999) *The Triumph of the Moon*, Oxford: Oxford University Press.

Hutton, R. (2001) *Shamans: Siberian spirituality and the Western imagination*, London: Hambledon and London.

Huxley, F. (1979) *The Dragon: nature of spirit, spirit of nature*, London: Thames and Hudson.

Ingold, T. (2000) *The Perception of the Environment: essays in livelihood, dwelling and skill*, London: Routledge.

Ingold, T. (2001) 'From the Transmission of Representations to the Education of Attention', in Harvey Whitehouse (ed.), *The Debated Mind*, Oxford: Berg.

Ivakhiv, A. (2001) *Claiming Sacred Ground: pilgrims and politics at Glastonbury and Sedona*, Bloomington, Ind.: Indiana University Press.

Jacobi, J. ([1964] 1978) 'Symbols in an Individual Analysis', in C. Jung and M.-L. von Franz (eds), *Man and his Symbols*, London: Picador.

James, W. ([1890] 1950) *The Principles of Psychology*, New York: Dover Publications.

James, W. ([1892] 1961) *Psychology*, London: Harper and Row.

James, W. ([1902] 1977) *The Varieties of Religious Experience: a study in human nature*, Glasgow: Collins.

Johnson, C. (2000) 'Putting Different Things Together: the development of metaphysical thinking', in K. Rosengren, C. Johnson and P. Harris (eds), *Imagining the Impossible: magical, scientific, and religious thinking in children*, Cambridge: Cambridge University Press.

Johnson, P. (2003) 'Shamanism from Ecuador to Chicago: a case study in New Age ritual appropriation', in Graham Harvey (ed.), *Shamanism: a reader*, London: Routledge.

Jones, A. (1996) *Larousse Dictionary of Folklore*, Edinburgh: Larousse.

Jones, P. and N. Pennick (1995) *A History of Pagan Europe*, London: Routledge.

Jordan, G. and C. Weedon (1995) *Cultural Politics: Class, Gender, Race in the Postmodern World*, Oxford: Blackwell.

Judge, W. ([1893] 1969) *The Ocean of Theosophy*, Bombay: Theosophy Company India.

Jung, C. ([1953] 1993) *Psychology and Alchemy*, London: Routledge.

Kaldera, R. and T. Schwartzstein (2002) *The Urban Primitive: paganism in the concrete jungle*, St Paul, Minn.: Llewellyn.

Kalweit, H. (1992) *Shamans, Healers, and Medicine Men*, Boston, Mass.: Shambala Publications.

Kapferer, B. ([1983] 1991) *A Celebration of Demons*, Oxford: Berg.

Kapferer, B. (1988) *Legends of People, Myths of State*, Washington: Smithsonian.

Kapferer, B. (1997) *The Feast of the Sorcerer: practices of consciousness and power*, Chicago: Chicago University Press.

Katz, R. (1982) *Boiling Energy: community healing among the Kalahari Kung*, Cambridge, Mass.: Harvard University Press.

Katz, R. ([1983] 1999) *The Straight Path of the Spirit: ancestral wisdom and healing traditions in Fiji*, Rochester, Vt.: Park Street Press.

Kelly, A. (1991) *Crafting the Art of Magic*, Book 1: A History of Modern Witchcraft, 1939–1964, St Paul, Minn.: Llewellyn Publications.

Kendall, L. (1988) *The Life and Hard Times of a Korean Shaman*, Honolulu: University of Hawaii Press.

Kenton, L. (1999) *Journey to Freedom: 13 quantum leaps for the soul*, London: Thorsons.

Kieckhefer, R. (1993) *Magic in the Middle Ages*, Cambridge: Cambridge University Press.

King, F. ([1970] 1990) *Modern Ritual Magic: the rise of Western occultism*, Bridport, Dorset: Prism.

King, F. (1975) *Magic: The Western Tradition*, London: Thames and Hudson.

Kitto, H.D.F. ([1951] 1968) *The Greeks*, Harmondsworth: Penguin.

Klaniczay, G. (1990) *The Uses of Supernatural Power: the transformation of popular religion in medieval and early-modern Europe*, Cambridge: Polity Press.

Knight, G. (1978) *A History of White Magic*, Oxford: Mowbrays.

Koerner, J.L. (1990) *Casper David Friedrich and the Subject of Landscape*, London: Reaktion Books.

Krech III, S. (1999) *The Ecological Indian: myth and history*, New York: W.W. Norton and Co.

Kuhn, T. ([1957] 1974) *The Copernican Revolution: planetary astronomy in the development of Western thought*, Cambridge, Mass.: Harvard University Press.

LaChapelle, D. (1995) 'Ritual is Essential', in A. Drengson and Y. Inoue (eds), *The Deep Ecology Movement: an introductory anthology*, Berkeley, Calif.: North Atlantic Books.

Lakoff, G. and M. Johnson (1980) *The Metaphors We Live By*, Chicago: University of Chicago Press.

Larner, C. (1981) *Enemies of God*, Oxford: Blackwell.

Larner, C. (1984) *Witchcraft and Religion*, Oxford: Blackwell.

Laughlin, C. (1994) 'Psychic Energy and Transpersonal Experience: a biogenetic structural account of the Tibetan Dumo yoga practice', in D. Young, J.G.Goulet (eds), *Being Changed*, Ontario: Broadview Press.

Leadbeater, C. (1987) *The Inner Life*, Wheaton, Ill.: Theosophical Publishing House.

Lee, J. (1999a) *Patrin*, (No. 1) Spring.

Lee, J. (1999b) *Shaman's Drum*.

Lee, P.(2000) *We Borrow the Earth: an intimate portrait of the gypsy shamanic tradition and culture*, London: Thorsons.

Leff, G. ([1967] 1999) *Heresy in the Later Middle Ages*, Manchester: Manchester University Press.

Leland, C.G. ([1891] 1995) *Gypsy Sorcery and Fortune Telling*, Edison, N. J.: Castle Books.

Leland, C.G. (1899) *Aradia, or the Gospel of the Witches*, London.

Leland, S. and L. Caldecott (eds) (1983) *Reclaim the Earth*, London: Women's Press.

Letcher, A. (2000) 'Virtual Paganism or Direct Action? The implications of road-protesting for modern paganism', *Diskus 6*, http://www.uni-marburg.de/religionswissenschaft/journal/diskus/letcher.html

Lévi, E. ([1913] 1982) *The History of Magic*, London: Rider.

Lévi-Strauss, C. ([1962] 1968) *The Savage Mind*, London: Weidenfeld and Nicolson.

Lévi-Strauss, C. (1979) 'The Effectiveness of Symbols', in W. Lessa and E. Vogt (eds), *Reader in Comparative Religion: an anthropological approach*, (4th edn), New York: Harper and Row.

Lévy-Bruhl, L. ([1910] 1966) *How Natives Think*, (trans.) by Lillian Clare. (Originally published as *Les Fonctions mentales dans les sociétiés inférieures*.), New York: Washington Square Press.

Lévy-Bruhl, L. (1975) *The Notebooks on Primitive Mentality*, Oxford: Blackwell.

Lewis, I. ([1971] 1989) *Ecstatic Religion*, London: Routledge.

Lewis, I. ([1986] 1996) *Religion in Context: cults and charisma*, Cambridge: Cambridge University Press.

Lienhardt, G. (1961) *Divinity and Experience*, Oxford: Oxford University Press.

Lindquist, G. (1997) *Shamanic Performances on the Urban Scene: neo-shamanism in contemporary Sweden*, Stockholm: Gotab.

Lipset, D. (1982) *Gregory Bateson: the legacy of a scientist*, Boston: Beacon Press.

Lock, H. (1981) *Indigenous Psychologies*, London: Academic Press.

Long, A. (1992) *In a Chariot Drawn by Lions: the search for the female in deity*, London: Women's Press.

Lonsdale, S. (1981) *Animals and the Origins of Dance*, London: Thames and Hudson.

Lovecraft, H. ([1951] 1974) *The Haunter of the Dark and Other Tales*, St Albans: Granada.

Lovelock, J. (1990) *The Ages of Gaia: a biography of our living earth*, Oxford: Oxford University Press.

Lovelock, J. ([1979] 1995) *Gaia: a new look at life on earth*, Oxford: Oxford University Press.

Luck, G. (1989) 'Theurgy and Forms of Worship in Neoplatonism', J. Neusner, E. Frerichs and P.V. McCracken Flesher (eds), *Religion, Science and Magic*, New York: Open University Press.

Luhrmann, T. (1989) *Persuasions of the Witch's Craft*, Oxford: Basil Blackwell.

MacCannell, D. (1992) *Empty Meeting Grounds: the tourist papers*, New York: Routledge.

MacCormack, C. and M. Strathern, (eds) ([1980] 1990) *Nature Culture and Gender*, Cambridge: Cambridge University Press.

MacEowen, F. (2001) 'Reclaiming Our Ancestral Bones: re-vitalizing shamanic practices in the new millennium', in *Shaman's Drum*, No. 58.

MacEwen Owen, F. (1996) 'Nemeton – healing the common wound and the re-enchantment of everyday life', in P. Carr-Gomm (ed.) *The Druid Renaissance*, London: Thorsons.

Macfarlane, A. (1970) *Witchcraft in Tudor and Stuart England*, Cambridge: Cambridge University Press.

MacLean, D. (1968) 'The Deva Consciousness'; 'The Messages', The Findhorn Community (eds) *The Findhorn Garden: pioneering a new vision of man and nature in cooperation*, New York: Harper and Row.

MacLellan, G. (1996) 'Dancing on the Edge: shamanism in modern Britain', in G. Harvey and C. Hardman (eds) *Paganism Today*, London: Thorsons.

MacLellan, G. (1999) *Shamanism*, London: Piatkus.

MacLellan, G. (2001) 'Dancing Between Worlds', in Alison Leonard (ed.), *Living in Godless Times: tales of spiritual travellers*, Edinburgh: Floris Books.

MacLellan, G. (n.d.a) *Talking to the Earth*, Chieveley, Berks.: Capall Bann.

MacLellan, G. (n.d.b): www.phhine.ndirect.co.uk

Malinowski, B. ([1948] 1954) *Magic, Science, and Religion and Other Essays*, New York: Doubleday Anchor Books.

Malinowski, B. ([1935] 1978) *Coral Gardens and Their Magic*, New York: Dover Publications.

Markham, I. (1997) *A World Religions Reader*, Oxford: Blackwell.

Marshall, P. (1995) *Nature's Web: rethinking our place on earth*, London: Cassell.

Matthews, C. (1997) *The Elements of the Goddess*, Shaftesbury, Element.

Matthews, C. and J. Matthews (1985) *The Western Way*, London: Arkana.

Matthews, J. (1993) *Robin Hood: green lord of the wildwood*, Glastonbury, Somerset: Gothic Images Publications.

Matthews, J. and C. Potter (1990) *The Aquarian Guide to Legendary London*, Wellingborough: Aquarian Press.

Mauss, M. ([1950 1972) *A General Theory of Magic*, (trans. by Robert Brain) London: Routledge and Kegan Paul.

McCormick, J. (1989) *The Global Environment Movement*, London: Belhaven Press.

McLaughlin, A. (1995) 'For a Radical Ecocentrism', in A. Drengson and Y. Inoue (eds), *The Deep Ecology Movement: an introductory anthology*, Berkeley, Calif.: North Atlantic Books.

Mead, M ([1930] 1965) *Growing Up in New Guinea*, Harmondsworth,: Penguin.

Meggit, M.J. (1962) *Desert People: a study of the Walbiri Aborigines of Central Australia*, Sydney: Angus and Robertson.

Melton, J.G. (1978) *The Encyclopedia of American Religions*, Wilmington, N.C.: McGrath.

Melton, J.G. (1986) 'New Age Movement', in *Encyclopaedic Handbook of Cults in America*, New York: Garland.

Melton, J.G. (1993) 'Another Look at New Religions', *Annals, AAPSS*, 527: 97–112.

Mendoza, R. (1995) *The Acentric Labyrinth: Giordano Bruno's prelude to contemporary cosmology*, Shaftesbury, Dorset: Element.

Merchant, C. ([1980] 1990) *The Death of Nature: women, ecology and the scientific revolution*, San Francisco: Harper and Row.

Merculieff, I. (1996) 'Western Society's Linear Systems and Aboriginal Cultures: the need for two-way exchanges for the sake of survival', in E. Burch and L. Ellanna (eds) *Key Issues in Hunter-Gatherer Research*, Oxford: Berg.

Merlan, P. (1991) Entry on 'Plotinus', in J.O. Urmson and J. Rée (eds) *The Concise Encyclopedia of Western Philosophy and Philosophers*, London: Routledge.

Merrick (1997) *Battle for the Trees: three months of responsible ancestry*, London: Book Factory.

Michelet, J. (1862) *La Sorcière*, Paris.

Michell, J. (1982) *Megalithomania: artists, antiquarians and archaeologists at the old stone monuments*, London: Thames and Hudson.

Middleton, J. ([1970] 1972) *The Lugbara of Uganda*, New York: Holt, Rinehart and Winston.

Miller, H. and P. Broadhurst (1998) *The Sun and the Serpent: an investigation into earth energies*, Launceston: Pendragon Press.

Miller, J. (1985) *The Vision of the Cosmic Order in the Vedas*, London: Routledge and Kegan Paul.

Monbiot, G. (1998) 'Foreword' to *Copse: the cartoon book of tree protesting*, Kate Evans, Wiltshire: Orange Dog Productions.

Morris, B. (1966) 'Hunting and the Gnostic Vision', *Journal of Human and Environmental Sciences*, 1 (2): 13–39.

Morris, B. (1976) 'The Unknown Ecologist', *The Ecologist*, 6: 262–264.

Morris, B. (1987) *Anthropological Studies of Religion*, Cambridge: Cambridge University Press.

Morris, B. (1991) *Western Conceptions of the Individual*, Oxford: Berg.

Morris, B. (1992) 'The Social Ecology of Murray Bookchin', in B. Morris, *Ecology and Anarchism: essays and reviews on contemporary thought*, Malvern Wells, Worcestershire: Images Publishing.

Morris, B. (1993) 'Paracelsus: magus and medic?', *The Rosicrucian Beacon* (Winter): 32–4.

Morris, B. (1994a) 'Matriliny and Mother Goddess Religion', *The Raven Anarchist Quarterly*, 25.

Morris, B. (1994b) *Anthropology of the Self: the individual in cultural perspective*, London: Pluto Press.

Morris, B. (1996) *Ecology and Anarchism: essays and reviews on contemporary thought*, Malvern Wells: Images Publishing.

Morris, B. (1999) 'Context and Interpretation: reflections on Nyau rituals in Malawi', in R. Dilley (ed.) *The Problem of Context*, Oxford: Berghahn.

Morris, B. (2000) *Animals and Ancestors: an ethnography*, Oxford: Berg.

Moses, J. (1995) Foreword to Michelle Jamal, *Deerdancer: the shapeshifter archetype in story and trance*, New York: Arkana.

Mosse, G. (1964) *The Crisis of German Ideology: Intellectual Origins of the Third Reich*, New York: Grosset and Dunlop.

Moura, A. (1999) *Green Witchcraft II: balancing light and shadow*, St Paul, Minn.: Llewellyn.

Moura, A. (1999) *Green Witchcraft: folk magic, fairy lore and herbcraft*, St Paul, Minn.: Llewellyn.

Murray, M. (1921) *The Witchcult in Western Europe: a study in anthropology*, Oxford: Clarendon Press.

Murray, M. ([1931] 1970) *The God of the Witches*, Oxford: Oxford University Press.

Myters, R.R. (1986) *Pintupi Country, Pintupi Self: sentiment, place and politics among Western Desert Aborigines*, Washington: Smithsonian Institution Press.

Naess, A. (1995) 'The Shallow and the Deep, Long-Range Ecology Movement: a summary,' in A. Drengson and Y. Inoue (eds), *The Deep Ecology Movement: an introductory anthology*, Berkeley, Calif.: North Atlantic Books.

Narby, J. and F. Huxley (2001) *Shamans Through Time: 500 years on the path to knowledge*, London: Thames and Hudson.

Nemeroff, C. and P. Rozin (2000) 'The Makings of the Magical Mind: the nature and function of sympathetic magical thinking', in K. Rosengren, C. Johnson, and P. Harris (eds), *Imagining the Impossible: magical, scientific, and religious thinking in children*, Cambridge: Cambridge University Press.

Nettle, D. (2001) *Strong Imagination: madness, creativity and human nature*, Oxford: Oxford University Press.

Newell, M. (1999) *Black Shuck: The Ghost Dog of Eastern England*, Hadleigh, Suffolk: Jardine Press.

Nichols, R. ([1975] 1992) *The Book of Druidry*, London: Thorsons.

Nightmare, M. (2001) *Witchcraft and the Web: weaving Pagan traditions on line*, Toronto, Ontario: ECW Press.

Noel, D. (1997) *The Soul of Shamanism: Western fantasies, imaginal realities*, New York: Continuum.

Noll, R. (1985) 'Mental Imagery Cultivation as a Cultural Phenomenon: the role of visions in shamanism', *Current Anthropology*, 26 (4).

Noll, R. (1996) *The Jung Cult: the origins of a charismatic movement*, London: Fontana.

Oldfield Howey, M. (1958) *The Horse in Magic and Myth*, New York: Castle Books.

Ortner, S.B.(1974) 'Is Female to Male as Nature is to Culture?', in M.Z. Rosaldo and L. Lamphere (eds) *Woman, Culture, and Society*, Stanford, Calif.: Stanford University Press.

Owen, A. (1989) *The Darkened Room: women, power and spiritualism in late Victorian England*, London: Virago.

Paxson, D. (1992) *The Jewel of Fire*, London: Hodder and Stoughton.

Pearson, J., R. Roberts and G. Samuel (1998) *Nature Religion Today: paganism in the modern world*, Edinburgh: Edinburgh University Press.

Penczak, C. (2001) *City Magick: urban rituals, spells, and shamanism*, York Beach, Me.: Weiser.

Pengelly, J., R. Hall and J. Dowse (1997) *We Emerge... The Origins and History of the Pagan Federation Including Excerpts from The Wiccan 1968–1981*, London: The Pagan Federation.

Pennick, N. (1995) *Secrets of East Anglian Magic*, London: Robert Hale.

Pennick, N. (1998) *Crossing the Borderlines: guising, masking and ritual animal disguises in the European tradition*, Chieveley, Berks.: Capall Bann.

Pinkola Estés, C. (1995) *Women Who Run With the Wolves: contacting the power of the wild woman*, London: Rider.

Plows, A. (2001) 'Earth Magics', *Dragon Environmental Network Publication*, Summer Solstice, Issue 01.

Plumwood, V. (1993) *Feminism and the Mastery of Nature*, London: Routledge.

Pois, R. (1986) *National Socialism and the Religion of Nature*, London: Croom Helm.

Porter, E. (1974) *The Folklore of East Anglia*, Totowa, New Jersey: Rowman and Littlefield.

Porter, R. (2001) *Enlightenment: Britain and the creation of the modern world*, London: Penguin.

Price, N. (ed.) (2001) *The Archaeology of Shamanism*, London: Routledge.

Raban, J. (1974) *Soft City*, London: Hamish Hamilton.

Raine, K. (1991) *Golgonooza City of Imagination: last studies in William Blake*, Ipswich: Golgonooza.

Raine, K. ([1970] 1999) *William Blake*, London: Thames and Hudson.

Ransom, J. (1938) *A Short History of the Theosophical Society 1875–1937*, Madras: Theosophical Publishing House.

Raphael, M. (1999) *Introducing Thealogy*, Sheffield: Sheffield Academic Press.

Rappaport, R. (1979) *Ecology, Meaning, and Religion*, Berkeley, Calif.: North Atlantic Books.

Rapport, N. and J. Overing (2000) *Social and Cultural Anthropology: the key concepts*, London: Routledge.

Raudvere, C. (2002) 'Trolldómr Rituals: practice and performance', in B. Ankarloo and S. Clark (eds), *Witchcraft and Magic in Europe*: Volume 3, *The Middle Ages*, London: Athlone Press.

Redfield, J. (1994) *The Celestine Prophecy: an adventure*, London: Bantam.

Renfrew, C. (1973) *Before Civilization: the radiocarbon revolution and prehistoric Europe*, London: Jonathan Cape.

Restall Orr, E. (1999) 'The Path of Inspiration', *Kindred Spirit*, No. 48 (Autumn).

Richardson, A. (1987) *Priestess: the life and magic of Dion Fortune*, Wellingborough: Aquarian.

Richardson, A. (2001) *Spirits of the Stones: visions of sacred Britain*, London: Virgin Publishing.

Rohde, E. (1992) 'Hekate's Horde: Parts 1 and 2', in S. Ronan (ed.) *The Goddess Hekate: studies in ancient pagan and Christian religion and philosophy*, Vol. 1, Hastings, Sussex: Chthonios Books.

Rohrlich, R. (1990) 'Prehistoric Puzzles', in *The Women's Review of Books*. VII (9).

Ronan, S. (1992) *The Goddess Hekate: studies in ancient pagan and Christian religion and philosophy*, Vol. 1, Hastings, Sussex: Chthonios Books.

Rosaldo, M.Z. and L. Lamphere (eds) (1974) *Woman, Culture, and Society*, Stanford, Calif.: Stanford University Press.

Rose, E. (1962) *A Razor for a Goat: a discussion of certain problems in the history of witchcraft and diabolism*, Toronto: University of Toronto Press.

Rosengren, K., C. Johnson and P. Harris (eds) (2000) *Imagining the Impossible: magical, scientific, and religious thinking in children*, Cambridge: Cambridge University Press.

Russell, B. (1946) *History of Western Philosophy*, London: Allen and Unwin.

Rutherford, L. (1996) *Shamanism*, London: HarperCollins.

Sabini, M. (ed.) (2002) *The Earth Has a Soul: the nature writings of C.G. Jung*, Berkeley, Calif.: North Atlantic Books.

Saler, B. (2003) 'Lévy-Bruhl, Participation, and Rationality', in Jeppe Sinding Jensen and Luther H. Martin (eds) *Rationality and the Study of Religion*, London: Routledge.

Salomonsen, J. (1996) '"I am a Witch – a Healer and a Bender": an expression of women's religiosity in contemporary USA', Unpublished Ph.D. thesis, University of Oslo.

Salomonsen, J. (2002) *Enchanted Feminism: the reclaiming witches of San Francisco*, New York: Routledge.

Samuel, G. (1990) *Mind, Body and Culture: anthropology and the biological interface*, Cambridge: Cambridge University Press.

Samuel, G. (1993) *Civilized Shamans: Buddhism in Tibetan societies*, Washington: Smithsonian Institution Press.

Samuel, G. (2004) 'Mind, Body and Culture Revisited 1: Rethinking the shaman', Leverhulme Lecture No.1, School of Oriental and African Studies, London. 8 March.

Sanders, A. (1984) *The Alex Sanders Lectures*, New York: Magickal Childe.

Schama, S. (1996) *Landscape and Memory*, London: Fontana.

Scholte, B. (1984) 'Comment on Paul Shankman's "The thick and the thin: on the interpretive theoretical program of Clifford Geertz"', *Current Anthropology*, 25: 540–542.

Schuman, M. (1980) 'The Psychophysiological Model of Meditation and Altered States of Consciousness', in J. Davidson and R. Davidson, (eds), *The Psychobiology of Consciousness*, New York: Plenum Press.

Seed, J., J. Macy, P. Fleming and A. Naess (1988) *Thinking Like a Mountain: towards a council of all beings*, London: Heretic Books.

Shallcrass, P. (1996) 'Druidry Today', in Graham Harvey and Charlotte Hardman (eds), *Paganism Today*, London: Thorsons.

Sheldrake, R. (1990) *The Rebirth of Nature: the greening of science and God*, London: Rider.

Sheridan, J. (1998) 'When First Unto the Country, a Stranger I Came: land, mammals and the rediscovery of place', in M. Griffith and J. Tulip (eds), *Spirit of Place: source of the sacred?*, Australian International Religion, Literature and Arts Conference Proceedings. Sydney: Berget, Sidgwick and Jackson.

Sikes, W. ([1880] 1973) *British Goblins: Welsh Folklore, Fairy Mythology, Legends and Traditions*, Yorkshire, E.P. Publishing.

Simmons, I.G. (1993) *Interpreting Nature: cultural constructions of the environment*, London: Routledge.

Sjöö, M. (1992) *New Age and Armageddon: the goddesses or the gurus? Towards a feminist vision of the future*, London: The Women's Press.

Smart, N. (2000) *World Philosophies*, London: Routledge.

Smith, J. (1978) 'The Wobbling Pivot', in *Map is Not Territory: studies in the history of religions*, Leiden: E.J. Brill.

Smith, K.F. (1992) 'Hekate's Suppers', in S. Ronan (ed.) *The Goddess Hekate: studies in ancient pagan and Christian religion and philosophy*, Vol. 1, Hastings, Sussex: Chthonios Books.

Solomon, R. and K. Higgins (1996) *A Short History of Philosophy*, New York: Oxford University Press.

Spangler, D. (1984) *The Rebirth of the Sacred*, London: Gateway Books.

Squire, C. (1912) *Celtic Myth and Legend*, London: Gresham Publishing Co.

Starhawk ([1979] 1989) *The Spiral Dance*, San Francisco: Harper and Row.

Starhawk (1982) *Dreaming the Dark: magic, sex and politics*, Boston: Beacon.

Starhawk (1990) *Truth or Dare: encounters with power, authority, and mystery*, San Francisco: Harper and Row.

Starhawk and Hilary Valentine (2000) *The Twelve Wild Swans: a journey to the realm of magic, healing and action*, New York: HarperCollins.

Stevens, A. ([1990] 1991) *On Jung*, London: Penguin.

Stewart, M. (1997) *The Time of the Gypsies*, Boulder, Colo.: Westview Press.

Strang, V. (1997) *Uncommon Ground: cultural landscapes and environmental values*, Oxford: Berg.

Sun Bear, Wabun Wind and Crysalis Mulligan (1992) *Dancing with the Wheel: the medicine wheel workbook*, New York: Simon and Schuster.

Sutcliffe, S (1998) 'Between Apocalypse and Self-realisation: "nature" as an index of New Age religiosity', in J. Pearson, R.H. Roberts and G. Samuel (eds) *Nature Religion Today: paganism in the modern world*, Edinburgh: Edinburgh University Press.

Sutcliffe, S. (2000) 'Wandering Stars: seekers and gurus in the modern world', in S. Sutcliffe and M. Bowman, *Beyond New Age: exploring alternative spirituality*, Edinburgh: Edinburgh University Press.

Tambiah, S. (1979) 'The Form and Meaning of Magical Acts: a point of view', in Willam Lessa and Evon Vogt (eds), *Reader in Comparative Religion*, New York: Harper and Row.

Tambiah, S. ([1970] 1985) *Buddhism and the Spirit Cults in North-East Thailand*, Cambridge: Cambridge University Press.

Tambiah, S. (1991) *Magic, Science, Religion, and the Scope of Rationality*, Cambridge: Cambridge University Press.

Tanner, A. (1979) *Bringing Home Animals: religious ideology and modes of production of the Mistassiri Cree hunters*, New York: St Martin's Press/ London: Hurst.

Tart, C. (1969) *Altered States of Consciousness*, New York: Wiley.

Tart, C. (1980) 'A Systems Approach to Altered States of Consciousness', in J. Davidson and R. Davidson, (eds), *The Psychobiology of Consciousness*, New York: Plenum Press.

Tart, C. ([1975] 1992) *Transpersonal Psychologies*, San Francisco: Harper.

Taussig, M. ([1986] 1991) *Shamanism, Colonialism, and the Wild Man*, Chicago: University of Chicago Press.

Taylor, C. (1989) *Sources of the Self*, Cambridge: Cambridge University Press.

Thomas, K. (1984) *Man and the Natural World: changing attitudes in England 1500–1800*, London: Penguin.

Thompson, E.P. (1994) *Witness Against the Beast: William Blake and the moral law*, Cambridge: Cambridge University Press.

Thorsson, Ö. (ed.) (1997) *The Sagas of the Icelanders: a selection*, London: Penguin.

Tompkins, P. (1997) *The Secret Life of Nature: living in harmony with the hidden world of nature spirits, from fairies to quarks*, London: Thorsons.

Tompkins, P. and C. Bird (1975) *The Secret Life of Plants*, Harmondsworth: Penguin.

Trimble, S. (1988) *Words from the Land: encounters with natural history writing*, Salt Lake City: Peregrine Smith Books.

Turner, E. (with William Blodgett, Singleton Kahona and Fideli Benwa) (1992) *Experiencing Ritual: a new interpretation of African healing*, Philadelphia: University of Philadelphia Press.

Turner, V. ([1967]1972) *The Forest of Symbols: aspects of Ndembu ritual*, London: Cornell University Press.

Turner, V. (1974) *Dramas, Fields and Metaphors*, London: Cornell University Press.

Bibliography

Turner, V. ([1974] 1975) *The Ritual Process: structure and anti-structure*, Harmondsworth: Penguin.

Turner, V. (1975) *Revelation and Divination in Ndembu Ritual*, London: Cornell University Press.

Tylor, E. (1873) *Primitive Culture*, London: John Murray.

Ucko, P. (1990) Foreword to P. Gathercole and D. Lowenthal (eds), in *The Politics of the Past*, London: Unwin Hyman.

Urmson. J. and J. Rée (1991) *The Concise Encyclopedia of Western Philosophy and Philosophers*, London: Routledge.

Valiente, D. (1962) *Where Witchcraft Lives*, London: Aquarian.

Valiente, D. (1978) *Witchcraft for Tomorrow*, Washington: Phoenix.

Valiente, D. ([1973] 1986) *An ABC of Witchcraft: past and present*, London: Hale.

Valiente, D. and E. Jones (1990) *Witchcraft: a tradition renewed*, Washington, Phoenix Publishing.

Van Gennep, A. ([1908] 1961) *Rites of Passage*, Chicago: University of Chicago Press.

Vitebsky, P. (1993) *Dialogues with the Dead: the discussion of mortality among the Sora of Eastern India*, Cambridge: Cambridge University Press.

Vitebsky, P. (1995) *The Shaman*, London: Macmillan.

Vitebsky, P. (2003) 'From Cosmology to Environmentalism: shamanism as local knowledge in a global setting', in Graham Harvey (ed.), *Shamanism: a reader*, Graham Harvey (ed). London: Routledge.

Vizenor, G. (ed.) (1995) *Native American Literature: a brief introduction and anthology*, Berkeley, Calif.: HarperCollins.

Von Franz, M.-L. ([1964] 1978) 'The Process of Individuation', in C. Jung and M.-L. von Franz (eds), *Man and his Symbols*, London: Picador.

Walker, B. (1983) *The Woman's Encyclopedia of Myths and Secrets*, San Francisco: Harper and Row.

Wallis, R. (2001) 'Waking Ancestor Spirits: neo-shamanic engagements with archaeology' in Neil Price (ed.), *The Archaeology of Shamanism*, London: Routledge.

Wallis, R. (2003) *Shamans/Neo-Shamans: ecstatsy, alternative archaeologies and contemporary Pagans*, London: Routledge.

Walsh (1990) *The Spirit of Shamanism*, London: Mandala.

Warner, M. (1994) *From the Beast to the Blonde: on fairytales and their tellers*, London: Chatto and Windus.

Washington, P. (1993) *Madame Blavatsky's Baboon*, London: Secker and Warburg.

Watts, A. (1981) *Tao: the watercourse way*, Harmondsworth: Penguin.

Bibliography

Weber, M. ([1922] 1966) *The Sociology of Religion*, London: Methuen.

Weber, M. ([1930] 1978) *The Protestant Ethic and the Spirit of Capitalism*, London: Allen and Unwin.

White L. (1967) 'The Historical Roots of Our Ecological Crisis', *Science*, 155 (3767): 1203–1207.

Whitehouse, H. (ed.) (2001) *The Debated Mind: evolutionary psychology versus ethnography*, Oxford: Berg.

Willis, R. (ed.) (1994) *Signifying Animals: human meaning in the natural world*, London: Routledge.

Wood, J. (1996) 'The Concept of the Goddess', in S. Billington and M. Green (eds) *The Concept of the Goddess*, London: Routledge.

Worthington, A. (2004) *Stonehenge: Celebration and Subversion*, Wymeswold, Loughborough: Alternative Albion.

Worthington, C. (1999) *Druids: A Beginners Guide*, London: Hodder.

Yates, F. ([1972] 1986) *The Rosicrucian Enlightenment*, London: ARK.

Yates, F. ([1964] 1991) *Giordano Bruno and the Hermetic Tradition*, Chicago: University of Chicago Press.

Yates, F. ([1966] 1992) *The Art of Memory*, London: Pimlico.

York, M. (1994) 'New Age in Britain,' *Religion Today*, 9 (3): 14–21.

York, M. (1995) *The Emerging Network: a sociology of the New Age and Neo-Pagan movements*, Lanham, Mad.: Rowman and Littlefield.

Young, D. (1994) 'Visitors in the Night: a creative energy model of spontaneous Visions', in D. Young and J.G. Goulet (eds), *Being Changed by Cross-Cultural Encounters*, Peterborough, Ontario: Broadview Press.

Young, D. and J.-G. Goulet (eds) (1994) *Being Changed By Cross-Cultural Encounters: the anthropology of extraordinary experience*, Peterborough, Ontario: Broadview Press.

Zipes, J. (ed.) (2000) *The Oxford Companion to Fairy Tales: the Western fairy tale tradition from medieval to modern*, Oxford: Oxford University Press.

Index

Index

Index